The **PRINT** *of*

The PRINT of the NAILS

The
CHURCH TIMES
Holy Week and Easter Collection

MARILYN McCORD ADAMS • JOHN BELL
STEPHEN COTTRELL • ANDREW DAVISON
PAULA GOODER • MALCOLM GUITE
RACHEL MANN • MARK OAKLEY
TIMOTHY RADCLIFFE OP • PETER STANFORD
BARBARA BROWN TAYLOR • ANGELA TILBY
SAMUEL WELLS • TOM WRIGHT
and others

edited by
HUGH HILLYARD-PARKER

CANTERBURY
PRESS
Norwich

First published in 2022 by the Canterbury Press Norwich
Editorial office
3rd Floor, Invicta House,
108–114 Golden Lane, London EC1Y 0TG, UK

www.canterburypress.co.uk

Canterbury Press is an imprint of Hymns Ancient & Modern Ltd
(a registered charity)

Hymns Ancient & Modern® is a registered trademark of
Hymns Ancient & Modern Ltd
13A Hellesdon Park Road, Norwich, Norfolk NR6 5DR, UK

British Library Cataloguing in Publication data
A catalogue record for this book is available from the British Library

ISBN 978 1-78622-424-8

Designed and typeset by Hugh Hillyard-Parker
Copyedited by Rosamund Connelly
Printed and bound in Great Britain by CPI Group (UK) Ltd

ACKNOWLEDGEMENTS

We are grateful to the following for permission to reproduce copyright material:
p.150 "Dawn Not Yet" from *The Collected Poems* by Elizabeth Jennings (Carcanet Press),
reproduced by permission of David Higham Associates.

The images on the following pages are public domain artwork downloaded from Wikimedia
Commons under its generic Creative Commons licence: pp. 8, 26, 28, 45, 77, 78, 91, 95, 112, 123,
127, 131, 139, 141, 156, 157, 167, 208, 213, 215, 216, 219, 220, 221, 224, 227, 232, 234, 237, 242

The following images are licensed under the Creative Commons Attribution licences indicated:
CC 1.0 Universal Public Domain Dedication: pp.3, 72, 152, 165

CC Attribution-Share Alike 2.0 Generic licence: p.148 Pauline Eccles; p.155 Patty O'Hearn
Kickham, Guelph, Ontario, Canada; p.178 deror_avi; p.186 Rod Waddington

CC Attribution-Share Alike 3.0 Unported licence: p.68 Doug Sim; p.188 John Stephen Dwyer
(Boston)

CC Attribution-Share Alike 4.0 International licence: p.116 Simon Alveranga

Provided by Alamy Stock Photo: p.13 Pixel-shot; p.22 Chris Hellier; p.38 PA Images; p.41 Lisa
Geoghegan; p.48 Jason Wells; p.83 Stuart Burford; p.106 Linda Johnsonbaugh Israel; p.183 Mark
Thomas; p.203 Geoffrey Robinson; p.205 Jon Bower Cambridge; p.228 Paul Melling; p.231 Art World.

Other images: p.87 Rob Floyd for Manchester Cathedral; pp.99, 171 Methodist Modern Art
Collection.

Contents

THE RESURRECTION

EASTER REFLECTIONS

WORSHIP AT EASTER

EASTER IN THE ARTS

Introduction

by **Paul Handley**

WHEN searching for theology, people look in the oddest places. By 'theology' here I simply mean a greater knowledge of God – I'm well aware that it's a rare Christian who goes in search of 'theology' as such. The first port of call is a church and, assuming they still follow some form of liturgy, that's theology straight into the artery. Hymns, too – though singing 'La-la-la' would sometimes be healthier than paying too much attention to the words. Bible readings, great – can't knock those, as far as they go. Sermons – let's just say that some of them can be brilliantly illuminating and thought-provoking, and leave it at that. Theological debate over the coffee afterwards – oh, if only!

A more discerning seeker will look out the right books. Why wait for your preacher to read something and regurgitate it from the pulpit when you can read it first? Increasing numbers are looking to podcasts and webinars, too, though the printed word still scores in my view; when I'm reading, I never know when I'll have to stop and think something through at my own pace rather than the author's.

Newspapers and news sites, perhaps for understandable reasons, get overlooked here. I would argue, predictably I suppose, that a knowledge of how the world works can furnish an intimate relationship with God. The news provides multiple examples of harm and rescue, damage and repair. Much of the time, God's hand is hard to detect, but then, our being confused and troubled is part of the human condition. All of the *Church Times*, then, I would argue, is theological. Some parts, though, are more obviously so, and this is what has been collected here.

There's one other thing about theology that many people don't realise. It dates. Each generation throws up texts that endure, but the tide of thought and understanding washes on relentless and excitingly. Theology is news, and sometimes even books are too slow to catch the wave before it moves on. Each year, as Easter approaches, we ask theologians what they are working on at present. Sometimes we suggest questions and themes that occur to us. Often they say, no, but how about something on this other thing.

The liturgical seasons are essential to this process, and Holy Week and Easter supremely. It is hard to contemplate reliving the confrontation, hostility, and pain that lead to the crucifixion. Must we really go through that another year? But the closer to God, the sharper the vision. On these pages you will find pieces that stare directly at unwatchable scenes in the manner of war correspondents. What they report is just as vital and arresting as something from a modern war zone.

But Easter is about resurrection, also. It is a generally accepted truth that good news is far harder to find and write than bad. Certainly, we have to work harder to persuade our theologians to write convincingly and creatively about the resurrection. I think we have succeeded, but I leave it to readers to decide.

There is a danger that articles pulled out of the *Church Times* from the past 20 years or so will have lost their edge. Our editor, Hugh Hillyard-Parker, has been diligent, however – one might say brutal – in choosing pieces that work at this moment, some perhaps better than when they were first published. It is exciting to see that they are still carrying out their theological task: bringing greater understanding about God.

Paul Handley has been Editor of Church Times *since 1995.*

Editor's note: all the pieces in this book first appeared in the Church Times *Easter editions, between 2000 and 2021. The year of first appearance is given at the end of each article.*

In the gardens of good and evil

Here and now, we can rediscover love, human and divine,
says **Martin Warner**

I HAVE to confess that this has not been a good Lent for me. It began before there had been a chance to recover from Christmas; the weather in the middle was cold and horrible; the school term has been hideously short; and my diary seems to be out of control.

But this is not an unfamiliar catalogue of excuses. I suspect that some of them are well rehearsed by those who heroically try to hold together a demanding job, family commitments, any kind of neighbourly, social or recreational interest — the things we call "a life" — and still manage some kind of Christian discipleship.

So now Holy Week confronts us. This is when I seek what releases in me the imaginative energy to experience and understand the folly of the cross as the wisdom of God. Here I patiently try to assemble what I want to say about failure, my own finitude, and the death of those I love and need. I hope to dump my distractions, and become able to feel again, spiritually.

It is often through familiar images that we are refreshed, as revelation reinvigorates well-worn places. The setting for important moments in the drama of the Passion and resurrection of Jesus is a garden — one that resonates with older scriptural associations. We begin in the garden of Gethsemane, and the betrayal of Judas (Mark 14.42-45), with its reminiscence of the betrayal of the eaten apple in the garden of Eden (Genesis 3.10-13).

We then move to the rock garden of Calvary, an outcrop of wasteland outside the city (John 19.17). Here we find overtones from Isaiah's vision of a wilderness, where transformation and healing will also be revealed by the God who comes to save his people (Isaiah 35.3-7).

But we end where we began. The man whom Mary of Magdala mistook for the gardener in the garden of the resurrection (John 20.11-16) is indeed Jesus. But, as the new Adam, he is the gardener into whose charge earth and the paradise of heaven are entrusted, just as God had settled the first Adam in Eden "to cultivate it and take care of it" (Genesis 2.15).

Over three sacred days, we shall enter each of these gardens, with their layers of association, seeking to find the God from whom we have a distant memory of hiding ourselves because of shame and nakedness.

What our gardens teach us is that we are not ultimately the prisoners of time, nor the conquests of death and despair. The first garden image from which I would draw that lesson is one of turned earth receiving the seeds of new life. Christina Baxter's intimate devotional writing in *The Wounds of Christ* (Zondervan, 2004) offers a profound reflection on Jesus's back, the part of his body harrowed by scourging and pressed on the wood of the cross for our salvation.

"The plowers plowed upon my back and made long furrows," Psalm 129 declares. And no less is the tilled garden a statement of struggle in the context of spiritual endeavour. John's Gospel directs our attention to this theme in words that herald the Passion: "Unless a grain of wheat falls into the earth and dies, it remains only a single grain; but if it dies, it yields a rich harvest" (John 12.24).

Living, as I do now, in the City of London, I miss the opportunity to cultivate a patch of garden. In the country, on cold, sharp days, ploughed and seeded fields make a statement about hidden life, a distant harvest-in-waiting, still fragile.

Calvary speaks to us about the flesh of Christ that is itself ploughed up and seeded in the process that will lead to the green shoots of the new creation. Here we are being told something important about flesh and embodiment: that it's the material in which eternal life is sown. This is why Thomas needs to touch the risen body in order to get his mind round the continuity between flesh and resurrection.

Here also is a lesson about the sowing of seeds for those who live in what W. H. Auden terms "the prison of [our] days" — in life locked up by the dictates of time. In Joel Hershman's film, *Greenfingers*, Colin (Clive Owen), a convicted murderer, finds recovery of dignity and purpose through seeds scattered on a bit of prison wasteland.

The prison ground is metaphorically ploughed, churned up by guilt, anger and despair. But, in this terrain, the seeds of beauty and hope that are sown enable Colin to win a prize for his garden, and say: "A prisoner was all I'd thought I'd ever be."

AS YOU MIGHT expect in a film, Colin falls in love, and it is in the garden of love that another Holy Week lesson is to be learnt. This year (2005) and again in 2016, the calendar works in such a way as to invite us to conflate two images, because the usual date for the feast of the Annunciation falls on Good Friday.

This will then not happen again this century. And we have two garden images for these two days. The first is the rock garden of the wilderness, in which waters break when the rock is pierced by Moses in order that the pilgrim people of God might have water to drink (Exodus 17.5-6; 1 Corinthians 10.4). The second is the enclosed garden of desire and union, which is described in the love poetry of the Song of Songs (4.12-15).

We are generally unfamiliar in the West with the tradition of a dry garden of rocks, but in the religious traditions of the Far East, there is much greater interest in the spiritual significance of stone. Not that this is entirely absent from the Christian tradition about the Passion: Matthew dramatically elicits an environmental response to the death of Jesus, commenting that "the earth quaked, the rocks were split" (Matthew 27.51).

Matthew's account continues with an image of holy people rising up from toppled tombs, rather like what appears to be a graveyard revolution in Stanley Spencer's painting *The Resurrection, Cookham* in Tate Britain. John depicts this outpouring of new life rather differently, using the sacramental symbols of life in blood and water flowing out of the side of Jesus.

This image of irruption in the dry, stone garden of Calvary links with an aspect of a different kind of garden, more familiar to us in the West — the enclosed garden. It is a popular late-medieval subject for artists, who paint a meditation on the mystery of Mary's virgin motherhood which the feast

What our gardens teach us: Annunciation, *attributed to* Petrus Christus, *c.1450, in the* Metropolitan Museum of Art, New York

of the Annunciation celebrates. In these paintings, water is significant, the sealed fountain, in Song of Songs 4.12, being a symbolic statement about potential awaiting its realisation.

Some may find the language of the Song of Songs disturbing, because from it medieval painters gather the delicate images of the enclosed garden in order to communicate refreshingly the power of human love. Their art reveals a capacity to include the beauty of the physical dimension of this love within the dispensation of salvation. The incarnation and the Passion — itself an ambiguous term in this context — of the Son of God direct all our loves towards perfection, so that none of them need be unredeemed.

The capacity for this inclusivity in medieval picture imagery may be found in a fluidity of symbolism which we have lost. For example, a red rose has been used in Christian art to represent Mary's paradisal purity. It is also the flower of erotic love, though a rose hedge is an allusion to exactly that love channelled by Mary, through grace and her freedom over her own body, into an act of co-operation by which God took flesh and became red-blooded. The red rose is also used to evoke the shedding of that same blood.

The theme of love lurks just beneath the surface of John's account of the crucifixion. It is the love of a marriage, evoked in the Gospel by the presence of Jesus and his mother at Cana, when the glory of the hour of exaltation on the cross was revealed for the first time (John 2.1-11).

The water turned into wine on that occasion prefigured the water and blood in which the new creation, itself a marriage between earth and heaven, came to birth. The Latin text of Jesus's final cry from the cross reads in English as "It is consummated," an allusion to marriage that Eric Gill brilliantly illustrated in a small drawing of the crucifixion, daringly entitled *Nuptials of God.*

There is much scriptural and theological material here that uses human love as a way of understanding the furnace of divine love in redemption. It is sad, therefore, that Christians do not often seem able to speak authentically about sex as a positive aspect of our vocation to life in its fullness.

This has become an area of anxiety and loss of confidence in the goodness of the nature of what God has made us to be. Perhaps we have become too grown up in our Christian culture, forgetting those strands of delight and play that can encompass suffering, and elicit faith, hope, and love.

IT IS IN a garden of play that I have chosen to locate the experience of the resurrection, a choice also determined by the coincidence of Easter and Christmas stories on 25 March, the day we celebrate the annunciation of the birth of the child who will suffer on Good Friday.

Oscar Wilde's story *The Selfish Giant* may appear sentimental, but its darker aspects are created by shadows that fall across our own time. The giant banishes children from his garden with a sign that reads: "My own garden is my own garden." As a result, the garden descends into perpetual winter, until the children get through a hole in the wall, and spring returns. Then the giant recognises his folly, and is moved by the pitiable child who is unable to climb into the tree in the furthest corner of the garden to release its branches from barren winter.

The conclusion of the story is set in the now benign, because transient, winter. The giant sees, however, in that furthest corner of his garden, a tree covered in blossom and fruit. In its branches sits that same tiny child, on whose hands and feet are nail prints — "the wounds of Love", declares the child, who invites the giant to his garden, which is paradise.

We are familiar with the words of Isaiah: "He was being wounded for our transgressions, crushed for our iniquities" (Isaiah 53.5). We are less certain, perhaps, of the application of them with graphic realism to the Christ-child. But it is hideously clear that the land, resources, funding and opportunity that should safeguard childhood have been seized by adults for their own profitable purposes.

Evidence of this is to be found in the exploitation of children — from the manipulation of their fashion and its branding, in an increasingly adult culture among young people who may lack the emotional resources to sustain its pressures; in the number of suicides among young offenders; and the disturbing incidents of teenagers charged with violent murder. And then there are the children of Africa: we hardly dare to list the wounds that they bear, while we adjust the iron chains of international debt.

It is precisely as a child that today the Christ suffers the most heinous crucifixion of famine, disease, poverty, and dispossession on the axis of the world's unequal distribution of its resources. Stamped all over the garden of childhood is a global message from the adult world: MINE.

Let's return to where we began: the out-of-control diary and life. This garden of play may have more to teach us about these than the other gardens do. If we adults have stamped "Mine" on the temporal benefits of the Garden of Eden in this world, the eternal garden of Paradise has a different message: PLAY.

If it is in the likeness of a child that we enter the Kingdom of heaven, then that's how some kind of innocence is recovered; how time is restored; how watching and wonder become normal modes of being; and play becomes praise, the pastime of the truly wise.

(2005)

Night of unity, night of sin

Maundy Thursday: **Robert Mackley** looks at the Last Supper

HOW DO you remember someone when they die? That is the urgent question that Maundy Thursday addresses. Jesus is about to die, and nothing will ever be the same again. It is true when anyone we love dies: we lose a part of ourselves, and they leave a hole that nothing can fill. We may get used to the hole, but it will never go away.

Bereavement is like starting to wear glasses: to begin with, everything looks different; over time, you get used to the change of perspective; but every so often you remember that you are wearing glasses, and that the world is different and always will be.

Jesus is making provision for the time after his death, and, with extraordinary sensitivity, he uses the ordinary and familiar to make that provision. He takes the Jewish paschal family meal, a meal that was at the heart of the disciples' lives and faith, and transforms it. He does not invent something out of the blue, but speaks to them of his impending death, and provides for them after he has died in the context of something they know well. Now is a time for the familiar and for directness: "Ah, now you are speaking plainly, not in any figure of speech!" John records the disciples saying (John 16.29).

Jesus knows that what people want more than anything is for their loved one to return — and if not to return, then for there to continue to be some connection with them. For the bereaved, doing something tangible (lighting a candle, visiting the graveside, arranging some flowers) becomes a vital way of connecting with the tangibility of the beloved who has died. It turns their wayward thoughts into something solid that they can touch and see and return to.

The Last Supper gives the disciples something tangible, too. They are to have this meal in memory of him. Each time they gather together, take bread and wine, and give thanks, they will remember him.

This is the Passover meal, however; and so they know that when they have this meal each year, they are not just sharing old Exodus memories of the Passover of the Angel of Death and the journey from Egypt to the Promised Land. They know that they are actively recalling this event. They know that at the Passover meal the Passover is real again. For the Jew at Passover, the opposite of remembering is not forgetting — it is *dismembering*.

So what must the disciples have felt as Jesus took this meal and applied it to himself? Would they have been thrilled that this meal would bring Jesus back into the present for them in future? Perhaps. More likely, however, is the usual keynote struck by the disciples — half in joy and half in fear, scarcely being able to believe what they are being told.

What were they being told? That the bread and the wine were Jesus's body and blood, and that they were to consume them. They were also being told more than that, however: they were to do this again and again ("as often as you do this"), and not because they were in danger of forgetting Jesus — how could they forget the one they loved? — but to unite themselves with him.

Maundy Thursday is supremely the day of unity. For the bereaved, the ashes on the mantelpiece or the body in the grave are a way of connecting with the deceased. The intimacy of the body is gone, but they long for it still. For the disciples, that unity is not to go — instead, it is to be intensified. The unity with Jesus that they have up to this point is human. The unity they will have with Jesus after his death will be divine as well.

They are to take his body and blood and make it part of them. The part of themselves that they have lost in bereavement is to be given back to them, and given back not just as it was, but with new depth — for by consuming his body and blood, they are not only therefore remembering Jesus, but they are remembering themselves.

Their unity with Christ will be such that, as they make him present to themselves in every subsequent supper, so they make themselves present, too. They will discover that, as they unite themselves with Christ, so they are uniting with each other, and even within themselves. They will be uncovering more and more not only of who Christ is, but of who they are, too. The mystery of their own lives will be revealed further and further as they "do this in remembrance" (Luke 22.19).

SO MAUNDY Thursday is about unity. It is Jesus's desire that his disciples may be one with him that makes him wash their feet — "if I do not wash you, you have no part in me" (John 13.8). This is not simply because unless the disciples share in Jesus's ministry of service, they cannot be with him; the unity is more intense even than that. There was one exception to the servants washing people's feet in first-century Palestine: that exception was the people's host, especially if he was a rabbi. Instead of his disciples or servants washing his feet, his wife would wash them. She would do this not out of servitude, but rather because by marriage they were one body, and no one had the right to touch her husband's feet but she.

Christ Washing St Peter's Feet *(1501), Hans Holbein the Elder,*
in the Städel Museum, Frankfurt am Main, Germany

Jesus, the rabbi, in washing his disciples' feet, therefore, not only offers an astonishing act of intimacy and humility; even more, he points them towards the unity of Christ and his Church, the Bridegroom and Bride. He behaves as the wife, so that disciple and master can both say: "This is my body." He is one body with his disciples; he is married to his Church; and so he gives them his Maundy, his *mandamus*, his new commandment: to love as much as Bridegroom and Bride love one another.

John omits the Last Supper from his Gospel, therefore, because he has other ways of illustrating the unity of which the supper speaks. The washing of the feet is one; the beautiful farewell discourses are another. Jesus speaks of his unity with his disciples in terms of a vine and its branches, and, in his prayer to the Father, prays that they may be one with him, just as he is with the Father. They make his body and blood part of them, that they may be in Jesus as Jesus is in his Father: "that the love with which thou hast loved me may be in them and I in them" (John 17.26).

The familiar paschal meal is being made strange, but at the same time Jesus is speaking directly, and explaining its significance. The long discourse that John describes is, in essence, an explanation of the meal — a thing so obvious to the Christians for whom John writes that he can omit the description of the meal itself. Unity is at the heart of this description, and it answers the deepest desires of the soon-to-be-bereaved. He says (in John 14.18): "I will not leave you desolate; I will come to you." The coming of which he speaks is twofold: first, the coming of the Holy Spirit; second, the Second Coming at the end of time.

Certainly, he will come at the resurrection — but only to go again at the ascension. The comings that the bereaved need are not temporary ones, but the coming of the "Counsellor to be with you for ever" (John 14.16). The Holy Spirit will be a further gift of unity, the gift of Christ again among the disciples, "to teach you all things and bring to your remembrance all that I have said to you" (John 14.26).

This is the night before Christ's death, however, and so Maundy Thursday is not only about unity: it is also about sin. For all his plain speaking and the power of the Passover meal to recall the past into the present, what Jesus is giving to the disciples is still sacramental. The outward form carries and connects with the inner reality, but they are not yet completely one. Although it will truly be his life that he will bestow in bread and wine, it will also be bread and wine and so a hint, a foretaste, a sign, a mystery, a gesture towards the future reality.

In heaven, there will be no sacraments; for they will see fully the Body of which they are a part. Now, there is death and sin to struggle against — the promise of Christ's presence is real, but it is also not yet complete. The unity of his disciples is real and also not yet complete.

So we turn to that other coming: the Second Coming, when sign and symbol will be no more because sin will be no more. Christ's presence will be utter and complete, and mystery — *sacramentum* — will give way to absolute vision. "For now we see in a mirror, dimly, but then we will see face to face. Now I know only in part; then I will know fully, even as I have been fully known." (1 Corinthians 13.12) That, above all things, is what Maundy Thursday is about.

Until then, however, there is Good Friday to be attended to ...

(2006)

9

Different from other nights

Jonathan Romain explains the significance of the Passover meal, and why it resonates so powerfully in even Jews who have lapsed

THE Jesuits reckon that having a child under their tutelage until he is seven years old will guarantee that he is theirs for life. The Jewish equivalent of this might be: hold a *Seder* (Passover meal) in your home annually and that alone will keep you Jewish for the rest of the year.

That is a slightly extravagant claim, but it is still largely true. There are many Jews whose synagogue attendance is abysmal and whose practices at home are non-existent yet who would be aghast at the thought of missing tonight's Passover celebrations — despite the fact that Passover is merely one of several important festivals in the Jewish year, and is arguably less significant than Yom Kippur (the great gathering for the Day of Atonement), or Shavuot (the Feast of Weeks, which marks the revelation on Mount Sinai and the giving of the Ten Commandments).

Four things make the Passover festival resonate so powerfully for even the most lapsed of Jews, while those who actively practise their faith regard it as one of the highlights of the Jewish calendar.

Passover celebrates the departure of the Israelites from ancient Egypt under the leadership of Moses, aided by the miracles and plagues recorded in the Book of Exodus.

Herein lies its first attraction. The Israelites of old are not only the spiritual ancestors of Jews today, but their direct forebears. The Exodus is not biography; it is autobiography. The Passover meal begins with the words: "We were slaves in Egypt": not "they" but "we". There is a real sense of personal identification.

True, there have been countless instances of intermarriage and rape down the centuries, but, by and large, there is a direct line of descent, and we feel the presence of an umbilical cord linking us to what happened in the land of Pharaoh.

The second factor is that, although there are Passover services in synagogue, the main way of observing the festival is through the special evening meal (Seder) at home, at which the story of the Exodus is narrated and symbolic foods are eaten. You do not have to make a special effort to go to the festival; instead, the festival comes to you. It is a domestic occurrence around the dining-table. This evening, Jewish people will be gathering in their homes.

Automatically, therefore, everyone is involved: the elderly relative who is not able to travel easily; the single person who does not like going out alone at night; the children who would otherwise be in bed; the secular Jew who is not interested in going to a place of worship.

Third, Passover may be about retelling a bygone tale, but it has a crucial message that is still fresh. Essentially, the festival records the first national liberation movement in history, that of the Jewish people. It acts as a model for every subsequent group denied freedom or suffering persecution. The stirring cry first uttered by Moses in the court of Pharaoh — "Let my people go" (Exodus 7.16) — has reverberated around the world ever since. It has been heard in the streets of Soweto, the gulags of the Soviet Union, and in Trafalgar Square on behalf of a variety of causes.

The legacy of Passover is the right to be free, a right not restricted to any one people or any one time. It has instilled a powerful sense of social action in the Jewish psyche, which has been reinforced by the command elsewhere in the Book of Exodus (22.21): "You shall not oppress the stranger, because you were strangers in the Land of Egypt." It is not just wrong to do so, but flies in the face of our own experience.

It is precisely because we know what it feels like to be persecuted that we should not put others in the same position. If ever there was a way of seeking to learn from history and avoid repeating its mistakes, Passover is that annual lesson.

The Seder ends with the words "Next year in Jerusalem", signifying the Jerusalem of our highest hopes, and reflecting the fact that Jerusalem is a Hebrew word meaning "city of shalom/peace".

So the fourth key attraction of the festival is that, although part of its narrative concerns brutality and suffering, it is optimistic in tone, and has a strong messianic streak.

It looks forward to a world redeemed, in which kingship reverts to God, and the values of justice and compassion reign supreme. There is a trust that next year will be better than this one, for all humanity; and that the world is slowly but definitely ascending in goodness.

THE WAY in which these lofty themes are expressed is two-fold. The Haggadah is a specially designed text that narrates the events from the time of the Israelites' entering Egypt, through their enslavement and liberation, until the crossing of the Red Sea.

The rabbis who created the Haggadah knew that a straight history could easily become dull, so they used various devices to enliven it. Thus it takes the form of a question-and-answer session, with the children being given a special part to play, both so as to engage them and to challenge the adults.

It is read around the table, with a senior member of the family (such as the grandfather) leading it, but with everyone else participating and taking it in turn to read sections of the narrative, either in Hebrew or in English.

"Why is this night different from all other nights?" they ask. "Why do we do this? Why do we not do that?"

Four set questions launch the response of everyone else present, although the children also have other special parts later, including opening the front door to invite in the prophet Elijah symbolically — both as a sign of hospitality and as a hint of messianic times.

The narration is also interrupted by four cameo characters who each ask a question about what is going on: the Wise Child, the Wicked Child, the Simple Child, and the One who does not know how to ask. They reflect the four types of Jew: pious, lapsed, ignorant, and confused — all of whom, remarkably, will be at the festive meal, and who each need a separate answer about the significance of the ceremony.

They are answered by giving the details of the story of the Exodus, but with the strong message that they should feel as redeemed as the Hebrew slaves, and that, but for the intervention of God, they themselves might still be in Egypt.

Psalms and songs also play a part, and it is highly traditional to put aside the set text and have a debate of one's own about various issues, ancient and modern, such as: was it moral for Moses to kill the Egyptian taskmaster? Who are the oppressed of today? How can we best honour our Jewish heritage?

THE OTHER method of expressing Passover is through food. There is a ban on eating all bread and other products involving the leavening process (such as cakes and biscuits) during the festival. Instead, we eat matzah/unleavened bread at the Passover meal and for the seven days of the festival (until next Wednesday).

This is a reminder of the haste in which the Israelites left Egypt, when Pharaoh suddenly changed his mind after the tenth plague and ordered them to depart immediately. It meant that the bread they baked did not have time to rise (Exodus 12.39). So, at breakfast or at any other meal, we are conscious of what happened long ago.

The Seder itself is full of symbolic foods, as each dish brings instant recall of particular events. Bitter herbs remind us of the harshness of slavery; salt-water tastes of the tears of those who suffered; green vegetables attest to the spring season at which the Exodus occurred; *haroset* (a mixture of nuts and raisins and apple and cinnamon, which is delicious, but looks like

Passover Seder plate with traditional food

brown sludge) resembles the mortar used by the Israelite slaves to build pyramids; roast egg brings memories of the burnt offerings used as sacrifices of thanksgiving.

THE RESULT is that we do not just tell the story, but re-enact it; we feel the bitterness and experience the hardship. Those who might find listening to history boring have to become participants. They not only have to pay attention, but are reminded that the gap between the Israelites and us is only a matter of dates. It could have been us; but for the events of those times, we might have disappeared from history and not be who we are today.

Despite the sense of exultation, there is also an awareness that others suffered, too, and that the cause of freedom had consequences for ordinary Egyptians. Wine is present at the Seder, as a symbol of joy, but, when we recite the ten plagues, we dip our finger each time into our glass and take out a drop of wine, lessening our pleasure and recognising their pain, rather than delighting in it.

Similarly, it is customary for Jews who were first-born to fast on the day before Passover — an act of solidarity with the Egyptian firstborn who died, and acknowledging the fact that no victory ever comes without consequences.

Passover is not just a biblical ritual dutifully observed, but a personal experience that encompasses a vast range of human emotions, and makes modern Jews feel they are a continuing part of that ancient march to freedom.

(2003)

13

Poet's corner: Maundy Thursday

Maundy Thursday is about everything that lockdown, last year, seemed to negate, says **Malcolm Guite**

THERE is something tentative and hesitant about the way we are approaching our second Holy Week and Easter still in lockdown. We are grateful not to be so utterly locked out of church and community as we were on that last strange Easter Day, but not quite sure how and where and whether to gather this time, how to keep company and at the same time keep safe.

There must have been some similar hesitancy, caution, and uncertainty for the first disciples about where and how to keep the passover with Jesus, about how to gather for that first Maundy Thursday. Our cautions and precautions are driven by anxiety about exposure to infection, theirs by fear of exposure to the authorities. The brooding threats of betrayal and arrest, gathering throughout Holy Week, must lie behind those mysterious, seemingly clandestine arrangements for obtaining the use of the upper room.

And yet they felt they had to take the risk; so much of the meaning of Maundy Thursday is bound up in the intimacy of personal exchange, the shared touch of the foot washing, a disciple leaning on Jesus's breast, the shared bread and cup, all being together and breathing the same air, all the things we have had to do without for more than a year: those little kindling contacts with one another, and, through the sacrament, with our Saviour.

In Linton, we won't actually gather in person till Easter Day, and then at a social distance, and everything will also be online. Yet even that small gathering is better than last year, when it was so hard to find the virtue in the virtual. I remember the shock of it, still so early in the strange new world of that first severe lockdown, when literally nothing was moving: the roads were empty, the planes all grounded, even the parks and playgrounds were deserted.

And, on that Maundy Thursday evening, when I should have been in church, I sat down instead and wrote this poem. Reading it again both takes me back and helps me to look forward.

(2021)

Maundy Thursday, All the World is Still

Maundy Thursday, all the world is still
The planes wait, grounded by departure gates
The street is empty and the shopping mall
Deserted. Padlocked, the playground waits
Against the day that children play again
Till then our sad refrain is just "refrain".

Maundy Thursday, all the world is still
And Jesus is at supper with his friends
No longer in the upper room, that hall
In Zion where the story starts and ends,
For he descended from it long ago
To find his new friends in the here and now.

Maundy Thursday, all the world is still
And Jesus is at supper with his friends
Our doors are locked for fear, but he has skill
In breaking barriers. With ease he bends
Our prison bars, slips past the sentry post
And joins us as the guest who is our host.

Maundy Thursday, all the world is still
But in cramped quarters on the fifteenth floor,
In lonely towers made of glass and steel,
And in the fierce favelas of the poor,
Touching with wounded hands the wounds he tends,
Christ Jesus is at supper with his friends.

Painting Gethsemane

A painter wrestles with a dark subject in a short story for
Holy Week by **David Hart**

GOOD afternoon, ladies and gentlemen. Thank you for coming to my exhibition. Please do understand, I'm a painter, not a talker. I have allowed myself to be persuaded to talk about this one work, on the easel here.

After a lifetime of painting ragged mountains, storms, dilapidated farmhouses, detached huts, shadows, how to talk about what at least began as a crowd scene? I shall try to take you through from that painting to what you see here. Not obvious, now, why it's called *Jesus in Gethsemane*. OK, *Jesus with his disciples was in a place people called Gethsemane*.

Here, look: olive trees, and, between them, some steps down — not far down, but into some seclusion; small stone steps, dandelions, you see, bluebells. My Gethsemane is a space left over from wartime bombs; a church was bombed near where I have my studio, hardly a trace of the building now, some steps, the single arch of a doorway, a yew tree, a few gravestones, the rest gone.

The bomb carved out a crater, about which more later. And you see, if you look here, one part of the garden, and another, where Jesus went after he'd said: "Wait here, I am going over there to pray." He didn't go alone, it says that he took Peter, and the two sons of Zebedee along with him, and it says that he began to be sad and troubled.

I hope that you can see how I tried to ease that moment into the present tense, make it present, show him being troubled and sad. If you look here, imagine him on a bright evening going into a bleak aura of darkness — I don't have the words, sorry — a darkness all of his own. He allowed it, welcomed it even, to allow resolution of it somehow, poor man. And there is a greyer shadow where the three disciples were, unable to keep still: you see a shivering grey.

IMAGINE what it must have been like for them to hear him say: "My soul is submerged into such sadness it is like dying." To indicate these words, I painted a splutter of light — not a splutter, I don't know, sorry — where he says as well: "Stay here and help me to wait and wait." This made me straighten the disciples into — I thought of wooden planks left to stand up without supports.

And then I experienced such a confusion about how to do this, one thing after the other. I'm talking days, weeks, spent working on it. Moving away from them, he fell with his face to the ground, and he shouted, and I heard it like this: "O unnameable my Father!", whom when he was a boy he had known from his teaching was the creator, the maker of all — was I AM THAT I AM, no more personal or defined a name possible — only now he says "Father". Why not "Mother"? I don't know why not "Mother", I would have cried for mine, I do now.

I hope you have seen what I have asked you to imagine, before I scrubbed it all out. When I went wandering again, to that place where the remains of the crater are, boarded over, as it turned out, under turf, I felt so drained I wanted only to lie down under the yew, let it spike me. Melodramatic? Yes, yes, of course, and true.

He said — and I think he said this quietly, soberly — "If it is possible, I want to escape this, but if you, I AM THAT I AM, Father, have marked me out for this." And did he, Jesus, hear yes, and whisper yes, or sigh only? How to paint this, to begin again? You see here now a wide open mouth. I thought: "And that's all;" it fills almost the whole canvas, then added an overflooding as well of dark cloud, the tiny specks of brightness, not stars but bluster, he is meeting I AM.

WE LIVE in time that is never the present — often tense, yes, sorry — which is only ever the past becoming the future. We are told and then, and then; it seems an incurable this, then that; so how to paint to make present everything that happened in that light-dark-light, if it's not to be a comic strip?

Look, I painted over and out the great open mouth, and over the darkening sky and the spots of light, do you see? All grey again. Then in bed, sleepless, I wished I hadn't.

Next morning, I knew I had been right to do it, the moment-by-moment was evolving into consequences. He returned to his disciples, and saw they were asleep. I saw him then as a force of nature. I would show him as storm, as storm in the form of a winged dark thing without boundaries, a hawk-angel bursting open the very air.

When he said, to Peter especially, "Couldn't you men stay awake to protect me, not even for an hour?", look, on the canvas now, a splash of his red voice, addressing shadows with splinter wounds for ears.

I was stopped again, held back. What if he had said it not in anger, but as gentle as gentle could be: "Couldn't you men, my friends, stay awake to protect me, not even for an hour?" So I made him a waif and stray who'd wandered away and got lost. He was crying, even.

The canvas becomes a confusion of tracks and loose doors, a nightmare of an arm here, some stray heads, eyes adrift, the sky as when the forecaster says, apologetically: "Watch out, today will be changeable."

And then I felt I was back in junior school, and I'd had my eye on someone's half-eaten pudding and custard, and they were looking away, and the teacher is behind me, and says: "Don't do it: you won't like yourself afterwards."

If not my talent, fill my stomach! Spare a thought for the disciples: "Not even for an hour?" They'd failed. They were confused, I was confused. They had wanted glory by association; I wanted, by enchantment or luck, to acquire more of the wherewithal and applause as a painter than I could ever — "Watch and pray so that you will not fall into temptation. The spirit is willing, but the flesh is weak."

Yes, yes, heard that a million times, but such lovely pudding and custard!

WORSE than stalled, I turned the painting to the wall, and for days walked, and walked — walked anywhere, wanted to give up this absurd dancing with shadows, get a proper job. Then, one stray bright afternoon, I had drifted back to the site of the bombed church, restless, mind elsewhere if anywhere, careless, wanted to feel careless; felt my feet touch wood under the grass, stamped on it a little, and it gave way.

I was on my back in the bomb crater — hard earth, dank smell, some sharp rock or remains of wall — seemed stuck, couldn't move, not badly hurt, I thought. Shocked, yes; alarmed, certainly. Tried to think whether I could haul myself out, started to panic.

An elderly woman came along, stopped, stood at the edge of what had opened up, looked down at me, knelt at the edge, and had hold of me. She was strong, with a will, had me almost hauled out, when she slipped. So there we were, half in, half out of this dank hole, holding on to each other.

We were lying awkwardly, me thanking her, she saying no, no, till a couple of young men in suits came by, looking puzzled, smiling then when we did — we smiled, we smiled! Of course we did — and get us out of here, please! — helped us out, all jollification.

The woman and I had a brief hug, brushed the earth off. I wanted to do something to thank her, she was shaking her head, smiling still, and went, looked back, waved, and as I stumbled home, I knew I would turn the large canvas and again confront it.

It has been handed on to us, scribe by scribe: "He went away a second time, and prayed." Why pass it on and tell it like that? The once would be good enough, anyway, for a painting. It nagged at me: the second time was more — desperate. What did he expect? Did he think that I AM THAT I AM Father would have had a change of mind? "Dad?"

No response whatsoever from I AM THAT I AM is recorded. No sound at all out of the Almighty Father. He wasn't listening? He heard and was indifferent? They — earthly — earthy — son and heavenly — hidden — father — being of one mind, was it that nothing needed to be said? How, facing the canvas again, to paint this? And whether to continue with that scrambled canvas, or to start a fresh one.

I HAD beome sick with the painting and overpainting, it was becoming ever more absurdly, as it seemed, game-playing. Take responsibility for it, man! Yes, but it had seemed given.

Now, in the story, a double bind: "My Who-is-and-who-knows Father, if you can't release me from this horrible crisis, except that I accept it." How to paint that?

Look now, all the disciples are snuggled up together fast asleep, and look, in a corner up to the right, a dove fixed in a broken cage is hanging from the sky, I don't know why.

Now, the whole scene is grey washed out again. Came the next day, and what I thought I wanted was a sepia photograph of Jesus running back to the disciples, a snapshot. He had, though, in every way gone further out, and now: "Are you still sleeping and resting? Listen, my time's up, this is it, the Son of Man is to be delivered into the hands of sinners. Get up! Let's go! Who is this coming? You know who it is, he has betrayed me."

And his sweat was like blood. And his sweat was like blood; what would you want to see on the canvas here now? I attempted a portrait, and I understood then the iconoclastic argument. Brushed it out.

But I am a painter. That image is now behind what you see here as a grey wash, and you can see also outstretched ragged hands. All this, while you have been looking at these hands. I shall take the canvas away, and paint over them.

Thank you for being here. No, no questions, please; honestly, I need a drink and some fresh air alone. Thank you for watching. Thank you.

(2014)

19

Patron saint of betrayers

If Judas was doing God's work, why the opprobrium, asks **Peter Stanford**

JUDAS ISCARIOT is not a typical subject of my usual car-journey chatter, but then Lord Archer is not your ordinary travelling companion. In 2007, the peer, bestselling novelist, and former Conservative politician, who was jailed for perjury, had published his fictional *The Gospel According to Judas*.

So, when I found myself recently, as part of a newspaper assignment, sharing a back seat with him, I confessed to being hard at work on a biography of Jesus's betrayer. "Let me give you a word of advice," he offered affably. "You won't make any money out of it. I'd assumed that Judas's name would sell books, but my book about him was the only one of mine that failed commercially."

My expectations of a financial return on a book are doubtless more modest than Lord Archer's, so I overlooked his guidance, and ploughed on with the book; but the assumption that had inspired his novel played in the back of my mind as I researched and wrote, and travel led to Italy and Jerusalem to complete the manuscript. For he was absolutely spot on. Judas's name is indeed one that still has a wide resonance.

IT IS undoubtedly wider than that of most of the other apostles — save, perhaps, Peter. And it is certainly wider, too, than the ranks of the congregations who will have listened this Passiontide to the Gospel accounts of Judas's betrayal of Jesus, his greed for 30 pieces of silver (apparently a paltry sum at the time), his infamous kiss, and the overwhelming shame that led him to his lonely suicide.

At its simplest, even in our secular and scientific times, when we are regularly told (and sometimes taunted) that religion is redundant, to call someone a Judas still has an extraordinary capacity to wound. In 2012, Bob Dylan gave an interview to the magazine *Rolling Stone*. In it, he was reminded of a famous concert, almost 50 years before, when, at Manchester's Free Trade Hall, a discontented member of the audience cried out, in the lull between numbers, to accuse Dylan of being a "Judas".

Behind the accusation lay a fan's fury that Dylan had swapped his acoustic guitar for an electric one. This change was taken as a betrayal (as change often is). What was most striking about the interview, though, was how much being labelled Judas still irked Dylan all those years later. He launched into a tirade in *Rolling Stone* against "wussies and pussies" who questioned his muse.

"These are the same people that tried to pin the name Judas on me," he said. "Judas, the most hated name in human history. If you think you've been called a bad name, try and work your way out from under that. Yeah, and for what? For playing an electric guitar. As if that is in some way equitable to betraying our Lord, and delivering him up to be crucified. [They] can rot in hell."

THOSE tempted to dismiss this as an isolated example of an over-sensitive artiste going off on one might like to consider as corroborating evidence the frequently heard chant of "Judas" in home football crowds when their one-time star player returns in the colours of their opponents. Or the occasion when the Australian Prime Minister, Tony Abbott, decried his erstwhile right-hand man, David Oldfield, before Parliament as his "personal Judas", when the latter defected to another party. Or countless other casual contemporary examples when the name of the renegade apostle is deployed as a weapon.

Those details of the Christian tradition that manage to translate into common parlance in an age when most people do not even go to church, tend to do so because their meaning is so clear, and, arguably, so clearly lodged in our collective subconscious after 2000 years. Everyone knows, for example, that "the Devil" is what you call someone whom you consider evil; "Mary Magdalene" fits a repentant sinner; and "the Virgin Mary" suits an individual who is blameless, self-sacrificing, and, possibly, virginal.

Does the same logic apply to Judas? Superficially, of course, it does. He is the arch-traitor. There is something in the human condition which makes us always quick to name and shame betrayal, and, when we do, we continue to reach for the name of Judas.

But is that all there is to him? A traitor's kiss, a pile of coins, and a corpse hanging from a Judas tree? The devil, as they say, is in the detail. In this case, literally. Traditionally, Judas and his deeds have been presented by the Churches as the actions of Satan's tool, the apostle so loathsome and treacherous that even being included by Jesus in the first eucharist was not sufficient to enable him to resist the devil's blandishments.

BOTH Luke and John, in their Gospels, attribute his actions to possession by the Devil, John in particular making the point that Judas had been easy prey for Satan because he was such an immoral, greedy character, capable even of stealing money from the apostles' common purse to feather his own nest.

Later, at the start of the Acts of the Apostles, when the 11 gather to elect Matthias as successor to the vacant berth left by Judas's death, Peter adds a new twist to Judas's devilish fate. The first pope revises Matthew's earlier haunting and plausible account of Judas's suicide, and so denies him whatever sliver of atonement might have come with taking his own life.

Instead, Peter insisted, Judas had spent his bloody money on a field — today's Hakeldama, or "Field of Blood", a barren hillside outside the walls of the Old City of Jerusalem — but then had no time to enjoy it, because he fell down on the ground, burst open, and his entrails poured out. It was as if the Devil within him could no longer be contained; a thought that gave subsequent Christian artists plenty of inspiration when they attempted — with a complete disregard for science — to combine both Matthew's account and Peter's in a single image grotesque enough to fit the most hated name in human history.

AT THE ancient French Roman Catholic shrine of Notre-Dame des Fontaines, a fresco cycle of the Passion was painted in primitive style in the 1490s by Giovanni Canavesio. His hanging Judas looks deranged, eyes flashing madly, half in fear, half in threat, his hair a spiky mop.

As he breathes his last, a miniature adult spills out of his open stomach, along with a stream of sweet-potato-like entrails. A golden-winged demon is on hand to catch the child, with the implication that it will continue Judas's treacherous legacy into future generations.

A legacy of treachery: Judas Iscariot Hanging from a Tree, Fresco (1492–1530) by Giovanni Canavesio, Chapel of Notre-Dame des Fontaines, La Brigue, France

Yet, even within the covers of the New Testament, there is another way of reading Judas. In this authorised version, he is less Satan's tool and more God's agent. The earliest of the writings to be found in the New Testament is Paul's first letter to the Corinthians. Here (11.23-24), he writes simply of Jesus's being betrayed (or handed over, depending on which translation you favour) to a hostile authority: the Jewish high priests and their officials.

But when, later, first Mark, then Matthew, Luke, and finally John came to write their Gospels, they decided that this faceless act of betrayal was not enough. They had to name the culprit and chose Judas.

WHY he stood accused is hard to judge. Paul, later in the same letter (15.5), makes plain that all 12 original apostles see the risen Christ. Paul apparently knew of no reason to exclude Judas from the chosen.

Perhaps the writer of Mark did, aware of a detail that had eluded Paul, but had been handed down through the oral tradition. Once he included it in his text, Judas's fate was sealed.

Or was Mark tempted by the symbolism carried in Judas Iscariot's name? Judases were commonplace then (Luke even lists another Judas, "son of James", as also being among the 12). In Hebrew, as *Judah* or *Yehuda*, it came from the verb "to thank" or "praise", but was also synonymous with the tribe of Judah, which, in Jesus's day provided the Jewish establishment.

Making Judas the betrayer among the 12, therefore, was a veiled way of reinforcing the guilt of the Jewish leaders for Jesus's fate, a process helped along by the fact that Yehuda and Yehudi, the Hebrew word for Jew, were so similar.

Equally, Iscariot — which has a harsh ring to it in English, I have long thought — can again be manipulated against the Jews. For the majority view among New Testament scholars (there are, inevitably, plenty of dafter explanations) is that Iscariot means "man of Qeriot" — a town south of Jerusalem, in Judea.

Judas alone of the 12 is identified by his place of origin; and, once again, this distinction made him, potentially, part of the Judean Jewish establishment, hence an easy channel into Jesus's inner circle for the chief priests brandishing 30 pieces of silver. By contrast, the other 11 apostles, and Jesus himself, were Jewish outsiders from Galilee, a place which many observant Jews in Judea regarded as beyond the pale.

FROM this wordy conflation of Judas with the Jews was to come centuries of bloody anti-Semitism, all the way down to the Holocaust in the 20th century. Judas's crimes became Jews' crimes — they were, Christians were taught, greedy, untrustworthy, the traitors inside every community. And that connection proved so potent that, across medieval Europe, each Maundy Thursday the Jewish ghettoes in Christian cities and towns would wait nervously indoors, in case the account of Judas's betrayal, heard from the pulpit, unleashed another wave of anti-Semitic violence.

Was that what Mark had intended when he was the first to name Jesus's betrayer? The fledgling Christian Church may have struggled with separation from its Jewish roots; but he could not have known what was to follow. Yet it took until 1965 for the Roman Catholic Church officially to absolve the Jewish people of the crime of deicide in the Second Vatican Council document *Nostra Aetate*.

HOW different it might have been had the betrayer not been named, as Paul intended. Part of his reticence seems to arise from a sense that the act of betrayal is not important in itself; that it is just one step on Jesus's journey to arrest, trial, death, and resurrection.

And that thought brings us back to the argument that Judas was, in fact, God's agent, and has been the victim these past 2000 years of an appalling miscarriage of justice.

Since, as Christians, we believe that an omnipotent God sent his beloved Son to be born in Bethlehem and die in Jerusalem to save our souls, then everything that happened during Jesus's life was pre-planned and God-given. It is even there, if you listen carefully this Easter, in the words of the Gospels themselves.

In Matthew, as Judas betrays him with a kiss to the soldiers in the Garden of Gethsemane, Jesus says: "My friend, do what you are here for" (26.50). And, in John's account of the Last Supper, just after Jesus has identified Judas as the one who will betray him, he tells the traitor: "What you are going to do, do quickly" (13.27). The clear implication is that Jesus knows exactly what the plan is, and what part Judas will play.

Such a thought probably won't stop football crowds chanting the name Judas, or even politicians accusing each other over the despatch box of being Judases, but it might just help Dylan soothe his anger. For, if Lord Archer gave me one important steer in writing my biography of the renegade apostle, an old Dylan song provided me with another.

A couple of years before that Free Trade Hall incident, he released an anti-war song, "With God On Our Side". One of the verses is all about Judas and his betrayal. "I can't think for you," Dylan sang in that unmistakable nasal voice. "You'll have to decide whether Judas Iscariot had God on his side."

(2015)

Judas, 'mine own familiar friend'

Pamela Tudor-Craig compares the record in scripture and art

THE Passion of Christ includes all the suffering humans can experience. Not only is there unimaginable physical pain, but mocking; the knowledge that those who love you most are suffering too, as helpless witnesses; that those who went around with you and on whom you depended have made themselves scarce — and even Peter, your appointed leader, has denied you to save his own skin.

Worst of all, one of those with whom you loved and shared everything, who has known you as only the inner band of companions could know you, has betrayed you — sold you for the price of a field with good clay under it. Had Christ known all along that Judas was his snake in the grass?

He could rebuke Peter fiercely, but he put Judas in a position of special responsibility, in charge of their resources, and never challenged him before the Last Supper. He then (Matthew 26.23 and Mark 14.20) identified his betrayer as the one who would dip the sop with him, immediately before he instituted the eucharist. The sharing that will go sour is juxtaposed with the provision of spiritual nourishment for the future ages of the Church.

John does not give the words of consecration; so the question whether Judas had already received the Host does not arise in his account. Luke puts the identification of the betrayer immediately after the consecration, but he identifies Judas only as having his hand on the table.

Are we justified in assuming that Christ had really cared for Judas — that he had the ambivalent attitude to him that distracted parents have towards grown children who have determined on the fastest route to ruin? Christ prayed for his disciples at the Last Supper: "While I was with them in the world, I kept them in thy name: those that thou gavest me I have kept, and none of them is lost, except the son of perdition" (John 17.12).

THERE are answers if we read the Bible the way my father used to read musical scores, "hearing" the full orchestral sound in his mind's ear as he turned the pages. No way can we can treat the Bible as a straight line from Genesis to Apocalypse.

The heroic task of synthesising the Evangelists into a single narrative thread has been several times attempted, most conspicuously by the ladies of Little

Kiss of Judas: detail of Giotto's fresco, c.1304–6, in the Scrovegni Chapel, Padua

Gidding in the reign of Charles I. The Concordance project has never quite worked out. In the 1980s, scraps of cut-up Bibles were found by Professor George Henderson in a drawer in the Pepys Library at Cambridge, where they had lain since the Cromwellians scattered the Little Gidding Community. In case they came in handy, the painstaking and scholarly women had saved spare "the"s and "and"s from the Bibles they cut up.

The Evangelists make up a quartet on their own, with the coda of Acts, and the commentary of Paul threading through them. Beyond and behind that lies the further dimension of the Old Testament, filling out the full symphonic texture.

If you use an old-fashioned Bible, there is that narrow margin, filled with cross-references in the tiniest writing down both sides of each page. These give the orchestration, the biblical equivalent of miniature scores. In listening for echoes, we know that the writers of the New Testament could depend on their first readers, especially the Jewish ones, on the Church Fathers, and indeed on the profound scholarship of medieval churchmen, to pick up the undercurrent beneath the line carried by the violins.

IT IS not by chance that it is Matthew, always the first to use the Old Testament cross-currents, who, having identified Judas as "he that dippeth his hand with me in the dish", records Christ addressing him in the garden of Gethsemane as "friend". The bass note lies in Psalm 41.9: "Yea, mine own familiar friend, in whom I trusted, which did eat of my bread, hath lifted up his heel against me."

There is another reverberation in the story of the betrayal. Those who have walked around the wall of Jerusalem, along the narrow valley served by the brook Kidron, to the Garden of Gethsemane have realised that Christ, who followed this sorrowful track on his last free night as a man on earth, was treading in the footprints of his ancestor, King David.

The account of the betrayal of David by his son Absalom begins with the shining loyalty of Ittai the Gittite, only matched among the disciples by John. Ittai refused David's advice to return to his own country since he had arrived "but yesterday". He would not desert his king just as David was leaving Jerusalem for exile in order to avoid conflict with Absalom: "'As my lord the king liveth, surely in what place my lord the king shall be, whether in death or life, even there also will thy servant be' ...

"And all the country wept with a loud voice, and all the people passed over, the king himself also passed over the brook Kidron, and all the people passed over, toward the way of the wilderness" (2 Samuel 15.19-23).

"He went forth with his disciples over the brook Cedron, where was a garden." (John 18.1)

In the thousand years since David's bitter retreat, the "wilderness" on the further hill had been colonised, and Christ was repairing to the Mount of Olives. Just beside the little stony stream, there is enough space on the further bank for a cluster of what look like late-Roman tombs. One of them, resembling Petra in its strange mixture of classical elements, is called the Tomb of Absalom.

As we all know, despite David's resolution to offer no resistance to his son, their armies engaged. Absalom was riding through a wood, "and the mule went under the thick boughs of a great oak, and his head caught hold of the oak, and he was taken up between the heaven and the earth; and the mule that was under him went away" (2 Samuel 18.9). As he hung there still alive, Joab thrust him through the heart.

Absalom had been the most beautiful of David's sons: "In all Israel there was none to be praised as Absalom: from the sole of his foot even to the crown of his head there was no blemish in him. And when he polled his head ... because the hair was heavy upon him ... he weighed the hair of his head at two hundred shekels" (2 Samuel 14.25-26). It is traditionally believed that this thick head of hair had entangled him in the branches.

There follows David's mourning, the most desolate lament of the Old Testament: "The King went up to the chamber over the gate, and as he went thus he said, O my son Absalom, my son, my son Absalom! Would God I had died for thee, O Absalom, my son, my son!" (2 Samuel 18.33).

Judas's death mirrored that of Absalom. He also "was taken up between the heaven and the earth"; for he hanged himself (Matthew 27. 3-10). Christ's disciples — Judas, his lost sheep, among them — in all their incomprehension, their jostling for rank, their cowardice and confused loyalty, were to Christ sons, the gift of his Father.

THE DEATH of Judas was seldom represented in medieval art, but there is one strange example. The scenes of the Passion around the transepts of the Lower Church of San Francesco in Assisi were painted by the Sienese artist Pietro Lorenzetti. Like his brother, the more charming Ambrogio, Pietro disappeared at the Black Death, which hit Italy in 1348.

His representations of Holy Week are among the most poignant ever painted. They include a dramatic version of Christ's encounter with Judas in the garden. The betrayer, striding violently across the foreground in his determination to display a brash familiarity, almost knocks over the Christ who would bless him. In total contrast, in the shadow of a staircase leading from the sanctuary to the friars' apartments, and seldom noticed by the visitor, there is a stark little fresco of Judas hanging from a beam of fictive architecture, a pathetic rag of despair (Matthew 17.1-10).

Medieval biblical scholarship was much governed by the principle of typology. Christ himself used it in referring to Jonah as foreshadowing his resurrection: "For as Jonas was three days and three nights in the body of the whale; so shall the son of man be three days and three nights in the heart of the earth" (Matthew 12.40). There are still insights to be drawn from following up the clues.

(2009)

Cost of betrayal: Judas's Suicide (c.1325–30), fresco by Pietro Lorenzetti (1280–c.1348) in San Francesco, Assisi (Lower Church, western transept, south wing)

The Kingdom of God is now or never

The West, says **Timothy Radcliffe OP**, looks to the future without hope, foreseeing only an endless war against terror. But if we can share the hope to which the Last Supper witnesses, we can offer the world something it longs for

THERE IS a crisis of hope in the Western world. Oliver Bennett, of Warwick University, has argued that, as we begin this new millennium, the West is suffering from a collective depression. We see violence in our cities, gang warfare, escalation of drug abuse; in the wider world there is growing inequality between the rich and poor, the spread of AIDS, the threat of ecological disaster, and, above all, clashes between religions and the spread of terrorism.

Hope is more than feeling cheerful. It is the belief that humanity is on its way to a future. It is the confidence that all that we live will be found to have ultimate meaning. Vaclav Havel, the playwright and former President of the Czech Republic, said: "[Hope] is not the conviction that something will turn out well, but the certainty that something makes sense, regardless of how it turns out."

When I was a child, after the Second World War, there was still the confidence, at least in my little world, that a story could be told about humanity's happier future. Every year the cars and the planes got faster. Countries were liberated from the British Empire; computers appeared on the scene, and they got bigger and bigger — until they became smaller and smaller. Even the food in Britain improved, and you could find frogs' legs and snails in restaurants.

But that was just the last echo of the optimism of our Victorian ancestors. As Charles Dickens wrote, "Time is rolling ... and the world is, in all great essentials, better, gentler, more forbearing, and more hopeful, as it rolls!" (*Pictures from Italy*, 1844). That confidence was lost in two stages.

First of all, after the fall of the Berlin Wall in 1989, we lost any story to tell of the future. As Fukuyama famously wrote, history has ended. We see the arrival of the Now Generation, which lives just for the present moment. Eat, drink and be merry, for we have no idea what will happen tomorrow. There may be merriment and big spending, but it is hopeless: the dream of humanity's future is lost.

Then there was a second moment, more than three years ago: 11 September. Now we do have a story to tell of the future. But it is worse than none at all, because it is the story of the war on terrorism, which promises nothing but violence.

One might say that our children are growing up with just two stories of the future. One is the war on terrorism, endless conflict; the other is the scientific story of the universe, stretching from the Big Bang to the Big Chill, when it will grow cold and dead. Neither story offers us a sense that our lives have meaning, and thus hope.

THIS IS, therefore, potentially a wonderful moment for Christianity. If we can find a way to live and share our Christian hope, then we shall offer something for which the world is thirsting.

So what do we have to share? Do we offer an alternative story of the future? We believe in the ultimate triumph of good over evil, the coming of the Kingdom, the end to all death and suffering. But the trouble is that we have no story to tell of how this may happen. We cannot look at the Book of Revelation and say, "Hi guys, it's OK. Five plagues down and two to go." We have no privileged information about what will happen to humanity in the next 1000 years.

I would say that it is good that we do not. The 20th century was crucified by those who knew the future story of humanity. The Soviet gulags murdered tens of millions of people in the name of the Communist road map to Paradise. In July, I visited Auschwitz for the first time. There is a big map that shows the railway lines from all over Europe leading to the extermination camp. The lines end at the gas chambers: literally, the end of the line. All that planning and mapping of the future ended in despair, and millions of dead.

A few months ago, I visited the Tuol Sleng genocide centre in Phnom Penh. This was one of dozens of places where Pol Pot's regime purified Cambodia of those who stood in the way of his road map. As the bishop, who lived through all this, said to me, "Everyone who spoke a foreign language, wore glasses, was educated or had soft hands died." A third of the population was killed. Every single Cambodian priest was murdered.

So in the past century we saw that those who know where we are going, and how to get there, often end by building the Killing Fields. Many people are deeply fearful that the war on terror may — in the process of becoming another attempt to impose a road map on humanity — lead to yet more slaughter. Our hope, then, is not the possession of a story, a road map for the future. It is to the Last Supper that we must turn to rediscover hope. But, paradoxically, that was also the moment when the disciples lost any story to tell of the future.

On the road to Jerusalem they had been sustained, surely, by some story of what was going to happen: the rebellion against Rome; the restoration of Israel; Jesus as a warrior King? As the disciples on the road to Emmaus said, "We had hoped that he was the one to redeem Israel." But faced with Jesus's Passion and death, they had no story to tell. In this moment in which this fragile community broke down, Jesus took bread, blessed it, and gave it to them, saying, "This is my body, given for you." And likewise with the wine.

Here is a paradox. The story of that Last Supper is our foundational story, the one in which we find the meaning of our lives. And yet it is a story that tells of the moment when there was no story to tell, when the future disappeared. Christians gather, as a community, around the altar and remember the moment when the community disintegrated: when Judas sold Jesus; Peter denied him, and the others mostly ran away. Our founding story is of the collapse of any story.

But the paradox is deeper than that. The documents that describe this event, the Gospels, appear to have been written at a second moment when the story of the future broke down. After the resurrection, the disciples seem to have pinned their hopes on another conclusion of the story: that Jesus would come again soon.

The Church was persecuted in Rome; Peter and Paul died; Christians betrayed each other; it seemed as if the Church was failing. Don't worry: Jesus is coming. But he did not. Not a hint. Again, a story collapsed — but that led to the writing of the Gospels, and our first extended account of the Last Supper. Jesus might not have come in the flesh and in glory, but he came in the words of the Gospels.

So we should know by now that hoping in the Kingdom does not give us a road map. Rather, it takes it away. In both cases, intimacy with the Lord grows as we lose our knowledge of what lies ahead. And so we should not be fearful of crises: the Church was born in a crisis of hope. Crises are our spécialité de la maison. The one that we are living through now is very small.

LET US LOOK at what Jesus did at this moment, because he commanded that we also do it, in remembrance of him. He took bread, blessed it, and broke it, and gave it to the disciples, saying, "This is my body, given for you and for all." What Jesus did was to perform a sign. Our hope is in a sign.

The Last Supper saw the clash of two sorts of power. There was the power of the political and religious authorities. But the story of Jesus is about another sort of power, the power of the sign and of the word. Jesus turns water into wine, opens the eyes of the blind and makes the dumb speak.

This is not a magical power, as if he were a first-century Gandalf. It is the power of meaning and of truth. As Jesus says to Pilate, "For this I was born, and for this I have come into the world, to bear witness to the truth. Everyone who is of the truth hears my voice." Pilate replies, "What is truth?" and notoriously does not wait for an answer. He does not need to, since he has the armies.

The Last Supper, then, is the clash of the power of brute force and the power of the sign; between the power of Pilate, and the power of the vulnerable man who takes bread and breaks it, and shares it in the face of death. Every eucharist is a celebration of our trust that, in Christ, meaning will triumph in ways that we cannot guess or anticipate.

This sort of power may seem ineffectual faced with the powers of this world, the powers of force and money. Especially it may seem so to us, who grew up in the world built on the Industrial Revolution. It was a world founded on the harnessing of the brute force of steam and coal, of electricity, ultimately of the atom.

This was linked with the triumph of imperial military powers competing to control the world. It was brute force at the service of a particular story: Western triumph. In particular, we English people were driven by a myth that we were God's chosen people, and force was justified in service of that myth. Now the Americans are heirs to that same myth.

But our world is changing. We see the signs of the ending of the Industrial Revolution. Its old heavy industries are largely finished. We live in a new world, which Zygmunt Bauman, of Leeds University, has called "liquid modernity". In this world, what circulates is not so much heavy goods as images, logos, symbols and signs.

In this new world, the strange Christian centring on the power of signs and symbols may not seem so silly, after all. If we can find signs of hope, then the world will be attentive, and transmit them around the internet in a jiffy. Think of that small and vulnerable figure in front of a tank in Tiananmen Square.

Of course, the terrorists who planned 9/11 understood this very well. The destruction was terrible, beyond words. But it was a most powerful symbolic happening. It used the symbols of modern communication, jet planes, to smash into the centres of military and business communication. Its violent symbolism spoke of non-communication, of the rejection of mediating words. That is why the effective responses can be only through other gestures that speak of creativity and forgiveness, and which gather Christians and Muslims into communion. Think of the firemen working in the ruins and giving their own lives.

One small example: some US Dominicans marked the first anniversary of 9/11 by holding a month-long fast of just water. There were brethren, sisters, and a lay Dominican. Others joined just for a short time, as I did myself, or for a couple of weeks. We camped in Union Square, just north of Ground Zero, and we spoke every day to hundreds of people who came to question us and read our pamphlets. Many Jews and Muslims joined us for prayers three times a day.

What astonished me was that the symbolic meaning of fasting was immediately understood, even by the young. And every day there were TV cameras and journalists to transmit it.

Admittedly it does not seem to have had much effect. There is no record of Bush phoning Blair to discuss cancelling the war because the Dominicans were fasting in New York. But I believe it is through a care for the meaning of what we say and do that we open windows for God's transforming grace in the world.

In *The Merchant of Venice*, Portia says: "How far that little candle throws his beams, So shines a good deed in a naughty world." It is part of our Christian faith that small deeds may reshape reality, because they may be a window through which we are in contact with the omnipotent Lord of the universe. The smallest deeds can belong to the Almighty God, speaking his word.

Jesus did not just make a sign. It was a creative and transforming act. He was to be handed over to his enemies, entrusted by one of his own disciples to the brutal power of the empire. He did not passively accept this: he transformed it into a moment of grace. He made his betrayal into a moment of gift. He said: "So you will hand me over and run away; well, I grasp this handing-over and make a gift of myself to you."

To hope is not just to bet on goodness being stronger than evil. It is not to say that God will have the last word, like the hero in a Western who gallops in at the last moment to save us. Our hope is in the infinite creativity of God, who brings good out of evil, and communion out of disaster.

WHAT are the creative signs that you can imagine or remember? My first is from the time when I was in Burundi during the ethnic conflicts between Hutus and Tutsis. One year I went to visit the community of Dominican nuns in the north of the country. It was a really dangerous trip. We were stopped by the army, who tried to prevent us from going ahead, because there were battles. We found a whole busload of people killed. We were shot at, I think. The country was brown and dead. All the crops were burned. And then, in the distance, we saw a green hill, and that was where the monastery was.

The nuns were both Tutsi and Hutu: it was one of the few places were the groups lived together in peace and love. They had all lost nearly all their families in the slaughter. Only one, a young novice, had been spared; and while we were there we had the news of the annihilation of her family, too. They always listened to the news together, so that they could share all that happened. Slowly people from all the groups came to gather in their church to pray, and to grow their crops in this safe place. It was a green place in a brown and burned land; and a sign of hope.

Another example is of a completely different sort. In 1966, Pope Paul VI and Archbishop Michael Ramsey celebrated together an ecumenical liturgy in St Paul Without the Walls, in Rome. They signed a declaration affirming their desire for unity. And then Paul VI asked the Archbishop to remove his ring, and slipped on to his finger his own ring, which he had worn as Archbishop of Milan. Ramsey burst into tears, and wore the ring for the rest of his life. It is the ring that Archbishop Rowan Williams wore when he visited Pope John Paul II.

Such gestures create community, and transform relationships. After 9/11, we have to use our imagination. What gestures might we make that will create community between Christians and Islam? What daring things might we do together?

THE Last Supper did not just point to the future. In a sense, the future broke in, then. What the disciples longed for was anticipated at that moment.

As Christians, we hope for eternity. But eternity is not what happens at the end of time. It is not what happens after we die. It begins now, whenever we share God's life; whenever we manage to overcome hatred with love. I wrote of the Now Generation as living only in the present moment, but this is not strictly true. It lives for what is just about to happen, for the gratification that is about to be given, for the purchase that is about to be made.

Hope means daring to find God's eternity glancing through the clouds now. To be hopeful is to live in the present moment. Meister Eckhart, the 14th-century Dominican, wrote: "What is today? Today is eternity." Over the entrance to the Deer Park Buddhist monastery in the United States is a sign that reads: "The Kingdom of God is now or never."

The celebration of the eucharist is a sacrament of our hope for the Kingdom. But the Kingdom is glimpsed now. We can rest in its celebration. The future is here.

So, if we are to be a sign of hope, then we must ask what signs we can make that will help us to have a glimpse of the future among us. The most moving Christmas vigil that I have ever attended was in Paris in 1995. It was the Christmas mass for the tramps, celebrated in a big tent in the centre of Paris. All the destitute, the homeless, and the bums were invited. A thousand came.

It was a celebration of intense, if sometimes befuddled, happiness. The altar was made of cardboard, to celebrate the Christ who was born for all those who live in cardboard boxes today. When Pedro pulled the cork of the wine bottle at the offertory, cheers rang out. Afterwards everyone was invited to a superb banquet. That was a sign of the Kingdom. That was a gesture that reached across the divisions of rich and poor, and spoke of the joy of the Kingdom now.

Anniversaries celebrate the passing of time. But hope is the virtue that keeps young. It is the virtue of eternal youth. St Augustine says that "God is younger than all else." We grow old, but God remains for ever younger than us. Hope expresses his eternal youthfulness, his ever-vibrant freshness.

Every year we celebrate our birthdays. We celebrate that we are one year older. But when we celebrate Christ's birthday, we celebrate the fact that God was born among us as a child. We will not celebrate, this Christmas, that Jesus is 2005 years old, but that he is newborn, always at the beginning.

The crisis of hope through which we are living is painful. But it is my trust that it will lead to a renewal of the Church, a rejuvenation. These periodic crises of hope are, for the Church, like the fire for the phoenix. We emerge again as younger.

What will this new, younger Church look like? I trust that it will be humbler, simpler, less optimistic, but more deeply rooted in hope; less clerical and more Christ-like.

I went back to Rwanda after the genocide. A Canadian Dominican who had worked there for 25 years took me to see the ruins of where he had lived. So many friends had died, and all his life's work seemed to be destroyed. We wept together. But the following Christmas he sent me a photograph of himself holding two Rwandan babies. And on the back he wrote, "Africa has a future." Because of the child whose birth we celebrate with each passing year, we can also say, "Humanity has a future."

(2005)

Keepers of the Queen's purse

No foot-washing, money that cannot be cashed — has the
Royal Maundy had its day? **William Whyte** thinks not

IN 1961, the people of Rochester gathered in the cathedral on the Thursday
of Holy Week. They were there to see the Queen participate in the Royal
Maundy service — an event that they believed had first been celebrated in
the city nearly 750 years before. This year (2010), the people of Knaresborough
will meet in their parish church on the Thursday of Holy Week to commem-
orate what they believe was the first ever Royal Maundy service, held there
exactly 800 years ago.

Maundy Thursday is a day that seems to inspire confusion, claim, and
counterclaim. It is a rich source of historical myth. We do not even know
for sure how it got its name: perhaps it comes from the Saxon word "mand",
which describes a sort of wicker basket in which alms and gifts of food
might be presented; or perhaps it originates in the medieval term "maund",
meaning "to beg".

Or it might be inspired by the word *mandatum*, taken from the moment
in John's Gospel where Jesus declares: "A new command I give you"
("*Mandatum novum do vobis*"). This, after all, is how the Maundy service
begins — although it has done so only in relatively recent times.

Not everyone calls it Maundy Thursday, either. In the north of England,
it was traditionally known as "Kiss Thursday", in remembrance of Judas's
final betrayal. For many medieval men and women, it was the Birthday of
the Chalice, in recollection of the Last Supper. Others knew it as White
Thursday, the day when the vestments were changed from Lenten purple.
Others, again, believed it was a time set aside to readmit penitents to the
Church, and called it Remission Day. To this day, it is also described as
Holy Thursday, Great Thursday, or even the Thursday of the Mysteries.

As this suggests, the problem with the Thursday of Holy Week is not
that it has been seen as unimportant, but that it has always had to mean
such a great deal. In the Middle Ages, it was one of the most complex days
of the liturgical year, having no fewer than seven separate services.

There was mass. There was tenebrae, in which deep silence is juxtaposed
with great noise, and the church gradually vanishes into darkness with the
extinguishing of candles. There was a service for the reconciliation of
penitents, and another for the blessing of oils. There was the stripping of

the altars, and the giving of a loving cup. What we now know as the Maundy service was only a small part of the day.

THE Maundy itself had two elements to it: the *pedilavium,* or washing of feet, and the giving of alms. The origins of both stretch back in time, and are probably now unrecoverable. Given the example Christ gave by washing the disciples' feet at the Last Supper, it is not impossible that it is an extremely ancient observance. It is mentioned by many of the Church Fathers, and by 694 the Council of Toledo had firmly fixed the *pedilavium* as an important feature of Holy Thursday. It is likely, too, that Augustine brought the practice to England in about 600.

But the washing of feet was never confined to Maundy Thursday. In some English monasteries, before 1066, it was carried out weekly, or even daily. Oswald, the saintly Archbishop of York, is reported to have died in 922 "whilst according to the usual custom he was observing the usual Maundy before the feet of the poor". This does not mean, however, that he expired in Holy Week — he practised the *pedilavium* every day during Lent.

Nor was the giving of gifts on Maundy Thursday always confined to monarchs. Great nobles and churchmen also doled out alms. One of the great disputes between Catherine of Aragon and Henry VIII was whether she could "keep her Maundy" after their divorce.

In the end, in 1536, Henry relented — although he made it clear "The King is content if she does not keep it as Queen; if so, she and others would be guilty of high treason." So Catherine was free to give gifts to the needy, but only on condition that she did so as a private individual.

As the rivalry between Rochester and Knaresborough suggests, the origin of the Royal Maundy is particularly ambiguous. Indeed, if the service performed at Knaresborough in 1210 was the first of its kind (and it seems likely that it was), then it was a somewhat unpromising event.

RECORDS show that King John doled out 13 pence to 13 paupers on the Thursday before Easter. John was not, of course, a famously religious figure, and critics have even suggested that the number 13 was chosen as a cabbalistic act against the Pope. It seems likely, however, that that effort was intended to demonstrate his piety as he acted in imitation of Christ.

A similar impulse doubtless shaped the pious Edward II's decision, about 100 years later, to introduce the *pedilavium* to the Royal Maundy Service.

The Royal Maundy now has nothing to do with the washing of feet, and only a little to do with almsgiving. The only relics of the *pedilavium* are the linen towels worn by the officers attending. The charitable aspects are also merely symbolic: the Queen hands out two small purses containing the

Queen Elizabeth II distributing the Maundy money during the Royal Maundy Service at St George's Chapel in Windsor

coins — one for every year of her life — to a hand-picked group of elderly people. The coins are specially minted for the occasion, and it is a considerable honour to be chosen to receive them. But the money is limited, and none of those who receive the coins are dependent upon them.

After 800 years, Holy Thursday is now marked — by the monarch at least — by a Maundy that has no foot-washing, and an almsgiving in which the alms are simply tokens. One might, indeed, be forgiven for thinking that it is an event that has had its day.

SUCH a view was certainly taken in the 18th and 19th centuries. No monarch participated in the Maundy Thursday service from 1698 until 1932. The revival of the service is due, more than anything else, to the current Queen, who displays more enthusiasm for it than almost any of her predecessors.

She has used it as an opportunity to travel around the country: since 1957, the Royal Maundy has moved to a different city each year. It has consequently become part of the modern monarch's armoury: in the same way as opening a hospital or visiting a school, it shows that she is in touch.

Ambiguous in its origins, uncertain in its meaning, and constantly hijacked by secular themes, a cynic might see the Royal Maundy as not merely outdated but actively unchristian. It was a means of asserting royal power in the

Middle Ages, and has become yet another photo opportunity in the modern world. Yet such a negative response would, I think, be a mistake.

FOR one thing, the Royal Maundy reminds us about the importance of power and hierarchy in the Bible. In our egalitarian world, we are inclined to play down these themes — rejecting talk of kings and rulers in favour of a sort of Republic of Heaven. We are also tempted to look at the events of Holy Thursday through the same distorted lens, focusing on Jesus's washing of the feet principally as a sign of equality and self-abasement.

In doing so, we ignore his words, "You call me Teacher and Lord — and you are right, for that is what I am," and we disregard his actions. Washing the disciples' feet against their will was an act of power, proof of his authority over them. The monarchs of the past were better able to see this, and that is why they were willing to kneel down before the poor each Maundy Thursday. It did not diminish their dominance — it demonstrated it.

In the second place, the changing meanings of the Maundy illustrate a wider truth about Christian worship. They reveal its capacity for reinvention and reinterpretation. On Maundy Thursday this year, a service first performed 800 years ago will be re-enacted — despite the fact that its imminent demise was predicted nearly 150 years ago.

What's more, it will be watched by a larger group of people than ever before. It will mean something new, and be different from the previous occasions, but none the less it will draw on a tradition that goes back centuries. In an age in which faith itself sometimes seems threatened, the service now stands as a symbol of both continuity and change: proof of Christianity's ability to transcend time and be reimagined in each generation.

We should rejoice in the ambiguities of Maundy Thursday; for, just as it did for those who went before, it offers us a space to innovate — the opportunity to create something new out of something very old.

(2010)

This Easter

for they were afraid – Mark 16.8

by **David Scott**

This Easter I shall paint
the walls a Jerusalem colour:
the green hill, the cockerel's crimson throat,
the purple pillar; and time will
fall into hours, the third, the sixth,
the ninth, into ethereal time.
It could be any time as I walk through town,
sensitive yet unbodied, feeling the weight
of the lowering of Christ, and smelling
the sacrificial hot-cross buns.

Why am I so keen to stay with death
and sorrow, so cautious of the light,
and all that yellowness? I am with the women,
falling off the end of the Gospel,
afraid. This year I may learn to fall
and not fear, and find myself lifted
to watch the face of forgiveness rise
with such silence and uncanny grace,
that with the thrush, high in the holly tree,
I will sing, **unique … unique … unique.**

(2002)

Word from Wormingford

Not mad, noble *Lepus*,
Ronald Blythe says

CLIMBING the high ground above the house, we find four hares about their amorous business, to us "mad", but to them in very heaven. They actually occupy a square of field, boxing about in separate corners, and are so absorbed in their ungainly courtship that they fail to see three humans and a dog until we are within yards of their love. Then — off in four directions.

"*Lepus*!" I want to call after them. "That is your name. Take no notice of all the things we men have burdened you with, that you can change your sex, that you can sleep with one eye open, that you are able to dance in time to music, that you herald a death, that you attend the goddess Freya. Let us be honest, like John Clare, and, if we must, describe you as "tasty".

"But he frequently saw what we are seeing now:

The timid hares throw daylight fears away
On the lane road to dust and dance and play.

"What you have done this April noon is to halt us, too, in our tracks. Given us pause. Your watchers have been baffled by your innocence, your limping towards your fate."

Richard Jefferies marvelled how hares would "come as it were to meet people on country roads" and continued, "Of all sport, if a man desires to widen his chest, and gain some idea of the chase as it was in ancient days, let him take two good greyhounds and 'uncouple at the timorous flying hare', following himself on foot.

"A race like this over the elastic turf of the downs, inhaling with expanded lungs air which acts on the blood as strong drink on the brain, stimulating the pulse, and strengthening every fibre of the frame, is equal to another year of life." These are the words of a young consumptive.

Someone else is being hunted all this week. Passiontide — *passio* = suffering. Someone else is being terrorised, brought down, raised high. Sad hymns allow us no more than a glimpse of his redemptive suffering, first mental then physical, then both at once during the climax of his pain.

The readings are dark, but stabbed through with brilliant light.

Who is this? None other, says the writer of Hebrews, than "the effulgence of God's splendour and the stamp of his being". What, we ask ourselves, "this poor creature sweating blood as he comes to the inevitable result of his teaching!" We learn that "he hid" before he arrived where he would be tracked down.

And what have we learned since then? If you look at the screen, only new ways to be cruel. The Gulf's questions and uncertainties increase by the hour as the three desert-bred faiths interlock with destruction and their politics become more questionable. How awkward for those who make war these days that channel after channel ensures that we see every bit of it. Could journalism finish fighting? Eventually? The reports are unsparing.

It is very cold at night. Bottengoms is a celebrated frost pocket and the hares' field shines as white and stiff as a cake under a slice of moon. But the greengage blossom is well out of it and should survive, being sheltered by naked oaks. My neighbour arrives cockahoop, having successfully patented a tool for planting bulbs, and can now advertise it on the internet.

Two elderly ladies pass the time of day — the daughters of farmworkers from over the river, the latter pretty well near-mythic people in our countryside in 2003. Did they see the hares?

(2003)

Hands that do nothing stay dirty

Good Friday: Pilate could have done something,
says **Samuel Wells**. So can we

ON Good Friday, all eyes are on Jesus. But I'd like to suggest that some should be on Pontius Pilate. The cross of Jesus is the condemnation of the world and the vindication of God. And no one is more condemned than the man of conventional power, Pontius Pilate.

Matthew and Mark portray Pilate as an expert political manipulator, who succeeds in disposing of an apparent threat to his authority while at no stage appearing to shoulder any culpability for doing so. Luke's account suggests that Pilate underestimates Jesus, but that Pilate disposes of him in order to maintain his alliance with the Jerusalem authorities. John presents the starkest narrative, in which Jesus is the light of truth that exposes the emptiness of Pilate and the profound betrayal of the Temple leadership.

These readings transform our understanding of Jesus's death and the reasons for it. The political option Jesus represented is no remote or abstract ideal: it is a live option today. Here I shall highlight two moments in the story of Jesus and Pilate which demonstrate the heart of God and the emptiness of the Roman world.

The first is the moment when Pilate washes his hands (Matthew 27.24). It is a moment that has passed into proverb and cliché, and become part of the vocabulary of self-justification. But it must not be forgotten that it is a charade. Pilate wants the crowd to believe that Jesus's death is no responsibility of his. (He has succeeded in persuading untold numbers of the Gospel's Christian readers of his spin on Jesus's execution.) But he is the governor. He has absolute power. Jesus has come before him, and he disposes of Jesus.

So the first thing the Passion narrative teaches about politics is to be very sceptical about anybody who wants to sigh and say: "Really, there's nothing I can do." There is plenty that Pilate can do – but he has established at the beginning that Jesus is a threat, so everything that he does from then on is directed to destroying Jesus. Washing hands is just a cynical smokescreen.

But what about the more charitable reading? In the more charitable reading, Pilate has his hand forced by the fanaticism of the crowd. In this case, the fault still lies with Pilate. Pilate has no reason to let the crowd force his hand. This is not a democracy (even though the crowd scene falsely suggests it is): he is the governor, and no one in Judaea can oust him.

The second lesson of this narrative is that those in power do no good by failing to realise the power they have. Power is not wrong, or bad, or inherently corrupt: it is given for a purpose – to reflect the truth, to set people free – and only becomes sinister when it is not used for the purpose for which it has been given.

Few people today have a monopoly of political power in the way Pilate had. But many people have overwhelming power in smaller spheres – families, churches, voluntary organisations, neighbourhoods, businesses, hospital wards, classrooms, building sites, football stands. Such people need to learn from the Gospel accounts of Pontius Pilate.

It is deeply manipulative to set someone up to be crucified, and at the last minute so arrange things that one can deny all responsibility. It is no use allowing others to prevail upon you through persistence, passion, or emotional blackmail, if you are in a position where you alone have the power to be just.

Who has such power? The shareholder has the power to oust directors who will not steer their company in the ways of fair and sustainable practices. The voter has the power to unseat a government or local authority that mishandles power. The trustee has the power to intervene in a voluntary organisation that is being turned into the poodle of its chief executive.

The union member has the power to invoke restraint on oppressive practices or harassment in the workplace. The shopper has the power to purchase fairly traded goods and shun the products of corporations that mistreat their staff or environment. The football fan has the power to speak to the police about racist chanting in the stands.

On one housing estate, there was a large empty field, fenced off by the county council. Local residents had often asked to be able to use it for sport and recreation, but there were always civic reasons why it was not possible – mostly referring to the debris on the park and fears of litigation.

One morning, two local parents arranged for a street of children to clear the park of cans, bottles, and other litter. They made sure the newspapers were aware. They did not tear down the fences, but they carefully dismantled all the local authority's reasons for keeping the fences up. Soon soccer matches were being played on the field.

The council seemed to be able to find money for equipment after all. It became obvious that plans to sell the park to a large retail developer would be politically disastrous. Those two parents began with a bottle clear-up. Within weeks, they had a youth movement. It turned out they were not as powerless as everyone initially thought.

It is no use saying: "Really, there's nothing I can do." Politics begins when I realise that there is plenty I can do. Discipleship begins when I realise that what I must do is to do what Jesus did.

John's account of the meeting of Jesus and Pilate shows the emptiness of Pilate's "inside", of the "inside" of his regime in Judaea, and ultimately of the "inside" of the whole Roman Empire. It is summed up in his question: "What is truth?"

Pilate is running a ruthlessly efficient machine. It makes the common people powerless subjects, and the social, political, and religious élites willing quislings; and it makes him exceptionally wealthy. Like most ruthless bureaucracies, it doesn't pause too long to ask the question why. The justification for almost every venture is that it will maintain the status quo.

Pilate's world is not so far from today's world as may at first appear. What they have in common is that truth is a difficult thing to talk about. On a famous occasion, Alastair Campbell intercepted a telling question to

What is Truth?
*(Christ before
Pilate), 1890,
by Nikolay Ghe,
Tretyakov Gallery,
Russia*

45

Tony Blair with the unforgettable words "We don't do God." In other words, please don't dig down to the truth issues. We're trying to run a bureaucracy that keeps most people happy most of the time. It gets us re-elected. Don't unsettle the equilibrium by asking why.

This incident displayed vividly how public life in Western democracies has settled for an instrumental notion of truth. Something is true if it works: it gets you to the next place. No one ever discusses what the last place is.

For example, in Britain people work very hard so their children can go to the best school. They either work hard to get a good salary to pay school fees, or they work hard to earn enough money to buy a house in the catchment area of a good state school, or they work hard to argue with the education authorities to get their child into such a school.

At the best school, pupils work hard to get to the best university. Once there, people work hard to get the best results. The best results enable them to get the best jobs. But what are the best jobs? The ones that make enough money to send one's children to the best schools, of course.

This is what I mean by an instrumental notion of truth and value. It is a circle from which I cannot escape, until I find a different way of defining the word "best".

For Pilate, all that was to be hoped for was more of the same. Jesus asked him why. He had no answer. Jesus stretched Pilate's imagination further than it was able to go, and Pilate snapped, and went out to resume his merciless taunting of the Jerusalem authorities.

Pilate couldn't imagine an order not founded on the threat of violent military force, a competition Rome would always win. But Jesus pointed to an empire not founded on force – an emperor who set his people free, a life not bounded by death. And he called this "the truth". You can see Pilate's brow furrowing, the eyes finding it hard to focus, the solid legs beneath him beginning to shake.

Does Jesus stretch our imaginations? Do we allow him to challenge our instrumental notions of truth? Do we take the risk of letting him dismantle the deftly prepared high-tech presentations that tell us how to make our companies, organisations or families richer, safer, fitter, stronger? Does it suddenly begin to strike us that we are Pilate in this story, saying to Jesus: "Don't disturb my carefully-ordered world. Don't look at me like that. I'm not powerful. I'm not a manipulator. I'm not a person who finds it best to avoid asking why. I'm not. I'm not. I'm not … Am I?"

(2006)

A journey through silence

In a Good Friday reflection, **Paul Cowan** considers silence
and its abusive and redemptive power

AT THE beginning of the year, with about 50 other clergy, I was invited to join the Archbishop of Canterbury for a three-day pilgrimage to Auschwitz-Birkenau. It was to be an opportunity to reflect on the nature and reality of human evil, and what this means for the mission, pastoral care, and leadership of the Church.

As we walked through the snow from the retreat centre where we were staying to the camp, in temperatures well below zero, I wondered how anyone could have survived even a single winter. We filed under the notorious entrance sign "*Arbeit Macht Frei*" ("Work sets you free"), and the conversations quietened and then ceased entirely. It felt impossible to comprehend the enormity of what happened in the place, despite the best efforts of our guides.

Before the visit, I was encouraged to read Lamentations. Predicting that I would struggle to concentrate, I decided to read the text aloud, and was struck by the power and urgency of the lament, the raw honesty of its questioning. I found myself reading at a pace and adding a sense of protest to my inflection: "Is it nothing to you, all you who pass by? Look and see if there is any sorrow like my sorrow, which was brought upon me, which the Lord inflicted on the day of his fierce anger."

As Jesus carried his cross to Golgotha, how many "passed by"? How many of his followers and friends fell silent, and hid themselves away? Acts of compassion and empathy, of walking alongside in solidarity — endeavouring, with Simon of Cyrene, to share the burden — are always costly, yet Jesus taught us that it is in this sacrificial place, among the poor and suffering, that we will find holy ground.

I ALSO read Laurence Rees's book *Auschwitz*, and came to appreciate more deeply how invasion and occupation brought a fear that had the power to silence entire nations. A pernicious silence enveloped not only those who were herded onto cattle trucks, but also those who "passed by": the neighbours who watched it happen. Martin Luther King once said that "in the end, we will remember not the words of our enemies, but the silence of our friends". Silence, or certainly the lack of an opportunity to speak, is often the experience of victims of injustice.

Barbed wire at Auschwitz

Clearly, silence is not always a holy state. Throughout history, abusers of power have found ways to quell the prophetic voices that call for justice, love, peace, and the protection of the vulnerable. As King Amaziah said to the prophet Amos, "O seer, go, flee away to the land of Judah, earn your bread there, and prophesy there; but never again prophesy at Bethel."

Jesus's disciples, too, were silenced by the power of the oppressor: we remember Peter, overcome by his fear, denying any connection with Jesus. I wonder how many people across Europe in the past century have fallen silent, minimised, or denied their relationship to the despised and persecuted "other", and, with Peter, have carried a crushing secret guilt?

And, overarching the silence of the individuals, there is the terrible sense of God's silence, both at the cross and on every other occasion of human suffering before and since. The cry of "Where are you?" echoes throughout the Hebrew scriptures. How often have we cried out for divine intervention, but heard nothing; prayed for an end to the horror, and yet the sun goes down on yet another day of suffering?

'My God, my God, why have you forsaken me?'

YET, as the group of clergy continued through the camp, I had a growing sense that I was walking on holy ground — even though this feels like a strange thing to write about a place of industrialised evil. The camps are more than a museum: they give voice to those who were not heard, and who died here in secret.

How necessary the silence suddenly seemed in giving us space to hear the voices of others, especially as we embarked on a Stations of the Cross walk around Birkenau camp. Our guide, the Revd Dr Manfred Deselaers, a Roman Catholic priest, encouraged us to listen in four ways: to the voices from the earth, to the voice of our own hearts, to the voice of the other, and to the voice of God.

This four-fold exercise in listening is perhaps a good framework for a rule of life, and one that resonates with our three Anglican sources of authority, which call us to listen attentively to Scripture, tradition, and reason.

If we are to honour our Anglican foundations, we need to learn pathways to a holy silence that listens to God through Scripture; through the voices of the saints who have gone before us; and through our hearts, our reason, and the voice of the other — particularly the marginalised, the vulnerable, and those with whom we passionately disagree.

The disciplines of counselling, arbitration, and mediation also rely on the ability to listen well — disciplines that we have recently been nurturing, and need to continue to develop in the Church as we struggle with contentious issues.

I wonder what the voices of the Auschwitz earth would say to us in the Church of England today? Saints past and present, we are all God's children, with a voice to be listened to and honoured.

THE silence we kept that day in the camps was not only wholly appropriate in response to the evidence of such appalling suffering, but also the only way in which any of us could encounter God that day in such a place; for "silence is the way God speaks to us," St John of the Cross said.

A former CBS anchor, Dan Rather, once found himself unprepared for a television interview with Mother Teresa. "When you pray," he asked, "what do you say to God?"

"I don't say anything," she replied. "I listen."

He tried another tack: "Well, OK, when God speaks to you, then, what does he say?"

"He doesn't say anything. He listens."

The interviewer looked bewildered. For an instant, he did not know what to say.

"And if you don't understand that," Mother Teresa went on, "I can't explain it to you."

As I look back on the way I prayed as a young adult, I am reminded of the prophets of Baal trying to light a fire. The few gaps I left were an attempt to squeeze responses out of God. But I have since learnt to treasure silence, and surrender my need for God to dance to my tune.

In juxtaposition to the prophets of Baal, Elijah encountered God in the "sound of sheer silence". Job's friends were doing well in support of their suffering friend, until they stopped listening and started talking.

There is, at both Auschwitz and the foot of Christ's cross on Good Friday, a deep sense of holy ground that must be approached in silence. Each serves as a mirror, starkly revealing our personal and corporate brokenness and potential for evil. Might it be that there is holy ground to be found by all who venture to sit in compassionate silence in places of suffering? In the present day, standing near me in the world, who are the people whose voices I need to listen to?

'Behold your son. Behold your mother.'

UNSURPRISINGLY, many who arrived at the camps as people of faith rejected the God who appeared to be utterly silent. Others continued to find solace and strength from their faith while surrounded by evil.

Eliezer Wiesel's account, in his book *Night,* of witnessing a child being hanged strikes at the heart of the matter: "Behind me, I heard the same man asking: 'Where is God now?' And I heard a voice within me answer him: 'Here He is — He is hanging here on this gallows.'"

After this experience, Wiesel writes of his desire to reject God, but that he still finds himself praying. There is, somewhere deep within him, a flicker of faith that refuses to be extinguished. Indeed, I have seen this incredible inextinguishable flame time and again throughout my ministry, in people who have suffered dreadfully in their lives.

Martin Scorsese's film *Silence* is the story of suffering at the hands of fellow human beings, in which torturers try to force a Jesuit priest, Fr Rodriguez, to reject his Christian faith. The film continually takes us back, through Fr Rodriguez's memory, to the image of an icon by El Greco of the face of Christ at the time of his crucifixion.

The wonder of an icon is that it can speak to us in different ways at different times, giving enough to nurture our devotion while leaving space for our individual prayers and journey — and so the crucifix is a mirror that reflects humanity's propensity for evil, and yet also a window through which we see God's limitless love.

It is tempting to gloss over the pain of Good Friday with a conclusion that hints at the joy and celebration of Easter Day, just as it is tempting to join Job's friends in the jump to comfortable answers and explanations.

But Good Friday is a day to remain alongside those in dark valleys, who need the freedom and space to contemplate — even rage at — the God who is absent, yet always present; the God who can be rejected, yet never escaped from; the God who is silent, yet never stops whispering to our yearning hearts.

'Father, into your hands I commend my spirit.'

(2017)

Power of healing is placed in our hands

We are called to live out Christ's defeat — and thus become his co-redeemers, says **Steven Shakespeare**

"YOU KNOW you'll always be on the losing side ..."

I remember the conversation even today. I was 18 years old, still at school. I had decided to go away and do theology at university, much against the wishes of some members of my Christian Union, who felt I would be forced to ask too many questions. It was a nervous, exciting time, and I was feeling the first stirrings of a vocation to ordination.

I shared this with a friend who was not a Christian. He obviously thought I was crazy. Why would anyone want to front a declining, discredited institution? Why put yourself in the position of "always being on the losing side"? I can't remember what I said at the time. I doubt it was very profound. But the question has stayed with me, slumbering.

IT WAS recently prodded into wakefulness again. I took a visiting theology professor to meet church and community activists in Everton, near where Liverpool Hope University has a campus, to discuss justice and empowerment. The local parish priest, who has been involved in community action for many years, was talking about the contribution Christians can make. He said: "We have to learn to fight losing battles."

It made me sit up and take notice. Here we were, talking about how people could overcome the dead hand of fatalism and learn to act for themselves, to speak with confidence. And suddenly we were talking a different language, about loss and failure. What was going on?

I ADMIT to being allergic to the rhetoric of failure that some Christians seem to be in love with. "All pain, no gain" is a version of the gospel that is envious of success, dismissive of achievement, and self-indulgent in its pessimism. When self-sacrifice is made the beginning and end of religion, all God's delight in creation is snuffed out.

If we develop a martyr complex, it becomes easy to believe that suffering is good in itself. It's a seductive idea, but also a dangerous one. It feeds the attitude that if the poor put up with their lot, if women accept a beating from their partner, if gays force themselves to be celibate, then they will all be more Christ-like. The pain will purge them, make them holier.

But Christ didn't come to nail us to a cross and leave us there. His Passion is also a protest. It exposes the machinery of sadism for what it is: power at the service of fear.

Our conversation in that inner-city community centre was about a different kind of power. Christians had no monopoly on struggles for dignity and justice, for decent housing and healthcare. What they brought to the table was an imagination shaped by the cross and resurrection. They were willing to fight losing battles, not because they loved failure, but simply because it was the right thing to do. It was the process of struggle that gave them a new heart, a new identity — and a glimpse of what real victory meant.

IT IS no secret that the theology of atonement — of how Jesus's death reconciles us to God — is in a tangle. The Reformers sought to free Christians from the idea that they could earn or buy salvation, and emphasised the free initiative of God. The Son takes the punishment for our sins on himself, and we do nothing to deserve that offer of grace.

The problem is: what comes next? How do we live? Unfortunately, a new religion of puritanical, obsessive moralism can rush in to fill the vacuum. I have seen how vulnerable students join intense Christian groups that try to police their behaviour, and warn them that, if they are not good and pure, God will abandon them to the devil.

It is a sad irony that the most extreme forms of belief in election and predestination can lead to the most anxiety-fuelled attempts constantly to "please" God and prove oneself worthy of God's love.

Arguably, this is a by-product of the lingering idea that God always demands a price for forgiving us. God's justice demands blood, sacrifice, and pain. And even when we are told that Jesus has paid the price, fear and guilt can still set the agenda for our faith.

WHAT IF we started from a different place? What if we did atonement theology from the streets surrounding that community centre? How would it look?

We would have to begin by listening to the real lives of people, before imposing our theological theories. And we'd have to understand that one of the problems is that, too often, people in such situations feel that things are "done to" them. Decisions are taken without consultation; stereotypes are peddled without knowledge. A theology that makes people simply passive, and then anxious to please, will not be a theology of liberation.

Paradoxically, it's the idea of fighting a losing battle that helps us here. For that is what Jesus did: he lost. But in the process, he fought and struggled, so that a new freedom from violence and oppression came into being. He fought, not through force, but through refusing to submit to and be defined by the political and religious establishment. He would not become a pale reflection of their fear and domination.

SO, Jesus resisted. And his strange victory called a new kind of community into being. That community is called to a new way of life, which is not simply about being good, or desperately trying to recruit people to shore up its power. It is first and foremost called to be a community that knows it is accepted, and which ultimately, therefore, has nothing to fear.

Think of the imagery used in the New Testament for this new community. It is God's family, no longer slaves but free men and women, children and heirs of God. It is Christ's body, intimately linked to him. It is a place of gifts, where the Spirit dwells.

The Church is an empowered community, which does not need to be anxious about its identity.

PERHAPS the most radical dimension of the Christian faith is that God calls us to share in the work of salvation and healing. God places the divine image within our shared humanity. Men and women are called to be fruitful not only by producing offspring but by creating places to live, tending the earth, telling stories, and making art.

If we are co-creators with God, we must also be co-redeemers. That may sound like a dangerous lapse into "salvation by works", but we need to be freed from the limitations placed on our imagination by past disputes. The Bible clearly gives the people of God a key role in being a light to the nations, ministers of reconciliation, stewards of the mystery of grace.

Sometimes we can't quite bring ourselves to believe that God is revealed in the way that Christianity affirms. We're quick to summon again the God who controls everything and leaves nothing to chance. The Bible suggests something different: a God who takes risks, a reckless and passionate lover who wants us as partners, not pawns.

Atonement cannot happen without us. It cannot happen without communities who live out the power of Christ's defeat, and the victory of his servant-hood. In a world obsessed with targets, numbers, and the outward trappings of success, that is the astonishing gift the Church can still name, and celebrate, and live.

(2007)

'Ransom, substitute, scapegoat, God: is there one doctrine of the atonement?'

No, says **Ben Pugh**, there are only theories

WHAT is the Nicene Creed's doctrine of the atonement? Can you recite it? No. That is because there isn't one.

The creed tells us that there was an atonement: that — for our salvation — Christ came down and was incarnate of the Virgin Mary, was made man, suffered under Pontius Pilate, was buried, and rose again. But it does not tell us how such events achieved our salvation, or even what salvation is. The result is open season where doctrines of the atonement are concerned.

Over the course of two millennia, the question of atonement has been a chance for the brightest of minds to set to work making the gospel message intelligible to each new generation. The result is that atonement theology — in my view — is the seam within our ancient tradition which is, by far, the richest to mine.

Theories of atonement fall into four main types. In chronological order of their emergence they are as follows:

Christus Victor

THE *Christus Victor* theory of atonement consists of two distinct approaches, both emerging within the first couple of centuries of church history, and holding sway until the Middle Ages.

1 *The ransom-to-Satan theory*

This theory believes our main problem to be our captivity to Satan. The atonement is a victory over Satan which procured our release. So far so good. Difficulties arise, however, when God is depicted as deceiving the devil by letting him think that he had the "ransom money", so to speak. When Jesus died, the devil thought that he had him firmly in his grasp. After all, that was the deal. Little did he know that Jesus could not be held by death, and would soon escape. The devil had already agreed to release all humankind in exchange for the Son of God. Now, he is left with neither. The title of the Rolling Stones' song "Sympathy for the Devil" takes on a whole new meaning here.

Elaborate metaphors were used to describe the deceiving of the devil, such as the fish-hook metaphor: the frail humanity of Christ was the flesh of the bait, the invincible divine nature, the hook that caught the devil and brought him to land; or the mousetrap metaphor: his humanity was the cheese, and his divinity the trap. But, as well as the idea of God's deceiving the devil, there is also the assumption that the devil had some kind of legal right, or authority, over humans which even God could not contravene.

There is a biblical basis for seeing the cross as a victory over Satan, although it is not extensive: Colossians 2.14; Hebrews 2.14; Revelation 12.11.

2 *Recapitulation*

With this theory, it is as though Adam were the chairman of a corrupt company. He tars us all with the same brush. Humanity PLC is a dysfunctional organisation, and we are all caught up in its systemic problems. Jesus comes along and becomes the new chairman. Everything that Adam did Jesus undoes. Everything that Adam failed to do the Second Adam does. Adam was disobedient; Jesus is obedient. He even dies our death in obedience to God.

This has a much clearer biblical basis. In particular, there is the whole Pauline notion of our participation in Christ: Romans 5.12-21; 1 Corinthians 15.45-50. This participation can be read both ways: the Son of God unites himself to human nature, thus potentially renewing the whole human race; but we also become partakers of the divine nature. He descends into our humanity, suffering our frailties and dying our death, but then he takes us up into his resurrection and glorification. And so death's hold over us is destroyed, as we now find ourselves caught up with the immortal and incorruptible God.

Objective theories

THERE are basically two of these:

1 *Satisfaction*

This theory was set out by St Anselm. He was the Archbishop of Canterbury in the reign of William the Conqueror's successor King Rufus. After a few years of falling out with him, Anselm took some time out and wrote *Cur Deus Homo?* ("Why the God-Man?") in 1099. His argument went as follows. We have all robbed God of the honour that is due to him. For that honour to be fully repaid, something greater than all creation needs to be offered in compensation — our situation is that serious. No one but humans must pay it, but only God has the power to. Only he could offer something so valuable that it is the equivalent to everything in creation. The debt is total; the obligation to pay it is total; the power to pay it is zero.

What better solution, then, than that God should become human, and, in that human nature, pay the debt? This is the reason for the God-Man. That he should offer himself is more than enough to satisfy divine justice;

so, in fact, it merits a reward. The Son has no need of such a reward, so freely bestows his merit, his reward, on all those who believe in him.

In this model, God is fully himself, both in his justice and in his mercy, fully expressing both attributes at the cross, resulting in an all-sufficient solution to the human predicament. Gone are the bargains with the devil — Anselm loathed all such ideas. God shows himself to be the sovereign of his world. The closest thing to a biblical text directly supporting the theory is Hebrews 10.12,14, where the writer emphasises that Christ's single offering was utterly sufficient.

2 *Penal substitution*

This phrase means that Jesus died to bear the penalty for my sins, hence "penal", and that he did this in my place, hence "substitution". The bearing of penalty implies that God needed to punish sinners, and that something actually happened to Jesus on the cross which was accepted by the Father as an equivalent to this punishment. Substitution goes beyond representation, pointing to the idea that, on the cross, Jesus was doing something without our participation — and, indeed, to spare us.

Penal substitution, which originates with Martin Luther's Galatians commentary of 1535, parts company with Anselm's satisfaction theory in two ways. First, the direction of travel has changed: in Anselm, the Son freely offers himself *to* the Father; in penal substitution, the Father pours out his wrath and judgement *on* the Son. Second, the aim is different: in the satisfaction theory, judgement is averted; in penal substitution, judgement is absorbed.

The clearest New Testament support for a fully penal view of the atonement would be 2 Corinthians 5.21 and Galatians 3.13, although many parts of Isaiah 53 are susceptible of similar interpretation.

Moral influence

A CONTEMPORARY of Anselm was Peter Abelard. His writings were driven by two concerns: one was an interest in romantic love. Love letters to his beloved Héloïse have been preserved to the present day. A second concern of his was with ethics. Much of his writing is on this subject. So, when he came to the atonement, the two ideas flowed together: the cross changes our ethical behaviour because there, in the crucified Christ, we come to understand something of God's love for us. This love motivates us to change the way we live. This is how we are saved from our sins. That Christ's death impresses us with the love of God, and inspires in us a life of dedication to him, is indeed a scriptural truth: Romans 5.8 and 2 Corinthians 5.15. The moral-influence theory was wholeheartedly endorsed by theologians within the German liberal tradition of the 19th century, who were all repulsed by penal substitution.

Non-violent atonement

WE NOW come to a fourth, and very recent, way of looking at the work of Christ. This approach has been dominated by the French literary critic René Girard, who was converted to Christianity by reading the Gospel accounts of the crucifixion. He brings two fresh insights to these accounts.

First, there is "mimetic desire": desire that is brought about by imitating other people. We desire something, for example in an advertisement, because others have made it look desirable. We mimic other people's desire. But Satan then puts what Girard calls "stumbling-blocks" in the way of some of our strongest desires, so that we cannot obtain those things. Mimetic rivalry ensues, in which we see others as a threat. As this process carries on, and frustrations intensify, whole communities can become enflamed with violence. It is a war of all against all.

Satan's next tactic is to offer an answer to the cycle of violence which he himself caused, and here is the second insight. Satan presents to the community a marginal person who is slated as being the true cause of all the unrest. The whole community then turns on that person to destroy him or her. It is now a war of all against one. A temporary peace is achieved by this. This is called the "scapegoat mechanism".

In the Gospels, we see Jesus fully absorbing all this community violence, but, crucially, it is not God who does the scapegoating. In non-violent atonement theories, God is not violent. He is on the side of the victims of scapegoating. Christ was then vindicated by his resurrection, thus fully exposing our scapegoating tendencies for what they really are.

But we are not saved by a sacrifice: people have been trying to achieve that from time immemorial. We are saved from sacrificing. We are saved from the very idea that the answer to bad violence is good violence, which we see never-endingly played out in global politics (and Hollywood) to this day.

WHY did Jesus suffer under Pontius Pilate? The answer is not simple, any more than the human problem is simple. Learning the full breadth of atonement theories might be compared to learning the piano. To begin with, we might only ever play the "Chopsticks" of our tradition, but then we discover Rachmaninov. Suddenly, there are some huge, fat chords to enjoy. And a concert pianist will become attuned to a vast range of mood in a piece: some movements requiring quietness and subtlety, others requiring pomp and vigour.

Perhaps our task is not necessarily to work out which theories are wrong or right — although, undoubtedly, some are stronger than others. Perhaps our task is to listen out for what the culture needs us to play, boldly, or to soft-pedal. But only the complete range will equip us for that. I encourage you to broaden your range this Easter. Play some fat chords. Discover the soft pedal. Preach the good news.

(2018)

In the shadow of Good Friday

Rod Garner reflects on the religious significance of
Samuel Beckett

SINCE his death in 1989, Samuel Beckett's fame has continued to rest on his plays, in particular *Waiting for Godot*. First performed in Paris in 1953, it remains one of the most significant plays of the 20th century. It is a tragicomedy in two acts, in which nothing happens except a frenzied and relentless conversation between two tramps, waiting for a stranger (Godot) who never arrives.

The play distils Beckett's bleak view of existence, and exposes the emptiness and fears that attend human wanting and waiting. *Godot* is about killing time and clinging, however tenuously, to the belief that deliverance may be just around the corner. If not today, then perhaps tomorrow ...

Beckett's friend and publisher, John Calder, described him as a writer searching for meaning in the world, but "unable to come to any conclusion about purpose or believe in any creed". An Irish Protestant, Beckett was familiar with the Bible, and traces of it inform his work.

St Augustine was another influence: the first part of his famous aphorism "Do not despair — one of the thieves was saved; do not presume — one of the thieves was damned" found its way into Beckett's first novel, *Molloy*.

The Church, however, held little appeal for him. He rejected the "very small God" of Christian worship, who took credit for the good things of life but "was never blamed for the multiple evils of the world". It is more than coincidence that Beckett began to formulate the idea behind *Godot* after the Holocaust and the absent God who ostensibly permitted it.

IN PRIVATE, Beckett was courteous and compassionate, given to long silences, and revered by the actors who performed his plays. He was also generous and brave. In 1969, after winning the Nobel Prize for Literature, it is understood that he gave away the prize money to struggling writers.

Having joined the French Resistance during the Second World War, he received two awards for his efforts in fighting the German occupation. Earlier, in Paris, he had been stabbed and nearly killed by a man who approached him in the street, asking for money. After recovering, Beckett visited his assailant in prison to ask him why he had attacked him. The man replied: "Je ne sais pas, Monsieur."

Beckett's pessimism and antipathy towards religion have complex origins. He was born on Good Friday, and never quite eluded its long shadow. At the age of 14, he went to the Portora Royal School, in County Fermanagh, before studying for his BA in European Languages at Trinity College, Dublin.

After relatively short spells lecturing in Paris and Dublin, he embarked on a period of restless travel through Europe, writing poems and stories and doing casual work in order to get by. The lost souls whom he encountered lurk behind the characters in his later novels and plays: bewildered individuals, just about surviving in a perplexing world.

Beckett read widely, particularly the writings of the 19th-century German philosopher Schopenhauer, who depicted life as a perpetual swing "between pain and boredom". Buddhism also interested him, with its insistence that all life was suffering which could be diminished only by the elimination of desire.

In contrast, the preaching and rituals of Christianity appeared verbose and insubstantial. Beckett saw part of his task to engage with "the questions the priests never raise", and to probe "where the human imagination quails or retreats".

IN THIS respect, Beckett continues to represent a legitimate challenge to forms of Christian proclamation which rest on unexamined assumptions and the need for certainty, especially in dark times. As a child of Good Friday, he is sensitive to the often unheeded cry of the maimed, confused, and inarticulate, and refuses to despair in the face of the void or the prospect of extinction.

Paradox surrounds him, and this represents part of his importance for religion. Apparently convinced that life is meaningless, he writes poignant, honest, and darkly amusing works that suggest the opposite. And, as noted earlier, he was prepared to risk his life to combat fascism.

Unable to leave the question of God alone, or to deny the attested human capacity to endure and hope in the face of calamity, he treats his memorable characters with sympathy, inviting his audience to do the same. In his play *Happy Days*, the central character, Winnie, is buried to her waist in a mound of earth which eventually threatens to engulf her completely. Despite the fact that she has little or nothing to feel happy about, no day passes without her trying to look her best and carry on.

BECKETT is a secular "man of sorrows", acquainted not only with grief, but with the reality of a seemingly ineradicable evil within ourselves. In his voice it is possible to hear intimations of Original Sin and the anguish of the first Good Friday — a world gone wrong, when innocence was betrayed, friendship denied, and goodness excised from the earth.

His plays lay bare the human predicament that preaching often fails to fathom or studiously ignores. Beckett's plays lack a saviour figure, but they serve as a terse and necessary reminder. If our gospel presumes to speak of the love and benevolence of God in a world polluted by innumerable ills, it must be earthed in the darkest areas of human life. However well-meaning, cheap proclamation and facile sincerity are not enough.

(2021)

O tree of beauty, tree of light

Suffering and grief are the price that love always has to pay,
says **Graham James**. God's love for us blazes out
from the cross of the dying Christ

AS A CHILD, I went to Newquay Congregational Church in Cornwall. I
didn't have a great deal of choice. My father was the minister.

Back in the 1950s, this church possessed something then rather unusual:
a large cross hung in the sanctuary. On the wood were attached three neon
strip-lights, one for the upright and two others for its arms on either side. I
suppose neon lighting was regarded as chic and contemporary at the time.
Even so, some people thought this cross rather tawdry, while others found
the idea of a cross from which light blazed forth strangely moving.

When I was 11, my family became Anglicans. Instead of the cross of
neon light, I found myself sitting in a church with a large crucifix. I gazed at
the figure of Jesus, hanging, dying, bleeding for the salvation of humankind.
I saw the cross in a new way. It was linked with human suffering. It was
clearly humiliating for any human being to die that way.

This was a different sort of light, the revelation of God's willingness to
suffer for me. I think I understood the crucifix long before I began to explain
it. I am not sure I can explain it even now. I expect God wants to be spared
being explained.

I remain glad that I first saw the cross as a blaze of light. Perhaps that's
why the crucifix never seemed morbid to me, as it clearly does to some.
Perhaps that's why I have always seen the cross as a symbol of God's love.
Over the years, I have come to realise that the connection between God's
love and Christ's suffering and death is far from immediately apparent.

Yet love and suffering are more intimately linked than we often think.
Love someone, and you can easily be hurt by them. Thoughtless acts or
cruel words cause special distress between lover and beloved. I have often
thought that marriage preparation ought to give attention to suffering, even
if it is liable to be parodied in the Les Dawson school of humour.

Love is often thought to be an immunisation against suffering or a protection from it: rather, it increases your vulnerability to it. We ought to
remember that grief is always the price of love. It is those who love and care
for no one who are peculiarly protected from the pain of bereavement, and

from much other suffering, too. Those protected in this way can pay a terrible price. They are also unlikely to know much joy or delight.

Jesus recognised in his teaching that we are willing to suffer for the sake of those we love. Such human characteristics are a pale reflection of the divine life. A teenage boy looking at a crucifix nearly 40 years ago comprehended something of this. But how to express it? Artists have tried to do so over the centuries. The crucifixion of Christ retains a hold on the artistic imagination, not because of its special cruelty, but because it links suffering with love and with God. The themes of art and life are all rolled into one, though none of them minimises the horror of crucifixion. That remains.

"IT'S LIKE waiting to be crucified." A farmer was being quoted in a news report I heard about foot-and-mouth-disease. He was in an infected area, his livestock unable to be moved, and he and his family confined to the farm. It was as if life was suspended. There was a dark inevitability that all was not likely to be well. 1 suspect the reference to crucifixion was instinctive.

Crucifixion is a slow, agonising and public death. The impact in some of our rural areas on livestock, livelihoods, and even a way of life is slow and agonising — and public. There's a strange humiliation in it.

But what also struck me was the use of the word "waiting". I don't suppose the farmer was seeking to make a theological point, but this reference to "waiting to be crucified" had a powerful echo of W.H. Vanstone's *The Stature of Waiting* (published by DLT in 1982, and still in print). It is just possible the farmer might have read the book, but more likely he was reflecting on the passive state of being the powerless victim. It reminded me of Vanstone's image of Jesus as the waiting figure. Human experience and divine grace were at work while he waited.

I remember, when I first read this book, that what he said about Jesus was so obvious I wondered why I had not noticed it for myself. Jesus waits for his arrest in the Garden of Gethsemane; he waits silently for the crowds to decide his fate before Pontius Pilate; earlier he waits for 30 years until the time is right for his brief public ministry to begin. Put bluntly, Jesus does a lot of hanging around.

Except during his public ministry. Vanstone notices that, in Mark's Gospel, the ministry of Jesus is recorded in short, sharp sentences. Jesus is active. He's a man doing a great deal — telling parables, healing the sick, teaching his disciples. Jesus is a man with a mission, keen to get on with things. Yet in the Garden of Gethsemane all this changes. To record the events, Mark even changes his vocabulary. Jesus becomes passive. The storyteller keeps quiet.

I remember that the first time I played the part of Jesus in a dramatised reading of the Passion during a Holy Week eucharist, it struck me how little Jesus has to say. There I was, the celebrant of the eucharist, usually so talkative at the altar, reduced to saying only a few words. All the action was going on around me. It was an accurate reflection of the fact that after his arrest, Jesus hardly speaks at all. He is, in every sense of the term, "handed over".

Waiting to be crucified: there are plenty of refugees, asylum-seekers, innocent people all over the world caught in the crossfire of political and racial tension, who must feel that they are handed over. Some shout. Most become quiet. They have not become indifferent to their fate — nor did Jesus.

IN OUR Holy Week liturgies, this rapid change of mood, so noticeable in the Gospels, is captured most vividly on Maundy Thursday evening. The eucharist of the Last Supper is celebrated joyfully. It isn't the equivalent of the last meal of the condemned man, eaten alone. There's no reason to assume there wasn't plenty of conviviality in the upper room.

But betrayal is imminent, and at the end of our Maundy Thursday liturgy there is a swift introduction of a more sombre mood. Altars are stripped, the church becomes bare, and a watch of prayer begins.

"Will you not watch with me one hour?" We remember that, after Jesus was arrested, his disciples "forsook him and fled". It is very soon after that intimate meal that Peter denies Jesus. It is very soon after his closest followers hear Jesus say "This is my body" and "This is my blood" that they run away. The intimacy of loving friendship is quickly followed by betrayal.

At the heart of these events lies the paradox of human and Christian experience. We know that joy is often mingled with sorrow; that faithfulness is frequently marred by disloyalty; that celebration and tragedy are sometimes strangely linked. The proximity of these things in human life is reflected in Christ's Passion and death.

A FEW miles outside Monmouth there lives a small community of nuns. Their life is simple and contemplative. Their chapel is both impressive and yet very plain. Since they are the Society of the Sacred Cross, a big crucifix hangs on the east wall. It's a very peaceful place, and a host of people find spiritual refreshment by sharing the lives of the sisters. There is refreshment and light that comes from being there, and I don't think this is unconnected with the fact that the community's focus is on the Cross. These nuns are not spared the darker side of human existence.

Back in the 1970s, Philip Toynbee, one of the most respected literary critics of his generation, fell under this community's spell. His spiritual journey during the final years before his death from cancer in 1981 is recorded in two books. It is in the second of them, *End of a Journey,* that you find some fragments of thought in which he struggles with the knowledge of his approaching death. He feared that the pain would render him querulous and miserable. Yet he longed that his faith in the strength and love of God might allow him to learn all he could from this experience.

I notice in his journal that he concludes a prayer: "through Jesus Christ, our brother and bringer of light". As he lies in his hospital bed awaiting death, it occurs to him that "Jesus wasn't just a bringer of light; he *was* a light."

He mused further. Jesus of Nazareth he describes as "that scarcely visible young man, from whom light streams forth into the New Testament, into the early Church, and into all later history …"

Is suffering sent that we may see God's light more clearly? That was something Toynbee struggled to discover as he lay dying.

He could not find a satisfactory answer. He could not believe that God was responsible for his cancer. But, equally, he was never convinced by the emphatic way that some of his friends, priests among them, declared that it wasn't, and couldn't, be sent by God. God could make too much good use of his suffering, he thought, for it to be wholly unconnected with him. His most mature reflection on this is worth pondering, written as it was less than three weeks before he died.

"I am as sure as ever that God does not send the savage and dehumanising afflictions that crush so many millions — and would of course, crush me. But I do find it hard not to feel that *some* hardships have a holy purpose, and not only a holy effect."

THE DYING of Christ on his cross is not merely an idea that has taken hold on the human imagination. It is not simply a story that has had a wholesome effect. It is an event in which we see the purpose and goodness of God moving in and through the world, changing it and redeeming us. It is through Christ's suffering and death that we discover the greatness of God's love. We don't have the capacity to repent and be renewed simply through our own moral resolution. God gives us grace to do so through Christ dying for us.

Christ's words from the cross are not dispassionate comments from a disengaged saviour. His passion and death was no easy accomplishment. It was a work of love. We glimpse God's love in his creation, but it has been finally revealed in Christ's passion.

That is why our Lord Jesus Christ is the light of the world, and the light blazes forth from his cross of love.

(2001)

63

An end of embarrassment

The foot of the cross is not a comfortable place to be,
says **Simon Jones**. But it is where we must kneel

The bishop's chair is placed on Golgotha ... A table is placed before him
with a cloth on it, the deacons stand round, and there is brought to him
a gold and silver box containing the holy Wood of the Cross. It is opened,
and the Wood of the Cross and the Title that hung upon the Cross are
taken out and placed on the table.

As long as the holy Wood is on the table, the bishop sits with his hands
resting on either end of it ... and the deacons round him keep watch
over it. They guard it because what happens now is that all the people ...
come up one by one to the table. They stoop down, kiss the Wood, and
move on ... Thus all the people go past one by one. They stoop down,
touch the holy Wood first with their forehead and then with their eyes,
and then kiss it.

SO WRITES the Spanish nun Egeria, who spent several memorable Holy
Weeks in Jerusalem at the end of the fourth century, and recorded what she
witnessed in a travel diary. In this passage, Egeria describes how the
Jerusalem Church observed Good Friday.

Remarkably, what that pilgrim experienced in the Holy City more than
1600 years ago will form the central act of devotion for countless Christians
this Good Friday, not least in the Church of England. Although our bishops
are unlikely to be found guarding relics of the true cross, in *Common
Worship: Times and Seasons* the displaying and honouring of the cross of
Christ, which can take many forms, stands at the heart of the Church's
liturgy on this solemn day.

For many of us, much of the Holy Week liturgy can be a difficult and
embarrassing experience: an outdoor procession with palm branches
observed quizzically by friends and neighbours; the removal of a shoe so
that our naked foot can be washed by a priest; and then, on Good Friday,
the invitation to leave our seat and come forward to venerate the cross of
Christ with a kiss.

But this embarrassment is not purely personal, caused by having to shed
our anonymous identity within a gathering of comfortable Christians to do

something individually or in public. At a much more profound level, it is also a spiritual embarrassment.

If we see our observance of Holy Week as a drama in which we are all called to be active participants rather than observers from a distance, then, as actors in the divine drama of salvation, the part that we are called to play on Good Friday is the hardest part of all. For on this day, as we survey the wondrous cross, we are confronted with the awful realisation that, in the Garden of Gethsemane, it was every one of us who, with Judas, kissed the Lord to betray him, and that what we see before us is the horrendous consequence of our action.

On Good Friday, that same Lord, now hanging helplessly from a blood-spattered cross, invites us to kiss him once again, no longer as those who would betray him, but as those who have resolved to take up our cross and follow him, in sorrow and in penitence, but also in hope and trust, as those who have been transformed by his reconciling love.

For the death of the Son of God has not only saved us from those sins which led him to a criminal's death, but it also frees us in the here and now to present ourselves to him as a living sacrifice.

THE LITURGY of Good Friday presents several opportunities to recommit ourselves to sacrificial living, not least in the prayers that, in *Common Worship*, follow the Proclamation of the Cross.

After the painfully individualistic encounter with the cross as the price of sin and source of salvation, the next part of our worship frees us from the preoccupation with ourselves as self-absorbed sinners by offering prayers that are explicitly directed towards others: the Church, the world and its leaders, the Jews, those who do not believe in Christ, and all who suffer. It is only after interceding for others that with them we are commended to God's unfailing love, praying for grace to lead a holy life in the hope of the resurrection.

ANY ATTEMPT to discover what sacrificial living might mean requires us to take as our starting-point the sacrifice of Christ. The priest and poet of the early 17th century, George Herbert, uses irony and paradox to great effect to fathom its depths in his poem "The Sacrifice".

This poem, the inspiration behind Samuel Crossman's popular Passiontide hymn "My song is love unknown", runs to some 63 verses; it is based on the Lamentations of Jeremiah and the Reproaches (*Improperia*), which traditionally form part of the Good Friday liturgy.

Each stanza, apart from the last, ends with the questioning refrain: "Was ever grief like mine?" This question is not an attention-seeking ploy for self-pity on the part of the crucified victim. Far from it: it is used again and again to highlight humanity's ingratitude for Christ's sacrificial death. These five verses come from the end of the poem:

> *In healing not myself, there doth consist*
> *All that salvation, which ye now resist;*
> *Your safety in my sickness doth subsist:*
>   *Was ever grief like mine?*
>
> *Betwixt two thieves I spend my utmost breath,*
> *As he that for some robbery suffereth.*
> *Alas! what have I stolen from you? death:*
>   *Was ever grief like mine?*
>
> *A king my title, prefixed on high;*
> *Yet by my subjects am condemned to die*
> *A servile death in servile company:*
>   *Was ever grief like mine?*
>
> *Nay, after death their spite shall further go;*
> *For they will pierce my side, I full well know;*
> *That as sin came, so Sacraments might flow:*
>   *Was ever grief like mine?*
>
> *But now I die; now all is finished.*
> *My woe, man's weal: and now I bow my head.*
> *Only let others say, when I am dead,*
>   *Never was grief like mine.*

In the first of these verses, it is only by refusing to save himself that Christ saves others: "Your safety in my sickness doth subsist." In the second, Christ's death is that of a common thief, and yet the only thing that he has stolen from humanity is death. And so it goes on. A king condemned by his own subjects, a wounded side bringing forth life-giving sacraments, our own wellbeing brought about by his agony: "Was ever grief like mine?"

When read in full, Herbert's masterful heaping up of paradoxes, verse after verse, points not only to humanity's continuing ingratitude and selfishness, but also to the saving mystery that should bring the Church to its knees at the foot of the cross.

If, in the course of our worship on Good Friday, the cross of Christ is to have any impact on our lives, then it must be because we acknowledge the paradox that Christ's death is both the result of our sin and the source of our salvation.

HERE the drama of the Good Friday liturgy can help us; for, however strange and treacherous it might feel, we need to add our voices to those of the crowd who had no time to listen to Pilate's frustrated question: "Why, what evil has he done?" and who shouted all the louder, "Crucify, crucify him" — just as, on the night of the Last Supper, we have to betray him with Judas, deny him with Peter, and, with the other disciples, forsake him and flee.

If we are not prepared to come with open eyes before the tortured body of our Saviour, to see the blood dripping from feet and hands and side, and to look him in the face as we confess the sins that have led him to this place of Godforsaken execution, then we will find it most difficult to experience the grace of salvation that flows from the lips of him who, with outstretched arms, prays: "Father, forgive them, for they know not what they do."

Our encounter with the cross, however embarrassing or uncomfortable it might be, releases us from the ingratitude highlighted by Herbert's poem, and provides a wonderful moment of reconciliation. This is a moment of grace, when we are invited to honour the Son whose crucified presence promises forgiveness of sin and accepts our sacrificial offering of love and thanksgiving.

This Good Friday, as we behold the world's salvation enthroned upon the wood of a cross, we can be encouraged by this undying act of sacrificial love and mercy to offer our lives to God in penitence and prayer. We can seek his healing, forgiveness, and the gift of new life, which is the promise of Easter.

Just as those fourth-century Christians, joined by Egeria, touched the relic of the True Cross with their forehead, eyes, and lips, so we can pray that, as we kiss the seat of divine mercy (either physically or imaginatively), the saving love of our crucified Lord may open our minds to respond to his call in our lives; may open our eyes to recognise his presence in the suffering peoples of the world; and may open our lips to bear witness to that life-giving death. So, we may fall to our knees and sing with penitence and with thanksgiving the words of Isaac Watts's hymn: "Love so amazing, so divine, demands my soul, my life, my all."

(2010)

The pity and the glory

Mark Oakley reflects on contrasting understandings of the cross

AS CHRISTIANS reflected on the cross in the New Testament period and over the later centuries, two apparently contrasting themes emerged. The first was the glory of the cross and its redeeming work: the cross as the workbench of salvation and the hope of humanity.

The second was the pity of the cross: the excruciating suffering; the death penalty given to an innocent man; the heartbreak of his family and friends.

In the course of the Good Friday services, both these perspectives come in and out of view, and — as is often the way in liturgy — we are not asked to decide between them, but, rather, to sit with them both and allow truth to do its work.

NO THEORY of atonement was ever declared by the Church to be definitive. In the creeds, we simply affirm that Jesus "suffered under Pontius Pilate, was crucified, dead, and buried". Because of this openness to interpretation, and the need to see in the dark, the poets of the world were drawn, early on, to use their imagination and help excavate some understanding.

The two themes of glory and pity were explored. One of the earliest Christian poems in English, from the early eighth century, can still be seen today, carved in runic form on a cross in Ruthwell, Dumfriesshire. It has been given the title *The Dream of the Rood*. "Rood" was once the only Old English word for the instrument of Christ's death. The words "cross" and "crucifix" came later,

Detail from the south side of the Ruthwell Cross (8th c.): Mary Magdalene washes Christ's feet

and the early English poetic and enigmatic mind was captured by this Rood of Christ.

In the 156 lines of the *Dream* poem (whose author remains unknown), the narrator describes a strange dream of a wonderful tree covered with gems. He is aware of how wretched he is in comparison, until he sees that, amid all the beautiful stones, this tree is stained with blood. The tree then speaks, telling us that it was cut down to bear a criminal, but that it was climbed by a young warrior who is Lord of mankind. The rood is not only vocal, but sentient.

Gradually, a mysterious identity emerges between the wood and the warrior, the rood and ruler. The revelatory climax is quickly reached: "All creation wept, King's fall lamented. Christ was on rood." The tree speaks not only for the cosmos, but as part of it, and then charges the narrator to share all that he has seen with others. The vision ends; and the man, left alone with his thoughts, finds himself filled with hope.

THE IMAGE of Christ in this poem is that of an Anglo-Saxon hero-warrior. The poet even uses for Christ a native phrase that is once applied to Beowulf. Christ is the young warrior actively stripping himself for the fight, hastening with resolute courage to climb the tree, who then rests — "limb-weary" after the exhaustion of single combat — watched over by his faithful followers.

In contrast, the cross remembers how it was pierced with dark nails, drenched with blood, endured many grievous wrongs from wicked men, was wounded with weapon-points, stood weeping, and was finally levelled to the ground. All the sympathy and pathos of the reader are directed towards the cross itself.

Suffering in this poem is caught up with victory, but over what or whom is not spelled out exactly. The impression given is that the victory interprets the suffering, but we cannot quite see how. All we do know from the poem is that the Passion is understood not as tragedy, but as a fulfilment of a divine purpose. Here is a Lord who does courageously what has to be done.

In some early Christian art, this is depicted by Christ climbing up a ladder on to the cross, freely taking on himself the cost of a saviour; shown like a fireman going up the steps to the window through which he will end his life. Here, Jesus is no helpless victim, he is a warrior-hero who — to use contemporary comparisons — is enlisted by God for a cosmic regime-change; a man giving his life as an enlisted peacekeeper. We are reminded of the combat that goes into shaping our soul for good or evil. Goodness does not just happen: it is fought for.

A FEW centuries later, thoughts refocused. From the 12th century onwards, such heroic images are less apparent. Instead of Christ the glorious warrior, we now find an intense meditation that starts with the suffering humanity of Jesus. Medieval piety was characterised by a revolution of feeling: a new interest in a more vulnerable figure of Jesus, and his human life and pain.

Spiritual writers such as Richard Rolle and Julian of Norwich focus on the bleeding wounds of Jesus as objects for devotion; but they are not now wounds incidental to a battle, but, rather, an expression of divine love and pity, which, in turn, awaken pity and love in the observer. The regal crown of Christ Victorious is replaced by a crown of thorns. The love of the saviour is fragile in its beauty.

People acquainted with wars and the plague see now a suffering and death that they understand only too well. Christ incarnates their own pain, and reveals the nature of God as one who comes alongside. Christ the King is now the Man of Sorrows — their sadnesses, as well as his own. We start to find carved figures of the wounded Christ detached from the cross, to enable the believer to focus on his pierced heart and his five wounds, described in one poem as the "wound words" that lie on the book of Christ's body that opens up to us the view into God's nature.

IN ART — not least in the rood screens that were being built — Christ's eyes now close in death. His skin turns white; the blood becomes visible; and, for the first time, the Virgin Mary and St John appear at the foot of the cross. The proximity of family and friends to this suffering makes it even more identifiable with. Tears are now a grace, not a disgrace.

In this period, poetry, music, and devotion begin to address the pain of Christ's mother, and to demonstrate direct compassion towards her. Emotionally, the poets are now so involved with the scene of the crucifixion that they are impelled even to address Mary herself and to compare her pain — her pierced soul — to that of her son. The hymn *Stabat Mater dolorosa* is a good example.

This empathy begins to make the crucifixion seem a contemporary event — a continuously present drama in which we are involved — and the prime emotion is now pity. The 15th-century mystic Margery Kempe tells our Lady to cease sorrowing, for her son is now out of pain, and writes that she takes her home and makes "a good caudle of broth to comfort her".

This is devout creativity, praying as though one were bodily present with Jesus's relatives, and it continues today in the poetry of the liturgy of Good Friday — a liturgy that, we sense, understands us more than we understand it. A liturgy of pity and of glory.

(2019)

Word from Wormingford 2015

Ronald Blythe is struck again by the freshness
of a medieval writer

HOLY WEEK. A soft gale troubles the bare trees. But it will not rain. Gulls land among the horses. The stream pours unseen to the river. The garden calls.

I reread Julian's *Revelations of Divine Love* in which, for me, there is an unparalleled account of the crucifixion — one that could only have been written by someone who had witnessed official torture. Also a slow dying. It comes after Julian's enchanting comparison of God's love to a hazelnut. "What is this? It is all that is made."

She translates medieval Christianity in a way that makes it acceptable to us, all these centuries later, and never more so than when she describes what happened on Good Friday. Without writers like her, "We do not know, we cannot tell, what pains he had to bear."

And yet her Christ is a gardener sent by his master to plant love in his creation, digging and banking, toiling and sweating, turning and trenching the ground, watering the plants the while.

"And by keeping at this work he would make sweet streams to flow, fine abundant fruit to grow; he would bring them to his lord, and serve them to his taste."

Although a young neighbour does most of the sweating and turning these days for me, I can look on the Bottengoms garden with some pride at the hard graft that created it, long ago.

In fact, I loved digging, especially in the kitchen garden, where the soil fell off the spade in delectable clumps, and robins followed me up and down, up and down, and the mower made its neat mark; and the excitement of deciding where the runner beans should climb this summer could be intoxicating. So when a friend came to tell me about his London allotment, my heart went out to him.

And when I visited the Garden Museum in Lambeth, its relics spoke more of human happiness than mere toiling and sweating.

Anyway, I have made a start. The white cat looks down at me from a tree. Nesting birds watch anxiously from ivy grandstands. Bluebells, their buds still near to their roots, perilously close to the badger setts, promise a show in May; and, altogether, I have made a start. Making a start is the thing. One cannot do it often enough.

How terrible it was that Jesus had to suffer in a garden — probably one that he knew and delighted in; one in which ancient olives were rooted in Jewish history: Gethsemane.

He had walked there after the Last Supper, accompanied by his disciples. He would have crossed the brook, Kidron, and descended the little valley between Jerusalem and the Mount of Olives.

It was springtime, and Julian of Norwich walked with Christ in Gethsemane. She was a young woman of 30, and was not well, but "thought it a pity to die". And rose from her bed because she had much to say.

It was 8 May 1373. It was then that she wrote her masterpiece. It became illegible with time, as we all do; but a modern scholar, Clifton Walters, brushed the grave-dirt from it so that we could find our way about in Holy Week, meeting the gardener and saviour, and be forced to comprehend his crucifixion, and attempts to uproot him, and then to arrive at his glorious flowering.

David Holgate's 2014 statue of Julian of Norwich, outside Norwich Cathedral

Life, where is thy sting?

A little more of the same for a little longer – is that all we yearn for? We must embrace death, as Christ did, argues **John Bell**

I BELIEVE in death, as a matter of fact.

Traditionally, euphemisms have been used in times of bereavement, out of kindness to the grieving relatives. I would defend such language as it struggles to deal with the mystery of our ending.

However, in the present context of the war with Iraq, the sensitivity surrounding the language of death verges on the status of taboo. There is a dysfunction in our discussions about war, if we believe that Iraqis are there to be killed and British soldiers are there to survive. The nation is invited to express disbelief that our forces, part of whose purpose is to engage in lethal warfare, should become victims rather than victors.

To make matters worse, euphemisms such as "friendly fire" or "collateral damage" suggest that pain is not felt, pulses do not stop beating, the theatre of war is of die comic rather than die tragic variety.

In the face of this, I believe in death as a matter of fact, and suggest that the retreat into euphemism is a symptom of that hedonistic disease that craves pleasure in all things even if that means turning bloody hell into entertainment.

I BELIEVE in death as an article of faith, for both the Bible and the Creed tell me so. "He was crucified, died and was buried." The Saviour of the world was a man of the world, who was not exempt from either the pain of grief or the experience of death.

How magnificent that in John's Gospel, which, like a film script, supplies details of movement, interaction and emotion, we discover that Jesus was not dispassionate in the face of loss, but was enraged.

When Lazarus has died, and Jesus eventually makes for Bethany, he is greeted by the sisters Martha and Mary, who exhibit a response to their erstwhile houseguest that is at odds with our expectation. Martha, who seems previously to have preferred housework to hospitality, states her faith in Jesus and in her dead brother's eternal security.

Mary, the former wide-eyed devotee, greets Jesus with the same salutation as her sister: "Lord, if you had been here, my brother would not have died."

73

But then there is no affirmation of faith in Jesus, only tears. So: "When Jesus saw her weeping and the Jews who had come with her weeping, he was moved with indignation and deeply distressed." (John 11.32-33)

What marvellous consolation, that Jesus should not regard the death of a friend as an eventuality that had to be dealt with, that the injustice of it all should anger him so much that he weeps in front of men and women!

Lazarus dies because he is fully human, and Jesus dies because he is fully human. There is no exemption from the consequences of mortality for the incarnate son of God. This has not been a ghoulish presence wandering around the Holy Land for 33 years; this has been flesh and blood that is fully limited. If we do not grieve for Jesus when he dies on Good Friday, perhaps we have never connected with him as the Saviour whose engagement with us is known first as a listener, teacher, debater, rule-breaker, foot-washer and friend.

Death is an article of faith.

YET IT IS also the pivotal dynamic of life. For if there is no death, there can be no resurrection. Jesus does not exit stage left into the tomb, to walk behind the props and appear on stage right a few minutes later, to the delight of the audience, which suspended belief during his absence.

Jesus goes into death and into all its seeming finality, and does this painfully but willingly, because he knows that only the life that is laid down is the life that will be resurrected.

All the teaching about self-denial; all the encouragement to leave the contingencies of earth behind in order to gain the kingdom of heaven; all the parabolic talk of seeds that must drop to the ground in order to produce a good harvest, or of branches that must be pruned in order that the vine will be more fruitful – all such documented discourse will not be vindicated unless Christ willingly goes to the cross and takes the sin of the world with him through death and hell.

Only thus can he and all things be made new, and forgiveness be breathed by one who has overcome the powers of iniquity. He accepts the fate that the wickedness of earth's people has plotted for him, and emerges — still visibly wounded by the world, but victorious over it.

We cannot believe in resurrection unless we believe in death. It is a dynamic prerequisite. And belief in the resurrection is vindicated only when we, like Jesus, integrate an acceptance of the necessity for death and of dying throughout our lives this side of time.

Christians are not famed for such an activity. We tend to hold on to practices, to organisations, to places that are clearly well past their useful or useable date. We will not let them die, and so our inner spiritual lives and our corporate congregational lives exhibit more of an antiquarian than a progressive-looking mentality.

Are we afraid to let the sterile devotional practices that no longer nourish our souls die? Are we afraid to let sparse, aged, and reluctant choirs step down? Are we afraid to let models of ministry better suited to the 16th century be consigned respectfully to history? Are we afraid to let go of language that suited our childhood, but confounds our children and grandchildren? Are we – am I – afraid to surrender the prejudices, the self-interested opinions, the cynicism clearly at odds with the gospel mandates of loving and forgiving, in order that God can do something new?

There simply cannot be any resurrection unless there is an acceptance of death and a willingness to let some things die. God cannot do anything in our souls, nor in our politics, if what we yearn for is a little more of the same for a little longer. It is as applicable to our desire for calmness of mind as it is for peace in the Middle East.

God will not grant us a quiet heart if we keep clutching the very things that are making us anxious. Nor will God give us peace if our nation presumes that, by dint of our imperial past, the supremacy of the English language, or advanced surveillance and military technology, we presume that our way, our culture and our rules should be binding on the rest of humanity.

If we move from the death of Lazarus to another of John's riveting accounts of Jesus's ministry, we find an interesting coda to the healing of the man who had been paralysed for 38 years. Having healed him incognito, Jesus leaves the pool of Bethesda, but later catches up with the man in the Temple. There he says to him: "Now that you are well, give up your sinful ways, or something worse will happen to you" (John 5.14).

As a result, the man, who now knows Jesus's name, does not rejoice in his health and praise his saviour; rather, he slinks off to the Jews who want to know the identity of the Sabbath-breaker. Here is one who did not want to lay down his crippledness, his marginal status, and his comfort in complaintiveness. Here is one who, despite mouthing a desire for betterment, was not prepared to risk the death even of his disadvantage.

I believe in death, willingly though painfully accepted, as the prerequisite for resurrection — primarily in Jesus, but also in us.

(2003)

Beside the cross with Mary

Christ's mother points us to the heart of the crucifixion,
says **Cally Hammond**

MARY STANDS at the foot of the cross, watching her son die. What meaning is there in this sorrowful mystery? We need to find a way to understand it, so as to make sense of Holy Week, and turn it to a wholesome purpose in our lives.

Mary stands there, not alone, but one of a milling, buzzing crowd; many people are watching Jesus die. Yet there is something qualitatively different about Mary's presence on Calvary hill. We need to make clear to ourselves what the nature of that difference really is. After all, we are talking about *Mary*, and, in all but the spikiest Anglo-Catholic congregations, there is an unease about letting our attention rest anywhere but on the cross itself.

If we start with what is uncontroversial: she is a mother, and her son is suffering. This we can all understand, and we grieve with her, and for her. As she sorrows for his cruel treatment and even crueller end, we grieve both for him, and for her: the one suffering unjustly (and to save us, too); the other enduring the unjust suffering of her own flesh and blood.

We might well remember the lament of an ancestor of Jesus, and perhaps of Mary, too. King David, in the agony of grief for a son who was anything but sinless, cried out: "O my son Absalom, my son, my son Absalom! Would God I had died for thee, O Absalom my son, my son!" (2 Samuel 18.33).

Experience teaches us that the hardest pains to bear are not those we face ourselves, but the ones we have to watch our loved ones enduring: our children going to school and for the first time coping with rejection because at home they get nothing but love and affirmation.

Friends or relations become ill, and suffer, when all we have to offer — we feel — is platitudes and awkwardness. Parents get old and frail, anxious and uncertain, where once they were calm and confident and capable. In this fact of human life, we find good reason to pay attention to Mary, as another human being just like us — which is what she is.

IF WE look at the commonest ways in which Mary is depicted in art at the foot of the cross, she is usually shown in one of two postures. The first embodies what I have just been describing: she gazes downward, away from Jesus, in a posture evocative of the inexpressible pain she is enduring, unable

Too hard to bear: Mary looks away from Christ in Jesus Consigning his Mother to Saint John *by an assistant of Fra Angelico, c.1450*

any longer to look on his suffering. Other people gather round to comfort and support her.

In the second, like the first, her position is lower than that of Jesus, who is lifted up. But, this time, her eyes turn upward to gaze on him.

There comes a turning point, a moment in most mothers' lives, when they really do have to look up, instead of down, into their sons' eyes, and one should not underestimate the emotional and physical impact of that experience. But this is something different.

The lifting-up of eyes is in itself a gesture of prayer. In John 11.41, at the grave of Lazarus, Jesus lifted up his eyes and said: "Father, I thank you that you have heard me." At John 17.1, he lifted up his eyes to heaven and said: "Father, the hour has come." In the parable, the tax collector who went to pray "would not even lift up his eyes to heaven" (Luke 18.13).

Lifting up the eyes should be a physical gesture with a joyful, spiritual purpose. It should connect us with the beauty and the love of God, in a gesture of instinctive reverence. Here at the cross, when we lift up our eyes, all that is before us is horror, misery, and humiliation.

This in itself is a microcosm of the paradox of the cross, and the paradox of the incarnation. Christianity is a very paradoxical faith.

Gazing upon suffering: Mary looks up towards Christ in this Crucifixion with the Virgin Mary, St John and St Mary Magdalene *(1617–19), painted by Anthony van Dyck, now in the Louvre Museum, Paris*

The gaze of Mary's eyes directs us straight to the crucified Jesus. He is at the centre, she on the periphery. So the lifting-up of her eyes to look towards him is a gesture with a powerful theological significance. It tells us how human beings can relate to the incarnate Son of God hanging on a tree. It is a way of saying "As I look to the crucified, and can endure, so can you. There is nowhere else our eyes can better turn. They must come back to this, come back to him. Do not turn, do not walk away. Watch with me."

So to enter into the sorrowful mystery of Mary at the foot of the cross, we must do what she does: put ourselves in the scene, at the cross, and lift up our eyes to the Crucified. Thus Mary is the one who points the way. She images us to ourselves; she shows us what we can and should be doing.

WHENEVER we want to reflect on Jesus in relation to Mary, it is helpful to clear the decks by making sure first that we know why this could be important or worthwhile. We should begin by asking ourselves two questions: "Who is Mary in herself?" (the "Protestant" angle, if you like); and "What does she stand for, or represent to us?" (the "Catholic" angle).

If she is merely a woman like any other, we can still discern from her responses to God and Jesus something about her. We can judge her in the same way as we judge any other Gospel character: obedience or disobedience; love or rejection; persistence or failure; encouragement or despair.

If she has a deeper meaning, if something about her place in the Christian story is unique, and sets her apart, we can be confident that when we give our attention to her, it will not be given unworthily or inappropriately.

When we pray with the Church in the liturgies of Holy Week, or on our own at other times of year, we make a choice to step into the crucifixion scene. But the first time that we decide to do so by deliberately taking a position with Mary at the foot of the cross, we want to be clear what it is we are choosing. We have to peel off all the layers of history and meaning and devotion and enthusiasm — and look at the facts.

There is her chosenness: God chose either at random or with a purpose, when he sent his son into the world to save it. Which is more likely? Of all the places, and times, and cultures, and women, God chose Mary of Nazareth. We do not know exactly why, but we do recall from Scripture quite a bit about how God chooses people, and what his priorities might be. They are not wealth, not lineage, and not seniority, at any rate.

We may not know why he chose her; but we find out fast that God was right, because of her response to the angel: "Behold the Lord's servant. Let it be to me just as you have said."

IN THIS FACT of being chosen, and in the vindication of God's choice in her response, we find the clue to the point of Mary for ourselves. She is there in the Gospel, and in the life and devotion of the Church, to teach us first what we are (beloved, chosen, unique), and what we can and should become (followers of Jesus, obedient to Jesus, ready to stand at the foot of the cross, prepared to follow even to death, and in faith that death is not the end). She stands for us.

This is worth emphasising because, when we move out of the joyful mystery of the annunciation, and into that of the crucifixion, what we see and feel is so different, and so overwhelming. The bare sight of the crucified is enough to sink us, to swamp us in horror and despair.

That is one reason why meditating on the episode as a whole is such an important exercise in prayer. I have imagined many things in my meditations on the death of Jesus. But I have never managed, and not even tried, to imagine the moment when Mary walks away from what she knows is the dead body of her son.

Art records for us iconic glimpses: the crucifixion, the deposition (when his body is taken down from the cross), the Pietà — Mary with the body of her son in her arms is a terrible counterpart of the baby she cradles with serenity and joy in so many statues and pictures. Yet art does not usually record the moment when his battered body was washed, laid out, anointed, wrapped for burial, and sealed in the stone-cold tomb.

I would be surprised if anyone has ever depicted Mary walking away from the graveside. Yet everyone who has ever buried a loved one knows the dreadful wrench of that betraying footstep. And many clergy will recognise the grim reluctance of the bereaved to face this point of disconnection, this letting go.

STUDIES of Mary begin, or ought to, from this point of theological principle: Mary is not worshipped. Her only purpose is to show the way to Christ (those who pray with icons will know her in this respect as the Hodegetria, the one who points the way).

Wherever she appears in the Gospels (and few as those instances are, they are more than any other individual character), her task is to point away from herself to her son. It is only in John's Gospel that her presence at the foot of the cross is made specific. The other Evangelists refer to many women present at the scene, and name a few, but do not mention her.

It is as if John has decided to complete the picture given by Luke. Where Luke depicted Mary's decision to say yes to God — her experience of the angel, the promise of the Holy Spirit's overshadowing, and her journey and becoming a mother — John shows her present at her son's departure from the world.

Luke is focused on her presence, proving Jesus was truly human at the beginning of his life; John makes the same point as Jesus hangs dying. This is flesh indeed. Her motherhood proves his humanity.

MARY looks up, gazing upon suffering, suffering herself. But the gaze is not equal. His understanding, his wound of knowledge, is infinitely greater than hers. He suffers in flesh and spirit; she in spirit only. But perhaps this distinction is not always helpful — the pain of grief is felt physically in the thudding heart, the choking breath, the sickness that destroys appetite and even the sense of taste.

I do not doubt that, if she could have chosen to suffer in his place, she would have done so. But it could not be so. Only he could taste the cup of suffering as he did, and only he can undo death as he will do on Easter morning.

At the annunciation, Mary stood for the firstborn of all the redeemed, because she accepted God's call. Here, at the foot of the cross, she is once again the first among the redeemed — the first follower of Jesus — the first Christian, that is, to endure the cross as a means to accepting the redemption he won for all humanity.

If we stand with her, if we are willing to learn from her, the sorrowful mysteries of this present time will certainly pass away into the glorious mysteries that will be revealed on Easter Day.

(2008)

Water and blood flow together

Samuel Wells considers why both blood and water flowed
from the side of Christ

THIS is a meditation on one of the more mysterious moments in the Passion account: the piercing of Jesus's side, and the outpouring of water and blood. John's Gospel does not waste words: each one counts. What do these words mean? There might be a clue in the hidden, but perhaps crucial, little word, "and".

One of the most privileged and tender moments you get invited into as a priest is to be with a person and their family at the moment of death. What I try to do is to touch the person's five senses, and gently offer each one back to God.

I touch the eyes, and think about what those eyes have seen; the ears, and reflect on what those ears have heard; the nose, and savour what that nose has smelled; the mouth, and dwell on what the tongue has tasted; and, finally, the hand, and consider what those hands have touched.

To touch the skin of a person's body after they have died is an intimate thing to do. It is terrifying, because it makes you realise how vulnerable each one of us is – because this moment will come for us all. But it also makes you ponder the intricate wonder of this person: how all the capillaries and nerve ends, organs, and brain cells that are now silent and still were once so busy for so long.

Our physical bodies depend on two things above all. One is water – we are each made up of about 60 per cent water. The other is blood – without the blood circulating around our bodies, nothing would function for more than a second.

Jesus had no nursing home or hospital side ward to die in. His execution was an extended and merciless form of torture. Once Jesus had died, John's Gospel records a significant event: "One of the soldiers pierced his side with a spear, and at once blood and water came out." (John 19.34)

It is an awesome event of atonement and salvation, judgement, death, and sacrifice; but it is also an intimate story of love and betrayal, physical pain, and emotional heartbreak. What is going on throughout the Passion narrative is an interweaving of awe and intimacy, of the grand cosmic story and the intense personal drama. I want to look at how all these things appear in this brutal moment shortly after Jesus's death, when the spear pierces his side, and out come blood and water.

THE FIRST strand is the background of this spear story in the ritual shape of the life of Israel. The day of preparation falls every Friday, and ends at sundown on Friday night. Passover falls once a year, on the 14th day of the seventh month of the Jewish calendar, which can be any day of the week.

John's Gospel points out that the day that Jesus was killed was an unusual day, because the way the calendar fell, it was both the eve of Passover and the day of preparation, a coincidence that occurred only every ten years or so.

The fact that it was the eve of Passover meant that the blood that appeared as the soldier pierced Jesus's side gushed forth just as the blood of the Passover lambs was being spilt. The fact that it was the day of preparation meant that those who had condemned Jesus wanted his body removed before the day of rest began.

All of this is told with repeated reminders that those who wanted Jesus dead could do nothing without the Romans' authority. Even the final spear-thrust into Jesus's side is carried out by a Roman soldier. So already we have the grand context of sacrifice and deliverance, and the earthier context of meeting legal requirements and avoiding the 24-hour sight and smell of a crucified corpse.

But all of these are focused in the reality of a Roman soldier who has control over Jesus's body, as surely as Rome had complete control over the land of Israel. Already, themes of politics, personal passion, and providential purpose converge on this single moment.

THE NEXT strand is the resonance of these events in the Scriptures of Israel. Most obviously, we recall the words concerning the suffering servant in Isaiah 53.5: "He was pierced for our transgressions, crushed for our iniquities; ... and by his wounds we are healed."

But, more subtly, we might reflect on the Greek word for "side", which is sometimes translated as "rib". It appears only here in the New Testament, and only once in the Greek version of the Old Testament. But that single place is very interesting. It is the moment in Genesis 2 where God takes the side (or rib) of Adam, and shapes it into a woman.

The creation of Eve in Genesis 2 represents not just the creation of woman, but the creation of society, of diversity, of the whole idea that human beings can share and give and pass on life to one another.

So what we have in this piercing of Jesus's side is not just the fulfilment of the prophecy of the suffering servant, but also an idea that what comes

out of Jesus may be the beginning of new life, a new society. When we recall Jesus's promise that from him will come streams of living water, we begin to wonder whether this is precisely what he was referring to.

THIS invites the weaving of another strand, which we might call the significance of these events in the life of the Church. Water and blood: it is hard to avoid the most obvious connection of this event to the two central acts of the Church's life: baptism and eucharist.

This moment on the cross is like Eve emerging out from the side of Adam, like a new birth – almost a new creation. Now it seems as if this is like the birth of the Church at the moment of Christ's death. And, in its birth, it is given the two sacraments that shape its life – the water of baptism, and the blood of holy communion.

A few verses earlier, Jesus had commended his mother to the beloved disciple, and the beloved disciple to his mother, with the words: "Woman, here is your son;" and: "Here is your mother." So here, at the cross, we are witnessing the foundation of the Church, with a new community, a new birth, and new sources of life.

THIS brings us to the last strand in understanding what the piercing of Jesus's side and the blood and water are all about. John's Gospel is fond of the word "and". In John 1, we get word and flesh, grace and truth. In John 2, we get water and wine. In John 3, we get spirit and truth. Here, we get blood and water.

I believe that that "and" is the clue to how we are to interpret Jesus's life, and how to interpret Jesus's death. When you touch a dead body, you get the delicate intimacy of realising that you are close to the fragility of another human being, perhaps one whom you loved deeply. But you also get a shiver of awe that this is death – cold, numbing, unavoidable death – and it is as scary close up, in flesh and blood, as it is far away in the language of oblivion and judgement.

I think that we can take these twin feelings to this moment of the death of Jesus. There is water – there is the way that Jesus's death gives life, gives hope, gives trust in the promises of God and the presence of the Holy Spirit. Yet there is also blood – there is pain, horror, brutality, ugliness, violence, and deep, deep fear. And John's account says "at once blood and water came out". They came out together. The cross is about water and blood.

THE SAME is true if we look back at Jesus's life through the lens of his cross. There is water – there are fountains of life, living water, healing, forgiveness, joy, and gladness. But there is also blood – there is hostility, betrayal, hatred, pain, adversity, and, finally, what looks very much like defeat.

On Good Friday, it is easy to make one of two mistakes: to look only on the watery Jesus, who saved us from our sins and made everything right between us and God; or to look only on the bloodied Jesus, who suffered in agony, and at the last believed that God had forsaken him. This is why the "and" is so important.

This is also why the last strand in understanding the water and the blood of Jesus's pierced side is the kind of life you and I are to live in faithfulness to the moment of Jesus's death. We could live a life that airbrushes out the blood, and sees only the water – a sunny life, that insists that everything always turns out for the best; that will not tolerate gloom; that fits the Jesus story into a positive and upbeat outlook on the world.

Or we could live a life that airbrushes out the water, and sees only the blood – a life of struggle, anger, and bitterness; a recognition that there really is hatred and enmity in the world; and that death comes to us all.

But to follow the Saviour from whose side at once came water and blood is to believe both that suffering and death are real, and that Jesus's death and resurrection have transformed suffering and death; so that they no longer have the last word. Because of the blood, what we see taking place on the cross is terrifying: it is real human death. But because of the water, we can look on it with hope, and not have to turn away our eyes in fear and despair. It is not the end of the story.

ONCE we have learned how to look at the glory and horror of the cross, we can look with new eyes at the most agonising sight in our own lives. We can look with new eyes at what we have brought about by our own foolishness; at what we cannot put right, for all our attempts to ignore it, deny it, distract ourselves from it, or resolve it.

We can dare to look at what we dare not look at very often: the truth about ourselves, our lives, our loves, our fears, our faith. And we can look with the searing honesty that is brought about by Christ's blood, and the unflinching courage brought about by Christ's water.

We can bring with us the tender intimacy of our own closeness to whatever it is, and the profound awe of how it connects to the suffering of Christ. We can dare to stay in that still place, a place of awe and intimacy, a place of water and blood, a place of grace and truth. This is the place of the "and". On Easter Day, we fling wide the doors, and feel the joy of glory. But on Good Friday, we stay in the place of the "and".

This "and" is the overlap between water and blood. It was a place that the disciples could not occupy, which is why they scattered at this crucial moment, and were not around to witness the scene.

They scattered because they wanted reality to be all water, and, when they saw the blood, they turned to fear and despair. But the heart of being a Christian lies in staying still, right in this moment, where water and blood come out together. Being a Christian means remaining in the place where hope and suffering meet.

This place, the place of water and blood, is the place where faith and fear overlap. It is perhaps the most difficult place to be. But this is the place where the Church was born. And this continues to be the place, more than anywhere else, where the Church still belongs.

The Church is, and always has been, most truly itself not when soaring in success, or when plunged in despair, but when success and despair are mingled like water and blood. It is a place of conflict, horror, and agony, but also of new birth, new community, and new sources of life. This place has a name. It is called the foot of the cross.

(2013)

Horror, admiration and outrage

A visceral response to the crucifixion is understandable,
but this needs to be transcended to find its true value in ministry,
says **Stephen Cherry**

THE FIRST WORD that springs to mind when I start to think about the cross is "horror". The sight of a life-size cross makes me think of the pain and the desolation of the one pinned to it. Medical accounts of what happens to a person strung out as a spectacle to horrify others horrify me.

I am not sure whether this is good for my spirituality or ministry. It puts many minor things in perspective, but gives me the chill feeling that the possibilities for suffering that lie ahead in my own life are limitless. It reminds me that I just do not know what is to come.

It is rare to think that. Mostly, I live with the assumption that my life will come to an end through natural causes, with pain reasonably under control. But the cross makes me realise how naïve this is: which again kindles my horror.

This horror draws out my "admiration". Whatever Jesus's attitude towards his own death — and we can let the scholars squabble — he must have known what to expect, after a certain point. He would have seen other men being crucified. It was not unusual under the Romans. And, because it was intended to intimidate, we can be sure that every effort would have been made to make a spectacle of it. It was the most public of public executions. You have to admire someone who does not run away from that.

Having experienced horror and admiration, my next reaction is "outrage". The killing of the wandering rabbi from the country, who had earned a reputation as a healer, is simply outrageous. And yet I wonder about my own outrage. It is a strong feeling, and yet it is not an emotion that is going anywhere. So the cross makes me cross; there is no merit in that. Indeed, the worst of ironies might be for the cross itself to blind me to the love that it is meant to represent.

I FIND it hard to get my attention away from the horror and outrage of the cross. I want to make more connections with life and ministry, but they are too easily eclipsed. The cross is just so vivid, so compelling.

The spectacle is so severe that identifying with it seems ridiculous. My life is lived in other places. My ministry is hardly touched by the horror and admiration I find here.

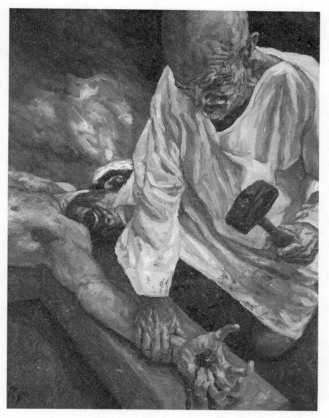

"A spectacle to horrify others": crucifixion, depicted in
Christ is nailed to the Cross, *one of the Stations of the Cross*
painted by Rob Floyd for Manchester Cathedral

Then I think of a holding cross. I have given many of these away. One lady in hospital, who was all but blind, called it her "little miracle", such was its power on her recovery. My dying father told me — with genuine surprise and sincere gratitude — that it gave him comfort.

One Sunday, a teenage girl came to our parish eucharist with her mother, and barked like a wild dog throughout. It was very alarming. I gave her a little time, and some prayer. Then I gave her a holding cross. The next day, I visited their flat. The cross had not left her hand. It was completely black. But she was much calmer.

I asked whether they had any occult or disturbing pictures or books. They had already cleared the pictures, but showed me some books, and asked me to take them away. One was *The Encyclopaedia of Serial Killers*. A few years later, I saw the girl again. Unrecognisable, she was fine.

NOW other words come to mind as I hold the cross in mind: "brokenness", in particular. "We break this bread."

Indeed we do, and know that the body was broken not only *on* the cross, but *by* the cross. Priests know the breaking of the body in ministry, because it is their hands that break it. We snap it dramatically but all too routinely. It is impossible to feel the pain and resonance of it time after time. It is just a wafer disc. It is just a bun. It is a just loaf in our hands.

Except that it is also the focal point of hopes and fears. It is the place where personal brokenness connects with the brokenness of all who gather, all who give it their attention in this sacred nanosecond of crack. And not only the brokenness, but the desiccated, crumbling brokenness of all we know about in others; and all we have heard of third- and fourth-hand; and all that we can imagine.

The brokenness of the universe is there in that one deft push of my two thumbs. Crack! The bread is broken for the life of the world. Not a nuclear explosion, but a spiritual one. It is a wonder that the windows don't fly out, or the walls tumble to nothing with the blast of it.

But it is much gentler than this. The cross brings nothing to shatter us any more. Rather, it gives us more healing and teaching than the young rabbi could ever share. And exorcism, too. The cross drives the demons away. It stills and calms us. That sounds forceful — but no force is here, only gentleness. Like the gentleness of forgiveness offered.

THEN there is friendship. "Today you will be with me in paradise." "Feed my sheep." A garden rather than a scruffy hill-top; that is the promise of the cross. Company, not isolation. The vertical pole grounds us solidly, and also points us to the heaven, which is open. The horizontal bar mimics the outstretched arm, the extended hand.

I take that hand, pierced, blood-stained, and torn as it is. I hold it firmly in one hand, reaching out with my other to share the love felt here with any who pass by.

In the end, then, the love that led to the cross becomes apparent through the cross, even if it is not the first aspect that arrests our attention. The horror and outrage of the cross have to be transcended if the true wonder of the cross is to be recognised and known in healing, if it is to become an engine of compassion and love.

The love seen on the cross, and felt as the cross is held, is amazing and divine not because of the depth of physical suffering, but because its power lives in those who let it touch their own vulnerability.

(2014)

Not quite so wondrous?

William Whyte considers the myths of the True Cross

THE ARTIST Piero della Francesca painted a cycle of pictures in the Basilica of San Francesco in Arezzo between 1452 and 1466. His subject was one of the great stories of the medieval Church: the legend of the True Cross.

Although people still queue to see the frescos, the True Cross is now something of an embarrassment to the Church, which tends to play it down as a part of the superstitious medieval cult of relics.

These objections, however, miss the point. The problem with the True Cross is not the relics associated with it. It turns out that, despite stories to the contrary, even if you were to put all the supposed pieces together, there is not enough True Cross to make a real cross. The problem is the story that surrounds it — the story that Piero painted nearly 600 years ago.

Since 395, when Ambrose of Milan first suggested it, Christians have erroneously claimed that the cross was rediscovered by St Helena, mother of the Emperor Constantine. On a pilgrimage to the Holy Land, so it is said, she founded churches, gave money to the poor, and — most importantly — set out to find the instrument of Christ's Passion.

A woman more interested in ends than means, Helena tortured a Jewish man — significantly called Judas — into revealing where the Cross was hidden. Predictably enough, it was buried at the site of the crucifixion: alongside the two other crosses mentioned in the Gospels.

Still undeterred, Helena solved the problem of which was the True Cross by using an experiment. A suitably grand invalid was found, and she was touched by each of the crosses in turn. The first two did nothing. But, as Rufinus put it in about 400, when the third cross was brought near, "the woman suddenly opened her eyes and got up."

Case closed. Helena had only to chop the True Cross up — sending much of it back home. As for Judas, he was apparently so impressed that he converted to Christianity, becoming, as a result, the future Bishop of Jerusalem.

Had any of this been true, Helena would certainly have been "the most successful archaeologist in history", as the Israeli journalist Amos Elon put it. Torture aside, she could certainly have given the people on *Time Team* a run for their money. Sadly, none of it is true. Helena does not even appear to have founded any churches, and the generous gifts she gave seem more likely to have been bribes than benisons, intended to secure the always-doubtful loyalty of the local soldiers.

The story about the discovery or, as the Church would put it, the Invention of the Cross turns out to be more inventive than one might hope. The likelihood is that the whole thing was made up in Jerusalem by a church and a bishop who wanted to stress the city's links with the imperial family.

THE DISCOVERY of the Cross is not the most remarkable, nor even the most important, story told. For Orthodox Christians, even today, the Invention is overshadowed by the Exaltation of the Cross. This is the second great story told about the Cross: a celebration of the moment when a Byzantine Emperor, Heraclius I, recaptured its remains.

The True Cross was lost to the Persians in 614, and regained 13 years later in 627. Returning it to Jerusalem, so it is said, Heraclius could not bear the weight of the wood — until, that is, he removed his crown, at which point he was able to lift or, more precisely, to exalt it.

The popularity of this story for the Eastern Churches is both undeniable and self-evident. It is still celebrated across the Orthodox world. In Ethiopia, *Meskel* (the Feast of the Cross) is one of the main events of the year. It links the True Cross to the true faith, and, more than this, it links military victory and Orthodox triumph to the wood of the Passion: a truly remarkable mixture.

Yet the Exaltation is nothing compared with the third and most encompassing story of the Cross: the extraordinary narrative of the *Lignum Crucis*. This found its final form in the *Golden Legend* of Jacobus de Voragine, written in the mid-13th century, and it set all these events within a much wider and still more remarkable frame.

Not content with retelling the stories of Heraclius and Helena, the *Golden Legend* sought to trace the origin of the True Cross itself. No ordinary piece of wood, the *Lignum Crucis* was the last remaining part of the Tree of Knowledge, the site and source of Adam's sin.

It turns out — or so Jacobus claimed — that, on his deathbed, Adam had asked his son Seth to plant the seed of the tree at his grave. Seth hurried off to the Archangel Michael, obtained the seed, and grew the tree, planting it in his father's mouth.

Generations later, Jacobus went on, Solomon chopped down the tree to make a bridge. The Queen of Sheba was about to cross it when a divine message reached her, prophesying that this wood would bring about the end of God's covenant with the Jews. Understandably alarmed, Solomon

The original Time Team: Discovery and Proof of the True Cross *by Piero della Francesca, from the fresco cycle* Legend of the True Cross *(1447–66), in San Francesco, Arezzo, in Tuscany*

destroyed the bridge and disposed of the timber — only for it to resurface in time for the crucifixion.

This story is, of course, even more absurd than any of the others. Yet it was also one of the most widely known and accepted legends in Western Christendom, and is illustrated in many books and churches.

The parallel between Adam and Christ; the link between the Tree of Knowledge and the Cross; the bridge between the Old and New Testaments — all these appealed to an imagination schooled in symbolism and in analogical reasoning. Our forebears were perennially interested in the patterns, types, and apparent similarities of characters in both parts of the Bible.

THE STORIES of the True Cross show just how hard it is to take the events of Easter on their own terms. The striking thing about almost all the legends that grew up is the extent to which they avoid the central fact that this was an instrument of death, of torture, and of suffering.

Remarkably, Piero della Francesca's fresco cycle at Arezzo tells the story of the Cross without once showing the crucifixion — and he was far from alone in this. The whole legend is a sort of displacement activity: a way of avoiding uncomfortable truths.

Further examination makes the matter even clearer, pointing out the way in which the cross was transformed from an instrument of death into a celebration of power. The Invention of the Cross is ultimately a story about imperial triumph. So, for that matter, is the Exaltation of the Cross.

Both show the Cross made meaningful by its association with emperors and empresses.

The *Golden Legend* is still worse. In its account, even the wood of the Cross cannot be ordinary. It has to be special wood from a special tree with a special place in history.

This attempt to redeem the cross is the real scandal of the old legend. What it does is to deny the awful reality of the crucifixion. By making the Cross a pre-consecrated piece of sacred timber, our predecessors sought to downplay the dreadful fact of Christ's being nailed to an ordinary piece of wood. By celebrating the cross through its association with the monarchy, it turned the evidence of agony into a piece of royal regalia.

Before we get too complacent about our modern and more sophisticated age, it is worth wondering whether we are any better equipped to face the awful reality of the crucifixion. Our Easter may not involve mysterious relics and ancient legends, but we have our own ways of avoiding the utter horror of the crucifixion.

Some get through Easter by ignoring it, and focusing only on the resurrection. Others do not look at the Cross as a place of human pain, but think of it only as a symbol. Still others are more concerned with the abstractions of theology than with the fact that Jesus actually suffered and died there: viewing the Cross as an unfortunate necessity for the atonement rather than as the instrument of utter abjection that it undoubtedly was.

Perhaps most do not think about it at all. The old legend of the True Cross may have been superseded — but we create new ones in every generation.

(2009)

The Saturday condition

The nothingness of Easter Eve has more to say than we allow,
observes **Peter Townley**

THE events of Holy Week and Easter should properly provide the framework for our Christian lives, but, perversely, Holy Saturday, or Easter Eve, is often given little thought or attention.

Holy Saturday is a day of waiting as we remember Christ lying in the tomb. Looking at this day with hindsight, through resurrection-tinted spectacles, it is hard to imagine the profound sense of bereavement, devastation, and dashed hope felt by the first disciples.

For most of us, perhaps, Holy Saturday is just another day of noise — our attention-sapping smartphones remain on, and we hunt for bargains in the Easter sales. In our rushed, technology-driven lives, perhaps we are no longer well equipped for the pause that Holy Saturday requires of us.

And yet, in his seminal book *Real Presences*, George Steiner writes of Holy Saturday as a day that holds within it much of the human experience: "There is one particular day in Western history about which neither historical record nor myth nor Scripture make report. It is a Saturday ... Ours is the long day's journey of the Saturday. Between suffering, aloneness, unutterable waste on the one hand and the dream of liberation, of rebirth on the other.

"In the face of the torture of a child, of the death of love which is Friday, even the greatest art and poetry are almost helpless. In the Utopia of the Sunday, the aesthetic will, presumably, no longer have logic or necessity.

"The apprehensions and figurations in the play of metaphysical imagining, in the poem and the music, which tell of pain and of hope, of the flesh which is said to taste of ash and of the spirit which is said to have the savour of fire, are always Sabbatarian. They have risen out of an immensity of waiting which is that of man. Without them, how could we be patient?"

The theologian Nicholas Lash agrees. In "Friday, Saturday, Sunday", the Aquinas lecture given at Blackfriars, Cambridge 1990, he says: "There is the sense that all prayer and expectation, all keeping of createdness in mind, occur on Saturday, in darkness illuminated from the pain of God, in watchfulness for the rising of the sun, in patience."

THESE thoughts, the ability to understand the "Saturday condition" of our lives, may help us to reflect on — and perhaps have more patience with — the many situations in the world which we struggle to comprehend. We are holding our breath in these days of uncertainty after the European referendum, as we wait to see how Brexit will affect our country and the rest of the European community, and as we come to terms with what it means to live in a world of "post-truth" and "alternative facts" after the presidential elections in the United States.

Likewise, within the Church of England, recent controversies about the Church's view of same-sex marriages and bishops opposed to ordaining women priests may need to be met with patient reflection rather than knee-jerk reactions and quick fixes.

In the silence of Holy Saturday, we also find the paradox of Christ's work — the mystery at the heart of our faith — in the fact that the tomb is the end of Christ's life, but also the place of his triumph. This tension is captured by the German-American theologian Paul Tillich, who writes of a witness at the Nuremberg war trials who spoke of escaping the gas chambers by hiding with other Jews in a cemetery.

While they were there, a young woman gave birth with assistance from an aged gravedigger. As the baby was born, the gravedigger was heard to pray: "Great God, hast thou finally sent the Messiah to us? For who else than the Messiah himself can be born in a grave?"

THE great Matthaean scholar John Fenton is reported to have told his students at Oxford that "the most obvious characteristic of God is his silence. He does not cough, or mutter, or shuffle his feet to reassure us that he is there."

But the silence of Holy Saturday does not mean that nothing was happening. Hans Urs von Balthasar reminds us that if Holy Saturday is about anything, it is about Christ's utter God-forsakenness and the completion of his *kenosis* (self-emptying), and therefore the boundless reach of his high-priestly ministry.

We live in the hush of our "Saturday condition", between these twin poles of Good Friday and Easter Day, and yet we begin to hear the first sounds of hope as Easter Day approaches. Paradoxically, this day of quiet expectation is expressed liturgically in many Orthodox churches on Holy Saturday morning by loud drumming on the pews, the ringing of bells, the scattering of rose petals, and the stamping of feet to symbolise the transforming Christ who breaks down the gates of Hades.

Out of the silence and expectant waiting, new life is born in a graveyard. As the Negro spiritual "Roll away that stone" by Richard M. Hadden has it: "Oh yes, jus' roll away that stone, brother, And let Lord Jesus out. Open your heart, brother, And let Lord Jesus in!"

(2017)

A slice of Rumsfeld pie

Holy Saturday is a time to confront the limits of knowledge,
writes **Mark Oakley**.

NOT long ago, I was introduced to something called the Pie of Knowledge.
It is a pie chart, such as we gazed on in maths classes, and it attempts to
describe your knowledge of things in relation to all the knowledge in the
universe by slicing up the pie into sections.

The first slice of this Pie of Knowledge is made up of those things that
you know you know. So, for example, this might be the plot of Jane Austen's
Sense and Sensibility, the name of your dog, or how to make sausage rolls.

Then there are the things you know you don't know: this may be a larger
slice, and include nuclear physics, the mating rituals of the firefly, or the
rules of polo.

The third slice contains things you know but have forgotten: let's say, the
age of the Archbishop of Canterbury, your grandchild's phone number,
what you had for dinner last Tuesday.

The fourth slice of the pie is very interesting: the things you don't know
you don't know. (I can't give you examples here, because that would mean
I knew.)

*Donald Rumsfeld's most famous quote
comes from a briefing he gave as the US
Secretary of Defense in February 2002:
"Reports that say that something hasn't
happened are always interesting to me,
because as we know, there are known
knowns: there are things we know we
know. We also know there are known
unknowns: that is to say, we know there
are some things we do not know. But
there are also unknown unknowns: the
ones we don't know we don't know. And
if one looks throughout the history of
our country and other free countries, it
is the latter category that tend to be the
difficult ones."*

The last slice is the things you think you know, but really don't. Family and friends might be better able to identify these for us, but it might include: why my neighbour is like he is; what it's like to be an archdeacon; or what this article is about.

For all human beings, the largest slice of the pie is the fourth: "The things you don't know you don't know". This slice probably makes up 99.9 per cent of the chart. The total knowledge of our universe is so vast that the sum of all human knowledge is infinitesimally small by comparison.

I AM struck, as I prepare to preach through the days of Holy Week, that those who make up our congregations fall into similar categories as regards our Christian faith. First, there will be those who know that they know — people who know the gospel of Jesus Christ with certainty, and are pretty sure where doctrinal boundaries are fixed. Should you step over one in your sermon, they will be ready to challenge you at the end.

Then there are those in church who know what they don't know. They are hungry, and want help. They feel they missed out learning about the Christian faith, or come from another tradition, and are intrigued, but not sure where to turn for trustworthy information.

Sitting somewhere near them will be those who once knew things, but have forgotten. They learned things when they were in Sunday school, or at school assembly, or maybe when they were churchgoers, years back, and have only now started to think about Christian faith again. They need their childish perceptions to be reframed and made resonant to the adult they have become.

Last, there are those who think they know the heart of the Christian faith, but actually don't. They have picked up the cheap slogan, or the populist caricature, or maybe they have confused the gospel for their own moral code or prejudices in an even more unapologetic way than the rest of us.

FAITH is always asking what it means to "know" God. Faith's knowledge is more akin to "believing in", trusting, than "believing that", as if there were some divine dotted line we could sew things up with if we signed up.

God communicates himself in a body-language. Jesus of Nazareth is the human face of God, open and visible; but, when Peter stood warming himself, and said "I do not know the man", he was telling the truth. He did not know — in the sense of completely understand — Jesus. There were plenty of things he had yet to learn.

As with all of us, there are things we don't know we don't know yet about God, Christ, life, and ourselves. Our Christian ancestors knew that they were engaged as members of "the way" not "the arrival". Peter's denial of Jesus was not, ultimately, about a factual knowledge of Christ's identity and purpose, but about losing the courage to trust him and continue a journey with him.

Over another fire later on, he was to be asked not "Do you know me?" but "Do you love me?" So, no matter which category in the congregation we fall into, we are all, when it comes to knowledge of God, a people of longing and desire. Without these, faith begins to die.

SO THE event and act of connection known as "preaching" is, to say the least, challenging. There is one category, however, that applies to everyone, including the preacher. None of us knows what we don't know. It means that the most effective preaching is done by those who take us to a place where we say "Oh! I never knew I never knew that. This feels fresh. It's dislocated me inside. This is making me rethink, re-feel. It's strange, new, and yet, somehow, it feels like home, too. I sense a hard little full-stop in me has just been changed into a comma. Could this be the gospel of Jesus Christ?"

Because of this, it is sad that preachers do not get the chance to preach during Holy Saturday. It is a day that nobody really talks about in the liturgical year. In church, it tends to be the day when the flower arrangers move in, and we start polishing everything in sight ready for the big day. Although there is a great deal to do, our busy activity on Holy Saturday might also reveal a disquiet that we have with what lies at its heart: our bereaved lives, and God's silence.

Perhaps we need to get busy and distracted on Saturday and seek, in George Steiner's phrase, "the immunities of indirection".

HOLY Saturday is a day of loss and felt absence. It reflects back to us something of our own losses — whether lovers, or certainities, or hopes — and reminds us that the life of faith can be one of devotion, but it can also be one of dereliction. It can be full of reverence one day, but also of rebellion at the pain of injustice the next.

More than 30 times in the Hebrew Bible is the phrase "*Hester panim*" used — the hiding of God's face — and Holy Saturday provokes us into admitting that there can be periods, short or long, when God seems dead and gone. Life feels like some shocked and reluctant walk away from his grave.

It is always tempting to translate this sense of spiritual bereavement as being our fault, a result of unfaithfulness to God. We sense that we do not pray correctly, or believe properly. We wonder if God is taking it out on us because we did something wrong.

So often, though, the silence of God is given to those who can faithfully grow in it. As André Neher points out in *The Exile of the Word: From the silence of the Bible to the silence of Auschwitz*, Abraham's reward for obeying God's voice was never to hear it again. When Jesus dies on the cross reciting a poem, Psalm 22, perplexed as to why God has forsaken him, never has he been more faithful, and never has God been closer.

Martin Buber wrote: "A divine eclipse does not mean God is dead." This is the other truth that lies deep in Holy Saturday. The silence, though real and presenting as absence, is where God does his deepest work.

Silence is God's last resort against our idolatry. It unpicks the full stops we have placed on him, and changes these also into commas, so that we understand that he is not a butterfly to be pinned down either by our cleverest or selfish thoughts — or even our ecstatic, Magdalene-like garden embraces.

THE silence of Holy Saturday is bereaved, but at its centre is liberation, rebirth, and hope. Not every fall needs to be final; it can be a fall into truth. Not every silence is empty; it can be where Gods shows us the poverty of our forces of habit, of thinking and relating, which deprive us of life worthy of his image.

Spiritually, we live our lives at a crossroads, a no man's land similar to the heart of Holy Saturday. We live at the point where a past that has affected us, and a future that lies open, meet in the present. When that point is forced into silence, we are invited to become vulnerable, because "nothing true can be said about God from a posture of defence" (Marilynne Robinson, in *Gilead*).

That poised silence is full of hope. It reminds us that God does not speak our language, our chatter. God does not make himself conveniently available for quick clarity, or easy answers. God is not a God of mouse-pad information, but of human formation, and — with the help of silence — transformation. God loves us just as we are, but he loves us so much that he does not want us to stay like that.

The grave-like quiet of Holy Saturday, even as we polish the lectern and buy the wine, is poised for as yet unseen things for us. It is true. We don't know what we don't know. It is called resurrection.

(2015)

Waiting for God to recreate

Holy Saturday: The paschal candle is lit, but first, darkness and chaos reign, says **Marilyn McCord Adams**

The Easter vigil consists of a series of rites of variable form, culminating in the first eucharist of Easter. The following order is envisaged here:

- the striking of a new fire and decoration of the paschal candle (outside or at the back of the church);
- the procession of the paschal candle to the front with the threefold declaration "The light of Christ!" and the lighting of the congregation's small candles along the way;
- the singing of the Exultet;
- the reading of Hebrew Bible stories — usually including the creation, the fall, the flood, Abraham's sacrifice of Isaac, the Red Sea crossing, and the dry bones — with collects and canticles; and
- the procession of the paschal candle back to the font for the blessing of the water and the renewal of baptismal vows.

EASTER VIGIL begins in darkness — the darkness of death that hovers over a battlefield when the fight is all over; the darkness of Sheol, where the souls of the elect are imprisoned in cramped quarters, deprived of enjoyments and unable to act; the darkness of creation unravelled, reverted to primal deep, where nothing is any longer, where nothing as yet is.

Flames in the darkness:
Easter Candles (Paschal Candle Procession),
1967, *by Eularia Clarke*

Easter vigil begins as sabbath is ending. All hell broke loose on Friday. The event, the Gospel story that our rites condense, the worst that a human being can come to, exposes the wreck and ruin of the whole human project, when the people of God crucify God. In the Synoptics, heavenly bodies avert their gaze. In Matthew's Gospel, shed blood of God pollutes the earth, which quakes and vomits forth its dead. The temple veil — hung to shield Israel from lethal close encounters with the Godhead — is torn from top to bottom.

Long before the tragic ending, there was a hopeful beginning, when God created the heavens and the earth, structured the environments, furnished them with plants and animals, and bestowed the gift of fertility. God embedded human beings in material creation, organically connected with the rest of the world — mud pies, but special because brought to life by the breath of God.

Life together with human beings in this material creation was what God wanted. God gave humans life as a gift. And because God knows that animal life is not self-sustaining, God cut a covenant, setting out a lifestyle of courteous consumption: human beings will be generously provided for, so long as they honour God as the source of life, and respect life in other creatures.

Neither life nor the necessities of life are entitlements. The sacrificial system reasserts this ritually by offering first-born livestock and first fruits (grain, wine, and oil) back to God. Limits to harvesting honoured God's image in others: the people of God were forbidden to glean fields to the very edge, to pick orchards and vineyards bare, to basket what fell to the ground, lest there be nothing for the poor or the sojourners to gather.

Likewise for cultivation: they were not to exhaust the land, but to give it a sabbath rest. Knowing how challenged humans are in evolving economic systems, God also mandated a jubilee year, when wealth would be redistributed, and lost patrimony returned to the poor.

In the Hebrew Bible, covenants were sealed with conditional blessings and curses. Courteous living in God's world would mean harmonious relations with God and others in a land of milk and honey. But if human beings refuse to behave as gifted guests, respectfully restrained in consuming what belongs to another, the whole cosmos will get radically out of kilter.

Acting as if we were entitled to life and to the necessities of life gives way to Darwinian grabbing and devouring of the lives of others. Feigned independence drives desperate expedients towards self-preservation. Alienation from divine purposes leads us to look elsewhere for help in our futile attempts to secure immortality for animal life.

Idolatry, bloodshed, rapacious consumption, and social injustice pollute land and temple, bring on warnings, and set curses in motion. God abandons sanctuary and city; the land vomits out the people into diaspora. Remnant Israel survives, wraith-like, deprived of embodied cultural existence in the land. New Testament apocalypses repaint the lurid consequences: wars and slaughter, crop-destroying plagues and tormenting diseases, poisoned and bloody rivers, fields reverted to wilderness, rolled-back heavens, and falling stars.

Friday encompasses all of this. Covenant bonds dissolve, the cosmos comes apart at the seams, because human desperation to live on our own has pressed on to its logical conclusion to slay the Lamb of God. The good news is that the divine divorce of Israel is never final; after a time and a time and half a time, God appears willing to begin again.

The good news is that Christ our Passover is sacrificed for us. "The life is in the blood," and Adam's race shed the blood of God in blasphemous self-assertion: "Our lives are our own; we don't need God to live!" But Christ meant it for good: in his human nature, Christ offers to God (to his divine nature) what Adam's race always owed — a life gratefully returned to its source. Blood shed violently cries out with Abel for vengeance.

But the martyr's blood poured out in sacrifice intercedes and makes atonement. Sprinkling it on us says that we live by the same life as Christ crucified, by a life returned to the hands of its Creator, by the power of an indestructible life.

WE HAVE waited a day. Holy Saturday recapitulates Israel's 40 years of wilderness wandering, Israel's 70 years of Babylonian captivity, and ages of waiting by the souls in Sheol. We are not waiting to be spirited out of this world to live as ghosts among the angels. We are waiting for our world to be recreated, for its fundamental structures to be laid down and redefined, so that we ourselves — embodied spirits — can be recreated.

By turning away from God, the source of life, human beings have made self and world a recalcitrant chaos. We are waiting for God to reorganise both by founding and recentring them in Christ.

The time is ripe to strike the new fire, to decorate and light the paschal candle. In the original creation, God begins by speaking God's Word to create light and divide light from darkness. Only on the fourth day does God gather up the light into discrete heavenly bodies — sun, moon, and stars — whose movements order time. In the recreation, Christ is the divine Word through whom all things were made and are remade. Christ yesterday and today, the beginning and the end, the alpha and omega, is the one in whom and through whom cosmos and persons acquire eternal significance.

In the recreation, the divine Word made flesh, crucified, and resurrected, is the one true light. The paschal candle insists: Christ is the light shining on in the darkness, the light that darkness cannot overcome.

As the paschal candle is processed forward, we are Israel, Christ the fiery pillar leading us out of our wilderness. Lighting our candles from his is already a declaration of consent, an appeal to Christ to descend into the hell we have made of self and world, and to bear it up, reorganised around the power of his indestructible life. Symbols give way to articulate speech as the sequenced Bible lessons rehearse our history. Each punctuating collect confirms our resolve, and furnishes broad hints on how to reframe our meanings in the light of Christ. The litany of saints — shining examples who show us how to do it — is sung as the paschal candle is processed back to the font.

In the original creation, chaos is watery; in biblical poetry, it is the haunt of Leviathan or Rahab, mythological monsters who resist the work of God. In ordinary life, water is a solvent that breaks down the structure of what is submerged in it. This property makes water not only a destroyer, but also a cleanser, when a body's internal organisation is stronger than its links with the dirt. In the original creation, bounded and separated water — contained in seas, flowing in rivers, falling as rain — is life-sustaining. But covenant curses take hold to poison rivers and bloody waters.

In the recreation, water must be purified, recontained, reordered. Old prayers over water explicitly send lurking demons packing. But the meaning is also in the action: the officiant exorcises the water of baptism by dividing it in the form of a cross. The cross of Christ enthrones human being, freely returning life to the source of life, freely choosing to live by the indestructible life of God.

Water from the side of Christ becomes the life-sustaining water of the apocalypse, flowing from the throne of God. Older ceremonies continue to sign the water with three crosses, to divide it and sprinkle it east-west-north-south to revive all four corners of the earth. Some rites still three-times plunge in the paschal candle, blow a *psi* for *psyche*, for life, for Spirit — to restore fertility to baptismal waters about to bring forth new life.

The cosmic framework is in place. The awaited moment has come. We descend into the water, not to rinse off or to freshen up, but to die. Our perverse desire for self-sustained and independent living is no surface blemish. It has penetrated to organise our selves at their very core. Baptismal waters must dissolve our deep structures, to allow the stuff of our lives to be recreated, recentred. We descend into the water for a radical makeover: to die to sin and to rise in Christ.

(2006)

How to live in Holy Saturday

To see the way the Anglican Communion dwells in tension over homosexuality is to know how to live together in self-contradiction, says **Luke Bretherton**

AS WE APPROACH Easter, we draw close to that time when God is divided. On Holy Saturday, we enter into that day when God was in self-contradiction. The Father gives up the Son as if accursed, and the Son gives up the Father as if godforsaken. Yet the mystery is that in the Spirit, God remains one. Nothingness, sin, evil, and death do not overcome God. Rather, out of God dwelling in death — God dying to Godself — new life, true life, resurrection life is born.

What, then, does it mean for the Anglican Communion to dwell in Holy Saturday, and to form an image of a God who gestates new life in death and self-contradiction?

It has become a theme of much contemporary theology to focus on the trinitarian nature of God, and its implications for the Church. In the debates about communion ecclesiology, one thing is clear. There is a rejection, on the one side, of a homogenising collectivism — we must all be the same, with no differences between us — and, on the other, there is a rejection of an atomising individualism — we are totally different and autonomous from each other, and so there is no necessity of relations among us.

In distinction from these two poles, a trinitarian theology of what it means to be human holds that, to be fully myself, I must be in relation with others, yet at the same time distinct. In other words, I need those who are not like me, in order to be truly human.

The current divisions over same-sex relations within the Anglican Communion seem to be a parody of the above. The opponents and advocates of same-sex unions are enemies. Each party in the dispute has established an oppositional identity wherein being opposed to the other side defines who "we" are. Each side sees itself as the same: we are the ones who are right; we are good; we are holy and righteous.

The temptation is to formalise this separation. But a trinitarian account of what it means to be human suggests that separation entails a false resolution of the conflict. Schism means that each side would relate only to those who are like it, and, at the same time, be unrelated to those who are different.

There is an obvious objection to the call to stay together. It is one thing to value those who are different from me — say, in ecumenical relations —

but what happens when the other is sinful? How am I to relate to those who are, to my mind, accursed by God because they propose immorality as virtue, and lies as truth? What am I to make of those who threaten the integrity of the Christian faith, and refuse to repent of their error? This, in essence, is the view of both sides of the debate. Each sees the other as being sub-Christian in its views on same-sex relations.

So how does a trinitarian view of what it means to be human address this problem? We must attend to what it means to live in Holy Saturday.

PLAINLY ASKING each side to stay together and simply tolerate each other is neither possible, nor, I would argue, theologically desirable. God does not tolerate us. God dies for us. God is humiliated, and risks annihilation so that we may be saved.

God's humiliation involves the most intimate of relations: the incarnation. In Jesus Christ, God knows us better that we know ourselves. And, in Jesus Christ, God dies because we kill him. This is what we contemplate on Holy Saturday. God becomes our enemy, whom we kill. For our sake and our salvation, Christ becomes a curse, and was made to be sin (Galatians 3.13; 2 Corinthians 5.21). In this process, Christ is forsaken by us and by the Father.

So, what does it mean for us to enter into Holy Saturday? A proper moment in our imaging of God is to be a body in self-contradiction. By living together in self-contradiction, we enter into death. To live in self-contradiction risks death because the truth is threatened, and each side risks being destroyed by the other.

Yet, in the midst of the rancour and darkness of this sepulchral time, we must remain together. While Holy Saturday feels like an eternity, we must wait, as one, for new creation from the chaos. While waiting, however, we must resist the temptation to sanctify the darkness, and mistake the tomb for a home and darkness for light. New life will come, and it is a very different form of life from the one we experience now.

We can better live through this Holy Saturday of our Church when we reflect on how Holy Saturday is, for the most part, our normative condition in this world. As Luther put it, we are simultaneously sinful and sanctified. That is, to be a Christian is to live in self-contradiction, yet be one. It is only in Christ, through the power of the Holy Spirit, that we are healed and perfected by the one who mediates between us and our selves. We do not have the power, wisdom or honour to do it in our own strength.

If, as Bonhoeffer argues, the Church is a form of Christ's presence in the world, we must reckon with being Christ on Holy Saturday. And perhaps being Christ on Holy Saturday means something like being an Anglican today.

(2005)

Poet's Corner: Holy Saturday

Malcolm Guite recalls a walk that he took one Holy Saturday

HOLY Saturday is a strange, in-between day. I've heard it described as the day we all hold our breath, poised between the grief of Good Friday and the hope of Easter

But I think it would be truer to say that it is the day when heaven holds our breath. For, on Good Friday, we see Christ, the second Adam, breathing his last breath, and ours, and entrusting it to heaven for safe-keeping. And that breath is held in heaven till he releases it afresh and renews us on Easter Day, when he breathes on us and says, "Receive the Holy Spirit". But, over the waiting space of Holy Saturday, there is a breathless hush.

We have our activities, of course: the children coming to make Easter gardens, while others decorate the church; and, for the more disorganised among us, there is the sudden realisation that there are still Easter eggs to buy.

I always try to find time, though, somewhere on that day, for a decent walk. Likely as not, the weather has been rainy, and I soon find my feet stuck in the miry clay, something pulling me earthward even as the birds sing overhead.

On Holy Saturday a couple of years ago, I headed into the woods with the dogs, seeking to clear my mind after an exhausting and exacting few weeks of life and ministry. I set out feeling burdened, feeling that I scarcely had the imaginative energy left to participate in this great re-enactment and celebration of the drama of our salvation.

For some reason, as a tinny and annoying background to more melancholy thoughts, I had Mott The Hoople's catchy 1973 hit "Roll Away The Stone" running round in my head. It is not a great work of art. Indeed, some might say that they had no business borrowing a gospel image to boost the chorus of a cheesy chat-up song, replete with lines like "We still got a chance Baby in love and sweet romance".

And yet, in spite of that, as I emerged from the thick of thickets, both outer and inner, and sensed the growing light behind grey clouds, on that tired Holy Saturday, the mystery of Easter opened up to me again, and even Mott The Hoople's little chorus was lifted into meaning.

I went home and composed, in the last light of Saturday, a villanelle for Sunday:

As though some heavy stone were rolled away,
You find an open door where all was closed,
Wide as an empty tomb on Easter Day.

Lost in your own dark wood, alone, astray,
You pause, as though some secret were disclosed,
As though some heavy stone were rolled away.

You glimpse the sky above you, wan and grey,
Wide through these shadowed branches interposed,
Wide as an empty tomb on Easter Day.

Perhaps there's light enough to find your way,
For now the tangled wood feels less enclosed,
As though some heavy stone were rolled away.

You lift your feet out of the miry clay
And seek the light in which you once reposed,
Wide as an empty tomb on Easter Day.

And then Love calls your name, you hear Him say:
The way is open, death has been deposed,
As though some heavy stone were rolled away,
And you are free at last on Easter Day.

(2019)

Replica in Nazareth, Israel, of the tomb of Jesus after his resurrection

Delight, and my fish stew

The resurrection is a game-changer, writes **Stephen Cottrell**

I WAKE up in a world where Christ has risen. That means I wake up in a world where sin, decay, corruptibility, and death do not have the last word. They are still all around me, and they appear to be Lord. But the presence of the risen Christ means that they are defeated. My destiny, and the destiny of all creation, is being gathered into the new creation of which, to borrow Tom Wright's phrase, the "incorruptible physicality" of the resurrection body of Jesus Christ is the first piece.

This changes everything. First of all, it means that I cannot view sin, decay, corruptibility, and death in the same way, ever again. I no longer need to fear them.

More than that, I have already passed through them, and beyond them. The baptismal promises I reaffirm at Easter, which is itself the great festival of initiation into the Church, is the declaration that, through my baptism, I have already died and risen with Christ. Therefore, although my earthly body will decline, and although I will still fall foul of the snares of sin, and although I will one day die, all this happens in the knowledge that I will also be reclothed. My death and dying have been shared by Jesus Christ, and are the necessary journey that I — along with the whole creation — must make.

And even when I sin, and even though it causes the same harm as before, and should elicit the same remorse, I also know that I am forgiven, that sin does not define me, that my truest identity and surest humanity are defined by the resurrection of Jesus Christ from the dead. This is where my humanity leads me: forwards to the new creation, and, here and now, the resurrection life.

And perhaps it is this knowledge of my forgiveness that changes my life here and now more than anything else. The resurrection of Jesus Christ makes me more merciful, more ready to go the second mile, and more concerned to share the goodness and beauty of God that I see in Christ. I discover what God has done in Jesus, and I discover what my own humanity could be.

It also changes my relationship with the world. I love it more than ever. I know that it, too, will be redeemed. Sometimes Christianity has been accused of promising heaven while disregarding the earth. The opposite should be true: the earth and all that is in it, and life itself, are the ingredients of heaven. They are not things we leave behind, but things to be transformed. Just as I cherish and care for the onions, garlic, tomatoes, parsley, and cod that will make the fish stew I am planning for supper, so I cherish the earth.

Even more disquieting, the promise of heaven has sometimes been used as an excuse for ignoring injustice and exploitation. Everything will be all right later, in heaven, is the empty promise sometimes made to the oppressed. The resurrection changes this. I see the Risen Christ, and I am enlisted in his programme of transformation. I, too, am called to roll away stones, break down barriers, wipe away tears, and raise the dead to life.

THIS new life and new hope breaks out not just once a year on Easter Day, but every day. Every day I can be transformed by God, and every day God's new life can be renewed in me, changing me and making me more like Christ.

But it is especially focused on Sundays, when I join with that rag-tag, barmy-army, muddled, broken, and "being transformed" gathering of every tribe and nation which is the people of God, the community of the resurrection, those who are being redeemed and renovated by Christ as we gather around the Lord's Table on the Lord's Day, and feast on his risen life.

For every Sunday is resurrection day; and every Eucharist is manna from heaven, rations for the journey, and a foretaste of the banquet at the journey's end.

In the resurrection, God's future comes rushing into our present. This is not just to calm our fears, though it is welcome reassurance in a world of so much horror, but to strengthen our resolve to work now for the heaven on earth that will be our future.

On that first Easter Day, standing in the dawning brightness of a new beginning, thinking all was lost, when actually all was about to be found, Mary Magdalene mistook Jesus for the gardener. Actually, she was right — he is the gardener; the new Adam, tending a new creation.

I wake up in a world where Christ is risen, and I am beginning again. I am part of this new creation. There is a smile on my face, a joy in my heart, and a spring in my step. Trees are coming into blossom. Dead seeds are rising. Even from the place where the nails were hammered into the wood, flowers are blooming. Behold, says the Lord, I am making all things new.

(2016)

What happened at the resurrection?

Tom Wright argues that Jesus bodily alive again
was exactly what the disciples saw

IN A DARK room, down an alleyway, four or five men hide in fear. Somehow they have escaped — it was a crowded festival, and the guards couldn't keep track of so many prisoners — and for the last three days they have been holed up. They know how it ended: their leader was dragged through the streets at the end of the triumphal procession, tortured, and executed. They had heard the shouting, full of blood-lust, celebrating the empire's destruction of its (supposedly) dangerous opponent.

The year is 70 AD; the empire is, of course, Rome; the dead leader is Simon bar Giora, whom the Romans saw as "king of the Jews". I've invented the escaped prisoners to raise the question: what would they think and do next?

If we were to believe one strand in New Testament scholarship, and quite a bit of popular thought both inside and outside the Church, they might suffer from "cognitive dissonance". They might find it difficult to come to terms with Simon's death. And (as a friend said to me the other day) the idea of resurrection was, in any case, "in the air". Mightn't they have begun to say that he'd been raised from the dead?

Or perhaps (corresponding to another regular theory about Easter), as they waited and trembled and whispered psalms, they had a new sense of God's presence. They felt loved and forgiven. They felt God somehow with them — or Simon himself with them. Perhaps one of them had a powerful vision of Simon himself, smiling and talking to him. Strange things like that happened in the first century, as they do today. This might have made them say that he'd been raised from the dead.

No. When we examine what first-century Jews believed about death, life beyond, and resurrection, these theories don't work. Many a Jewish leader was killed by pagans; in no case, except for that of Jesus of Nazareth, did anyone say thereafter either that he was the Messiah or that he'd been raised from the dead. Escape with your life if you can; find another Messiah if you dare; pray and fast and wait for God's fresh comfort and hope — but don't say he's been raised from the dead. He obviously hasn't been.

"Resurrection" had a clear meaning in the first century: a new bodily life after a period of bodily death. It never referred to "life after death", as it often does in today's misguided Christian usage. Still less was it a word for "His cause continues," or "He's gone to heaven". The word had this meaning for pagans, who, from Homer to Pliny and beyond, routinely denied that it happened (with Platonists insisting, in addition, that it was undesirable).

Many first-century Jews, nourished on Daniel 12 and martyr-legends, affirmed resurrection; many questioned it, or didn't bother either way. Judaism could also use "resurrection" language as a metaphor, not for a blissful life after death, but for the this-worldly concrete events of return from exile (Ezekiel 37), interpreted in this case as release from foreign domination.

Many things about early Christianity demand historical explanation. One such fact is that, with only a few small exceptions, virtually the entire movement, as it spread quickly across continents and cultures, embraced the Jewish doctrine of resurrection.

The Jewish belief was, though, modified in six striking ways:

1 Resurrection was one point among several on the Jewish spectrum of belief. It was virtually the only option in Christianity.

2 Resurrection was important in Judaism, but not that important. It was central and vital in early Christianity.

3 Jews saw "the resurrection" as a single event, happening to all at the very end. The Christians declared that it was a two-stage event: Jesus first; others later.

4 Judaism never described the resurrection body in detail. The early Christians insisted that it would be a transformed physicality: neither a mere resuscitation to the same kind of life as before (the new body would not suffer or die), nor an abandonment of the body to corruption and decay, while the "real person" (the soul, perhaps) went off elsewhere. That would mean that death was merely reinterpreted, not defeated.

Paul's language about the "spiritual body" in 1 Corinthians 15 has often been misunderstood. He doesn't mean "a person made of spirit", i.e. "a non-physical person", but "a new body *animated by* God's Spirit", as in Romans 8.9-11.

5 The Jewish metaphorical use of "resurrection" to denote "return from exile" virtually disappears in early Christianity. Instead, we find a different metaphorical use: to refer to baptism and holiness (e.g. Romans 6). "Resurrection" refers to actual persons and events, not simply to states of mind, even when used metaphorically (that is, when actual resurrection is not in mind). It remains anchored to two central

doctrines: God as creator and God as judge. God will put the world to rights, and will rescue creation from corruption, not leave it to rot.

6   No one in Judaism ever supposed the Messiah would be resurrected. This was basic to Christianity from the beginning: the resurrection demonstrated Jesus to *be* Messiah, and therefore the world's true Lord.

THESE developments were mutations from within Jewish belief, not transformations of Jewish ideas into a pagan framework. Together with the other extraordinary events of early Christianity, they force the question: why?

The answer all the early Christians gave, of course, is that Jesus of Nazareth was indeed raised from the dead. They clearly meant by this that, soon after his shameful, violent death, he was bodily alive again.

"Resurrection" did not mean that he had been "raised to heaven", as people sometimes say. They had other language for that. Nor did it mean, as some have urged, that, over a long period, they had an increasing conviction of Jesus's being "alive among them", guiding them, and so forth, without anything happening to his corpse.

It may be spring, but we should resist the call of the cuckoo at this point — *not* because we are clinging to old-fashioned dogma in the teeth of modern scholarship, but because serious historical investigation about what Jews and Christians said and meant in the first century rules out that interpretation. From the beginning they said, and meant, that Jesus had been raised bodily.

The stories they told are, of course, fascinatingly confused and elusive. How many women went to the tomb? Did the appearances happen in Galilee (as Mark seems to imply), in Jerusalem (as Luke says), or both (as Matthew says briefly, John more fully)? Piecing together the stories is like figuring out what precisely happened when Karl Popper met Ludwig Wittgenstein on 25 October 1946.

Some of the greatest minds of the day were present when Wittgenstein brandished a poker and then left the room, but they could never agree afterwards what exactly had occurred (see David Edmonds and John Eidinow, *Wittgenstein's Poker: The story of a ten-minute argument between two great philosophers,* Faber, 2001). Confused reports of surprising events don't mean that nothing happened.

The stories themselves are surprising in several ways. One regular theory suggests that they were made up many years later to legitimate or defend an idea of "resurrection" to which the Christians had come, not because of happenings three days after Jesus's death, but because of a combination of new-found faith, spiritual experience, reflection on the Scriptures, and Church controversy.

There are several features of the stories themselves, which make this virtually impossible:

1 Unlike the rest of the Gospels, not least the crucifixion narratives, the stories are devoid of biblical reference, allusion and echo. They read, not as reflective pieces mulled over with a Bible in hand, but as breathless, pre-reflective accounts. As dramatic anecdotes, they retain for ever (except for very light editing) the form and content had in their first, and then frequently repeated, tellings.

2 The stories all highlight the initial place of the women. By the mid-second century, Celsus was pouring scorn on them for this reason (women were not regarded as credible witnesses in the ancient world). But already by the mid-first century, the "official" account of "the gospel", as in 1 Corinthians 15.4-8, had screened out the women and inserted James the Lord's brother, a central early-Church leader who isn't mentioned in the Gospel resurrection stories.

   One might imagine one evangelist inventing stories about the women to boost their claims to leadership. We cannot imagine all four doing so, and so differently, unless there really were women who really did find an empty tomb, and whose testimony was discovered to be true.

3 The portrait of the risen Jesus is not at all what we would expect. He is "physical": he can eat, be touched, and leave behind not only an empty tomb, but, at Emmaus, a loaf broken but not consumed. But the same

A physical presence: The Road to Emmaus *(c.1516–17), by Altobello Melone, in the National Gallery, London*

stories speak of his not being recognised, his coming and going through locked doors, and finally his ascending into heaven.

Had Luke and John been writing (as many have asserted) to combat the idea that Jesus wasn't really human, they have shot themselves in the feet with both barrels. What the stories do *not* say is equally remarkable. Had they been invented on the basis of Daniel 12 (the best-known Jewish "resurrection" text), they would certainly have had Jesus shining like a star. Their portrait of Jesus is impossible to account for unless it reflects actual memories that surprised the early disciples as much as they surprise us.

4 Almost everywhere else in early Christianity, mention of Jesus's resurrection is closely linked to the Christian's future hope (final resurrection, after a period of being "asleep" or being "with Christ").

It is astonishing — and deeply challenging to half our Easter hymns and sermons — that none of the Gospel Easter stories so much as hints at that. The emphasis is on the most basic message of Easter: God's new creation has begun, and Jesus's followers are its agents, not just its beneficiaries. The stories don't say: "Jesus is raised, therefore we will go to heaven and/or be raised from the dead"; they say: "Jesus is raised, therefore we have a job to do."

SO, IF THE STORIES are early (albeit written down later), what can the historian say about them? The normal rationalising proposals, as we saw, fail at the level not of dogma but of history. History demands two things: that the tomb really was empty on Easter morning, and that Jesus's followers really did meet him alive again. How do we explain that? Historians often speak of "inference to the best explanation". The best historical explanation for the origin of Christianity is that the stories are basically true.

The shrill, relentless modernism that opposes this conclusion needs to be confronted head on. It isn't a "modern" discovery that dead people don't rise. Aeschylus and Pliny knew that just as well as Richard Dawkins. Modernist intellectual imperialism tries to do to the Christian gospel what modern geopolitical empires try to do to countries they imagine to be a threat. The resurrection grounds the Christian challenge to both.

Death is the last weapon of the tyrant: beware of those who want it to remain unchallenged. Jesus's resurrection, precisely because it is the start of God's new creation, is the foundation, not for an escapist, otherworldly theology, nor one wedded to outmoded dogma, but for one that generates and sustains the lasting work of God's kingdom within real human history. Resurrection is the ground of Christian hope for life before death, as well as beyond it.

(2003)

The cross was not enough

The resurrection is vital to our faith, says **Paula Gooder**

Therefore his faith "was reckoned to him as righteousness". Now the words, "it was reckoned to him", were written not for his sake alone, but for ours also. It will be reckoned to us who believe in him who raised Jesus our Lord from the dead, who was handed over to death for our trespasses and was raised for our justification.

Romans 4.22-5

A WHILE AGO, I had a conversation with someone who was a new Christian and was trying to make sense of what she had heard in church. She asked me what the resurrection was for. She had been coming to church for a while, and she understood nearly all of the Christian festivals (and Good Friday), but she simply couldn't understand why we needed Easter.

"Is it", she asked, "simply so that we can be cheerful after a long Lent and depressing Good Friday? Didn't Jesus do everything he needed to do on the cross to save us? Did he really need to rise from the dead?"

Such questions are dangerous ones to address to me, and she went away a long time later, weighed down with much theology — though not necessarily much wiser.

I was intrigued, however, that she should have picked this up so soon, because, on one level, she was right. One could be excused for thinking that the death and resurrection of Jesus were unconnected in terms of theology (the cross being about salvation, and resurrection about life now and in the world to come), and that the cross was, in fact, more important than the resurrection.

Throughout Christian history, great — and appropriate — emphasis has been placed on Jesus's death on the cross, as the means by which we enter into a new relationship with God, based not on law but on faith. Sometimes, however, one could be forgiven for wondering whether Jesus needed to rise from the dead at all, if everything has already been achieved in its entirety by his dying.

Would it have made any significant difference to salvation if Jesus died for our sins and remained dead? For me the answer is yes: it would make an enormous difference.

Scholars counsel against making too much of Paul's distinction in Romans 4.25 between the effect of Jesus's death (for our trespasses) and the effect of his resurrection (for our justification). Paul does not often make this distinction in his writings, and we should not overemphasise it here.

Nevertheless, his phrase in verse 25 reminds us that the death and resurrection of Jesus are intimately linked. If any distinction can be made between the two, then, roughly speaking, Jesus's death frees us "from", and his resurrection frees us "for": from our sins, for a life in Christ; from our old way of being, for new creation, and so on.

By and large, however, the death and resurrection of Jesus should be seen as a seamless whole, working together for our salvation. We need both Good Friday and Easter Day, death and resurrection. One without the other would be very much impoverished.

> *Do you not know that all of us who have been baptised into Christ Jesus were baptised into his death? Therefore we have been buried with him by baptism into death, so that, just as Christ was raised from the dead by the glory of the Father, so we too might walk in newness of life. For if we have been united with him in a death like his, we will certainly be united with him in a resurrection like his.*
>
> **Romans 6.3-5**

TRYING to explain baptism to a child is something of a challenge. I once overheard a conversation between a mother and her son at a baptism service, which rather summed up the problem.

It went a little like this: "Mum, why is that man putting water on the baby?"

"He's baptising her?"

"Oh, what is that?"

"He is welcoming her into God's family."

"With water?"

"Yes."

"If I have a bath, does that make me a part of our family?"

"No, you are a part of our family already."

"So he's washing her?"

"Yes."

"Why was she dirty?"

At this point, the mother gave up, and with clever sleight of hand distracted the child with something else. But the question remains. What does baptism do?

Being baptised into Christ's death and resurrection:
the font at Salisbury Cathedral

In Romans 6, Paul gives one of the best explanations of the nature of baptism that we can hope to find. In this passage, Paul sees baptism as a way of mimicking the death and resurrection of Christ.

In Paul's image, the water is to be seen as symbolising death and burial. As we go down into the water, we die and are buried with Christ; as we come out of the water, we rise with him into newness of life. In baptism, therefore, we come to share in the life of Christ, dying and rising with him, so that we might now live a new Christ-like life.

Paul's theology of baptism makes it clear that Jesus's resurrection is no longer just his resurrection, it is now the resurrection of us all. When Jesus rose from the dead, he opened up a new way of being in which the characteristics of our own future resurrection life (which will happen at the end of the world) are now available, in part, to those who are in Christ. When we are baptised, we follow in the footsteps of Christ, and enter that new creation.

This is where we begin to see that, rather than being an interesting historical event, Jesus's resurrection is something that affects everything that we do. "This risen existence", as R. S. Thomas so evocatively calls it, is not just Jesus's own risen existence, but yours and mine, too. We live resurrection lives — lives transformed by a new creation.

(2010)

What's the latest on the resurrection?

The empty tomb once proved a stumbling-block for some theologians, but this is now less the case, says **Andrew Davison**

WHERE is Christian theology today when it comes to the resurrection — and how did we get there? This might be the story of musing on the most glorious event in our redemption, but the tale is surprisingly muted — not least because theologians have disagreed about whether the resurrection really is primarily marked by glory.

A survey of theological approaches to the resurrection might start from Friedrich Schleiermacher's (1768–1834) thunderclap launch of liberal Protestant thought, *The Christian Faith* (1831). He could not see how the resurrection relates to redemption at all. Indeed, the link is "impossible" to see, and we could understand Christ perfectly well without even knowing about his resurrection. Schleiermacher did not dispense with the resurrection in his scheme; it simply does not play a prominent part.

In contrast, the resurrection was excised by the 19th century's more thoroughgoing radicals, such as David Strauss (1808–1874), who rejected it as part of their general rejection of all that is supernatural in the Gospel stories.

That period of Gospel research, or Gospel dissection, came to an end with the work of Albert Schweitzer (1875–1965). In the era after the First World War, there was a decisive turn away from this rather corrosive attenuation of the story about Jesus. As William Lane Craig has pointed out, however, the physical resurrection hardly gained a prominent place in what followed, either in the existentialist theology of Rudolf Bultmann (1884–1976), or in the neo-orthodoxy of Karl Barth (1886–1968).

BULTMANN emphasised the effect of the resurrection message on the believer. He thought that our emphasis should be on the proclamation of the resurrection, and its claim on us, not on anything that did or did not happen in the tomb. The resurrection is "a definitely not historical event" (*Kerygma and Myth*, English translation by SPCK, 1953).

Bultmann was right to emphasise that the resurrection is not some neutral fact: it is transformatory, or it is nothing. Less convincing was his sense that this proclamation could stand on its own two feet: an effect without a cause, we might say.

The message of resurrection has invariably been of influence because of a literal belief in a risen body, not in spite of it. Bultmann was right to ascribe more to the resurrection than the resuscitation of a corpse, but the early Christians clearly saw that already. Any wider significance was grounded, for them, in what the Greek word for resurrection, *anastasis*, means: Jesus "sat up".

This matters for us in space and time, because something happened in space and time. Often in 20th-century Anglican circles, even those who accepted the physical resurrection, such as the Doctrine Commission in its 1938 report, typically sought to distance themselves from anything that looked like naïvety.

For my part, I would say that the resurrection is true in wider senses only because it is first of all true in this "naïve" way.

Barth's weak focus on the resurrection is perhaps the most surprising lack in his entire theology (although his tendency to downplay the Holy Spirit and the Church are strong contenders). His wish to emphasise the sovereign freedom of God led him to underplay the place of the contingent particularities of history and humanity in God's work.

Just as the incarnation, for Barth, happened, despite there being "no point of contact" (on his view) between us and God, similarly, God touched the world in the resurrection "as a tangent touches a circle, that is, without touching it" (*Commentary on Romans*, English translation, Oxford University Press, 1933). The resurrection is "an event in history ... [that] is not an event in history at all".

Here, Barth was a child of the philosophical idealism of his times, which placed ideas above matter. Just such a background also lies, for instance, behind the resolutely Anglo-Catholic Oxford Library of Practical Theology, which included a volume on *Immortality* (1908), where reference to bodily resurrection, either of Christ or of the rest of humanity, is all but absent.

Within this perspective, however different the sources, the resurrection has become a "wholly transcendent occurrence", as Richard R. Niebuhr put it. Niebuhr, for his part, tended in the opposite direction, missing the radical newness or departure that the resurrection represents when he described it as "the confirmation of the order of creation and preservation of that which otherwise would be lost" ("Resurrection" in *A Handbook of Christian Theology*, eds Cohen and Halverson, Meridian, 1958).

THE critics of the 19th century had been driven by a certain account of history, which ruled out the supernatural as a matter of course. History remained a problem to be overcome for both Bultmann and Barth. Bultmann ducked from history into the abstraction to the all-demanding address to the hearer; Barth downgraded history in comparison with the sovereign distance of God from creation.

The historicity of the resurrection remained a "problem" within Protestant and Protestant-influenced theology for most of the 20th century. For a sense of this, consider how the topic is treated in theological reference works. The prevailing tone, in even quite Evangelical volumes, into the early 1990s, is either a note of relative anguish, or of defensiveness, at least if they seek to appeal to an academic readership.

In marked contrast, Roman Catholic reference works from this period treat the resurrection in a confident and upbeat fashion.

IN THE decades before 2000, when I came into theological training, "difficulties" over the resurrection were considered one of the principal struggles facing any candidate for ordination. Judging by my work in the Cambridge Theological Federation over the past four years, the situation today is entirely different. I would have difficulty finding a single ordinand who would not subscribe to the physical resurrection of Christ — or, indeed, have difficulty finding one for whom the resurrection was not the foundation for his or her vision of the world and of the Christian life.

Something has changed, and pride of place in restoring a central place for the resurrection in Christian thought and self-understanding belongs to another iteration of the "Quest for the Historical Jesus": the so-called third quest (1980s to present), in its most theological form.

N. T. Wright deserves particular praise, primarily with his *Resurrection of the Son of God* (SPCK, 2003). Biblical theology is at the forefront of what we can expect to be a wider return to the resurrection in theology. Doctrinal theology lags behind: the resurrection is still under-represented and "underplayed", relative to what we would expect from the prevailing tenor today.

Consider, for instance, the rise of "post-liberal" theology in the English-speaking world: a trend that is variously patristic, Thomist, and post-Barthian, and represented, in different forms, by Rowan Williams, John Milbank, or Stanley Hauerwas. Parallel to earlier in the 20th century (with Barth, for example), this represents a general return of confidence in Christian orthodoxy — expressed, for instance, in a new conviction about the doctrine of the Trinity — but this has not brought a proportional return of attention to the resurrection.

Certainly, we are no longer in the critical atmosphere of the 19th century, or even of the 1960s; but consult Milbank's nearest thing to a contribution to systematic theology, his brilliant volume *Being Reconciled* (Routledge, 2003), and we find that, while the resurrection is strongly affirmed when it is mentioned, it is not mentioned that often.

AT LEAST from an Anglican perspective, the resurrection does not feature in contemporary doctrinal writing as the central source of illumination, as it does, for instance, in the Orthodox East. Indeed, the resurrection does not even feature as prominently, or as "gloriously", in contemporary doctrine as it does, increasingly, in Anglican popular piety.

A principal reason is the significance that tragedy played, as a category, within resurgent Anglican orthodoxy in the latter decades of the 20th century. The foremost advocate was Donald MacKinnon, who could describe the resurrection as "the ultimate source of that peculiar tension between optimism and pessimism" (note: pessimism) that he judged to be "characteristic of Christianity" (*Borderlands of Theology and Other Essays*). Yes, Christ was risen, but he has risen as wounded, as "elusive and restricted", and (quoting Pascal and concluding his essay) he is "in agony unto the end of the world".

For a current worked example of this, consider the new altar in the Resurrection Chapel in the College of the Resurrection, Mirfield. One side represents the entrance to the empty tomb. The other three bear reliefs by Nicholas Mynheer of the meal at Emmaus, the women at the tomb, and the miraculous draft of fish.

The subjects were chosen, explicitly, to represent what might be called "emotional ambiguity" around the resurrection, but which could shade even further into that tragic "sadness of the resurrection" approach.

The former Archbishop of Canterbury, Lord Williams, was clearly influenced by this tradition of interpreting the resurrection with an eye to tragedy when he wrote that it makes God present "in all suffering, at the heart of suffering and even in death" (*Open to Judgement*, DLT, 1994).

Here, and in later writing, the emptiness of the tomb is his central image. The tomb is empty because Jesus has been "freed" to be "with us". That freedom, however, is more prominently the freedom to be with us in pain than it is freedom from the pains of death, and exhalation to reign in glory.

How theologians approach history is central. For Lord Williams, the emptiness of the tomb is an event in history. It must therefore remain both historical and empty. Too much historical reconstruction, in what he calls an "apologetic" vein, has us filling the emptiness, but neither will it do for us to entertain "a theologically dictated indifference to history" (*On Christian Theology*, Blackwell, 2000), where Lord Williams names Bultmann, although Barth would equally stand.

THE place of the resurrection in the twists and turns of theology over the past century-and-a-half is an ambivalent one, at least among Anglican and Protestant writers. Roman Catholic theology may have retained a stronger commitment to the physical resurrection and its significance in theology, but neither were RCs entirely isolated from those doctrinal and cultural influences. Hans Urs von Balthasar's *Mysterium Paschale* (English translation, T&T Clark, 1990), for instance, proceeds with greater gusto in discussing Holy Saturday than it does in discussing Easter Day

From the century before, 20th-century theologians had inherited theological doubts about the centrality of the resurrection within theology, and historical doubts about the resurrection as an event in space and time. The early-mid-century resurgence of orthodoxy, for instance in Barth, failed to place the resurrection centre stage in mainstream academic theology.

The same can be said of another turn to orthodoxy, at the end of the century and into our own, which we can put down to an attachment to a tragic vision as the proper sign of moral seriousness. Meanwhile, a new generation of scholars on the boundaries of biblical studies, doctrine, and history have begun to exorcise those twin doubts, theological and historical.

They have reasserted that the resurrection is the cornerstone of the faith, and they have questioned whether the canons of historical scholarship can foreclose the question whether it happened. All the same, we wait for systematic theologians to take up that conviction with the vigour that it deserves.

Where else, then, can we look? Pre-eminently, the liturgy guards the faith, witnessing to the resurrection, week by week. The Eucharist presents us with the Easter feast of the risen Christ, although that is not taught as often as it might be. Sunday is our day for communal worship because it is the day of resurrection – the eighth day, the first day of the new creation — which is taught even less often.

Neither should we underestimate the power of the Easter vigil to express the paschal mystery, nor underestimate the significance for the Church of England that this most remarkable of all observances is becoming the central liturgical event of the year for more and more members of the Church.

Doctrinal theology has a part to play — a part here that it has not quite managed to fulfil — but it is a secondary one. Theology might take up the resurrection into thought, but it is an event to which the liturgy bears the best witness: the liturgy, and the effects of the resurrection, displayed in lives restored to life.

(2014)

Night of weeping, morn of song

Mary Magdalene came to the tomb looking for a person,
not a reason, argues **Marjorie Brown**

WHY does anyone believe that Jesus was raised? Historical events cannot be deduced from abstract principles, or proved by logical argument. They require witnesses. Someone reliable must describe what happened. But what happens out of sight is a difficult story to unravel.

No one ever claimed to have seen Jesus rising from the dead. It is idle to speculate how a ruined and abused body, certified dead by those experts in judicial killing, a squad of Roman soldiers, came to be walking in a garden at first light.

We have witnesses to the death and we have witnesses to the risen Jesus, but we have no account of how the transformation took place. (Mel Gibson's Christ, quietly opening his eyes in the tomb and sitting up, with his wounds strangely airbrushed away, is on the level of a cartoon superhero, and need not detain us.)

The thing we are most curious about, the central fact of history if the gospel is true, is hidden from us. At his death, Jesus was laid like any human corpse in the secret darkness of a tomb. But in dark and hidden places God's power is astonishingly at work. We expect new life to emerge from a womb (though it always seems miraculous), but who expects it to come from a cold grave?

THE Gospels tell us that the initial discovery was a negative one: the tomb was empty. Jesus was gone. Even the small consolation of anointing his remains was denied to his friends. This added grief resonates with the heartache of all those who have lost the bodies of their loved ones in a tsunami or a terrorist attack, and bereaved parents whose dead baby was never placed in their arms.

Mary Magdalene, coming to the tomb on that thwarted errand of loving service, is the first witness to this absence, and she reports it to the disciples. Peter and John have a sort of race to reach the tomb and find out what is going on.

Having seen that she told the truth, they then (according to John's Gospel) do something that appears astonishing. They go home. They accept the extraordinary situation, and go back to their friends to ponder it. It seems that they have forgotten about the woman whose message alerted them to

Horror: Mary Magdalene (right) with Mary, the wife of Cleopas lament over Christ's body, terracotta figures from La Pietà (1462–63), by Niccolò dell'Arca in Santa Maria della Vita, Bologna

the news, and who not only ran to fetch them but accompanied them all the way back to the garden as well.

The next verse always raises the hair on the back of my neck: "But Mary stood weeping outside the tomb." That "but" is the hinge between the story of Peter and John's detective work, and Mary Magdalene's numinous encounter with the risen Christ.

Her primary emotion is not curiosity or fear; it is the profoundly human response of grief. Her purpose is not to find out what happened, but rather to seek the one she mourns. She is drawn to the tomb by longing for her Lord. She needs to be in the place where she last saw him, like any bereft wife or mother who makes a shrine of her loved one's room, or sits for hours by his grave.

When she does look into the tomb for herself, she sees rather differently from Peter and John. Where they had spotted only the discarded grave-clothes, she sees two angels, guarding the empty space like the cherubim on the Ark of the Covenant. They speak to her: "Woman, why are you weeping?"

And she repeats to them the message she has already given to the disciples, but with a slight variation: not "They have taken the Lord out of the tomb," but "They have taken away my Lord, and I do not know where they have laid him."

The gratitude for her healing that caused her to follow Jesus has deepened into love and devotion. She has already shown her courageous faithfulness when Jesus was arrested. When the hand-picked disciples who had been trained for leadership deserted him, she stayed at the cross. Here she is, a myrrh-bearer at his tomb as soon as the sabbath is over. Her actions are driven by grief and longing. She is passionate and steadfast.

"They have taken away my Lord, and I do not know where they have laid him." As soon as the words are out of her mouth, she turns around, and another mysterious stranger repeats the earlier question in the same words: "Woman, why are you weeping?"

Then he asks a significant follow-up: "For whom are you looking?" Surely her heart leaps in her at the sound of that question, so like the questions she has often heard the Lord ask: "What do you want me to do for you?", "Who do you say that I am?"

But the moment of utter conviction comes with the calling of her name and her answering joyous embrace. At the same moment as she addresses him by a deeply respectful Hebrew title, she does what no female disciple ever does with her rabbi, and throws her arms around him, or perhaps in a slightly more seemly fashion embraces his feet.

I am intrigued by the possibility raised by the New Testament critic J. H. Bernard that Jesus's next words to Mary may be a textual corruption. Rather than "*me aptou*" ("Cease clinging to me"), does he perhaps say "*me ptou*" ("Do not be afraid")? It would certainly be more in keeping with Jesus's usual style of speech.

Yet, whether she lets go because she is specifically told to do so, or because she feels a new courage and confidence, she readily departs with the message that has been personally entrusted to her.

PETER and John go home as observers of an inexplicable event, to puzzle it over with the disciples, but Mary Magdalene goes home in response to an intimate encounter and a special commission. She comes to the tomb carrying a pot of myrrh to anoint a dead man, but she sets down this gift for a corpse, and carries home instead the announcement "I have seen the Lord!"

Her earlier report was of an absence, but now she can witness to a presence. And the presence that so strongly drew her has now released her into new freedom of action. She has been transformed.

What happened in between? We are back to the hiddenness of God's mysterious action in raising Christ. All we can say is that it is not what happened to Lazarus, a calling back to mortal life. The French paschal greeting "*Le Christ est ressuscité*" is sadly misleading. The resurrection is not the work of a cardiac-arrest team, but a new creation by the power of the Spirit.

A transformation has taken place, and we can see it only by its effects. A grieving woman becomes the apostle to the apostles. A band of despairing runaways begins to preach the gospel. And the witness of those first disciples has enabled countless millions to see the risen Lord at work in our lives, too.

(2011)

Resurrection to the roots

The resurrection re-opens the gates of Eden and gives us the tools to start work, suggests **Simone Kotva**

IN THE 1980s, the ecological economist Eric Zencey pointed to close parallels between ecology and apocalypse. The way in which we speak about them can be surprisingly similar. By the '80s, environmentalism had already become the ersatz religion it is today, and part of its success lies in the way in which it employs ideas borrowed from Christian eschatology.

"Deep ecology", the most theologically inclined school of environmentalism, rests on a consciously spiritual narrative of fall and redemption. Humanity, having abused the gifts of nature, aspires to return to "a state of ecological grace ... a rich and participatory culture" in which there might be, not harmony with the Creator, but "harmony with nature".

The precedents behind this story of a return to the bosom of mother nature, or Gaia, are biblical. Nature is Eden, the lost garden; its contemporary advocates are latter-day prophets preaching the reconciliation of lion and lamb (Isaiah 11.6), and offering an apocalyptic vision of new things, even of planetary revolution: "And I saw a new heaven and a new earth: for the first heaven and the first earth were passed away; and there was no more sea" (Revelation 21.1).

The rhetoric might look similar to that of Christian eschatology, but there are significant theological differences between deep ecology and Scripture, differences often overlooked by critics such as Zencey. There may be echoes of redemptive grace guiding deep ecology's nostalgia for Eden, but they rest on a certain blindness to that event central in a Christological narrative of fall and apocalyptic redemption — the resurrection.

THE 17th-century metaphysical poet Andrew Marvell will serve as a good guide in this debate. At first blush, Marvell appears to be the prototypical deep ecologist himself. His pastoral evocation of Eden, a poem entitled "The Garden", portrays nature as a "green thought in a green shade".

But, although Marvell is often invoked as the quintessential nature poet, like St Paul he believed that the pivot of redemption involved more than a spiritual reunification with nature, and more even than the pagan mysteries that celebrated nature's cyclical renewal. Easter certainly draws on these, and, happily, "The Garden" repeats them.

For Marvell, redemption is, first of all, historical, begun with the cross and resurrection. It is an event in which nature becomes all too human, collaborating in the crucifixion of Christ. As Marvell writes in "Upon Appleton House": "Do you, *O Brambles,* chain me too, And courteous *Briars* nail me through". For Marvell, the cross is the loss of nature's innocence, as Wendell Berry, the influential American environmentalist, points out in a thought-provoking presentation of Marvell's eco-theological consciousness (*A Continuous Harmony,* 1970).

Developing Berry's insights, we might say that, instead of heralding a deep ecology of the "green wave" era, Marvell seems to anticipate the more recent, secular environmentalism that focuses, not on the cheery vision of Gaia, but on the "anthropocene". More sobering and scientific than deep ecology's "harmony with nature", the anthropocene describes the present age of the planet as one shaped decisively by humans, following a "death" of nature that calls to mind Marvell's guilty briars.

But although the anthropocene is rightly sceptical of religious overtones in earlier environmentalism, it none the less succumbs to its own, quasi-religious attitude, which is as foreign to the universe of Marvell as is deep ecology's visions of ecological grace.

Where spiritual environmentalism might be described as a Romantic nostalgia for Eden, advocates of the anthropocene easily come across as pessimistic Calvinists. Abandoning hope, we shoulder the burden of anthropocene guilt, attempting to minimise collateral damage, but with no illusions regarding a future revolution, as described by John of Patmos, or dreamed of by Marvell.

Marvell's briars acknowledge a fall from grace, infecting all of nature, but — unlike anthropocene pessimism — they do not proclaim this fall to be absolute, or irrevocable. Rather, their twisted beauty speaks of a place transformed: "Bind me ye *Woodbines* in your 'twines, Curle me about ye gadding *Vines,* And Oh so close your Circles lace, That I may never leave this Place."

With the stern anthropocene critics of deep ecology, we might forswear an easy hope for the environment; but if we reject the husk of a cheap ecological grace we need not also discard the kernel of Christological truth.

Marvell charts a precarious middle way for us here. So does Scripture. Its properly apocalyptic theology points us to the resurrection as the event which restores us to the work, rather than the place, of Eden.

ST JOHN writes of how, after Christ had risen, he disguises himself appropriately to Mary Magdalene as a gardener (John 20.11-18). The Church, as the body of Christ, is the inheritor of this work. It is the work given by God to the first human beings, restored by Christ to humanity in the imperative to establish the Kingdom of Heaven.

Lost innocence? Christian theology and ecological concern converge in
The Garden of Eden *(oil on canvas, c.1860), by Erastus Salisbury Field*

For Paul, Christ is even described as the "last Adam" to humanity's first, the one who recapitulates and renews all things —"things … in heaven, and … on earth" (1 Corinthians 15.45; Ephesians 1.10).

For Paul, as for Marvell, the apocalyptic return to Eden is not a literal retracing of paths, but neither is it merely a metaphorical image. Rather, it is historical, even shockingly material — Marvell's brambles and briars piercing the flesh of Christ, or the disciples healing the sick. Beyond deep ecology, we see that there is valuable work to be done.

Unlike the anthropocene, the mood is not irreversibly gloomy: the God of Marvell and Paul gives grace continuously, entering into history to inaugurate the work, and realise faith in the flesh. The newness of the earth proclaimed by the last Adam of the resurrection and apocalypse describes a transformation of the world through this labour.

With the resurrection, then, begins a time of participation, not in solitary dreams of ecological grace but in the present grace offered continuously by the Christ-like disciples who surround us, sweaty gardeners planting the lattice-work that will grow into the heavenly Kingdom.

In this sense, ecology can be said to be apocalyptic, but a truly apocalyptic ecology recognises the visionary also in the affairs of the ordinary, in the life of the spade, in the effects of the planting, gathering, and waiting, which exposes the roots of things, and prepares for the Kingdom.

(2016)

127

Making a meal of the resurrection

The risen Jesus walked, talked and ate,
says **Hugh Rayment-Pickard**

THE PASCHAL narrative begins with the Last Supper, a tragic farewell meal, heavy with talk of betrayals and a broken body. It was night, we are told, and the disciples were "very sorrowful". They sing a hymn at the end, but we can hardly imagine there was much joy in their voices.

For the Messiah who came eating and drinking, this is a grim repast, lightened only by the promise of a heavenly meal to come. Knowing that the band of disciples is already falling apart, Jesus prays that "they will all be one". But, in a few hours, they will all have deserted him, and he will walk alone to his death.

How would these feeble friends ever be able to sit down at the table of fellowship again and look him in the eye? There is something very final about the Last Supper — relationships are so damaged, it is hard to see how they will be restored.

It is perhaps because of this sense of ending that Albert Schweitzer, the German biblical critic, described the Last Supper as Christ's "last earthly meal". He isn't the only one to have made this absent-minded mistake. If you start looking for it, you find it everywhere. *The Oxford Dictionary of the Christian Church,* for example, says that the Last Supper was Christ's "final meal with his apostles".

For some reason, we forget that Jesus was resurrected to an earthly life, and that he has at least three more earthly meals after the resurrection: breakfast by the Sea of Tiberias, an evening meal in a village near Emmaus; and an impromptu snack of broiled fish with his apostles. Food is the most distinctive and consistent feature of the resurrection appearances.

These meals take us to the heart of the meaning of Easter, but they have drawn comparatively little comment from theologians. There are some weighty theologies of Easter which make no reference whatsoever to the post-resurrection meals. There is a collective Christian absent-mindedness that forgets that Jesus not only came eating and drinking, but continued eating and drinking after the resurrection.

Popular religion has always intuitively understood the importance of celebrating the resurrection with food. While the priests observe Easter with the more formal liturgies, ordinary communities and families around the world re-enact the resurrection life with seasonal food: eggs, breads, lamb and cakes.

We often disparage these practices as "folk religion", but ordinary life is sometimes more eloquent about religious truth than formal theology. Nothing speaks so powerfully of the joy of the glorious embodied life of the resurrection than a feast shared with others after the privations of Lent and Holy Week. The medieval townspeople of York liked the story of the resurrection meals so much that they embellished it — their Mystery drama shows Jesus eating "honey and fish".

ON GOOD FRIDAY, we spend three hours contemplating every aspect of the Passion narrative. We pore over the crucified body — the wounds, the blood, the sacred head sore wounded, the scourging, the painful steps along the Via Dolorosa. This degree of liturgical attention is never lavished on the resurrection story. The crucified body captivates us, whereas the resurrected body is taken for granted. In some churches, the crucifix is "adored" and kissed. We should perhaps balance this with an Easter liturgy to adore an image of the risen Christ.

However abhorrent, the suffering body is something we know only too well. The crucified body is ghastly, but not strange. By contrast, the resurrected body is uncanny and incomprehensible. By observing Good Friday with such thoroughness, we assume we are facing up to the most difficult and mysterious aspect of the gospel. But perhaps the opposite is true. Perhaps our scrupulous attentiveness to Good Friday is partly a form of avoidance. Perhaps the truly difficult thing is to embrace the resurrection life.

The Gospels record that the apostles found it difficult to accept Jesus's resurrected body. The accounts of the resurrection do not show them joyfully celebrating the risen Christ, but struggling painfully to come to terms with the event.

Cleopas and his friend had heard about the resurrection, but are still going around with "downcast faces". Thomas has just been greeted by the risen Christ, but is "agitated'; the women who go to the tomb are "scared witless". Most who hear about the resurrection simply refuse to believe it.

The resurrection joy takes its time coming, and has to seep through a thick layer of human resistance and disbelief. Luke expresses this beautifully in his curious phrase "they still disbelieved for joy, and wondered" (24.41).

It is also the ordinariness of the resurrection that fazes the apostles. They would probably have coped better if Jesus had appeared in a majestic theophany, with theatrical effects and a new mystical body. This, after all, was the messianic expectation that everyone took as read. Hadn't Jesus himself said that the son of man would come again, but this time with the angels and fireworks (Mark 8.38; 13.26-7)?

JESUS must have an "ordinary" body if the resurrection is not to cancel out the incarnation. If Jesus had been resurrected to an unearthly body, this would imply that his earlier body was unworthy or improper. The resurrection must complete the logic of the incarnation.

J.R.R. Tolkien (who was fascinated by the structure of the gospel narrative) argued in his essay "On Fairy Stories" that: "The resurrection is the eucatastrophe of the story of the incarnation." "Eucatastrophe" means the overcoming of catastrophe: in this case, the restoration of the incarnation after the disaster of the cross. The resurrection signs, seals and delivers the truth of the incarnate God.

So the resurrection narrative is all of a piece with the nativity: Jesus became the flesh of a boy from Galilee, and he was resurrected to the same flesh. The resurrection fulfils the incarnation by showing conclusively that Jesus was not merely wearing his body like a garment of skin, but he was, from beginning to end, living *in* his body, *as* his body and *with* his body.

The Gospels can hardly be more emphatic that the resurrected body of Jesus is his same human body. Thomas wants to be sure about this point and insists on examining Christ's wounds. These are like the scars and distinguishing marks that we used to register on passports: they prove that we are a named bodily person and not any other.

As well as eating, the Gospels underscore the message that the resurrected life involves walking, breathing, talking and touching. So Jesus cooks a meal, eats bread and fish, and breathes on the disciples. The resurrection life is not any other life, but this life, flourishing even on the far side of human violence. The life-after-death is none other than the kind of life we experience before death.

What is more, Jesus is not resurrected to some abstract state of living, but to a particular historical and cultural setting. His resurrected body speaks a language, follows social rules, and interacts with named human beings. Jesus was resurrected into the ordinary life of his friends.

There is a tendency to play down the ordinary and historical character of resurrection meals, and classify them, as Rudolf Bultmann does, as "mysterious" and "cultic". Karl Barth is another who sees the resurrection as essentially extra-ordinary and "not an event in history at all". But this reading does not stand up to examination. The resurrection meals are never set-piece occasions like the Last Supper, but spontaneous events that spring out of specific situations: an evening meal, a fishing trip, a visit. These meals are no more "cultic" than an average Sunday lunch.

Yet the resurrection meals carry an immense theological importance. Following Maundy Thursday, these meals are moments of forgiveness and reconciliation. They reinstate the bread-fellowship broken by disloyalty and

An average Sunday lunch? The table is set for Supper at Emmaus *(1601) by Caravaggio, in the National Gallery, London*

fearfulness. The Last Supper is a meal of dispersal, from which Jesus and his disciples are sent out to face the consequences of betrayal and violence. At the resurrection meals, Jesus presides over a gathering back together of the shattered company of apostles. The disciples are given the body of Christ at the Last Supper, but they receive it properly in the meals after the resurrection.

THE RESURRECTED Christ is the Christ of forgiveness. To mark this, the risen Jesus uses a new greeting of reconciliation wherever he goes: "Peace be with you." The atrocity of Good Friday and the hurt of betrayal plead for a resolution. God's response is the risen Jesus: forgiveness made flesh.

The bread shared at Emmaus and the fish barbecued at Tiberias are physical tokens of absolution. Rowan Williams — one of the few to acknowledge the "enormous importance" of the resurrection meals — argues that "to take food from the hands of Jesus after Easter is to receive from him the gift of his essential being" *(Resurrection,* DLT, 1982).

Another writer who could see the material essence of the resurrection was D.H. Lawrence. One of his oddest yet most charming stories is a late novella, *The Man Who Died.* It tells of a strange man who comes back from the dead. The point of this resurrection is to enable the man who died to live fully within his body. His former life had been dominated by the need to deny his body in order to fulfil his "mission". Now that his mission is complete, he can enjoy his embodied existence in all its purity and power. The "man who died" is not Jesus, but Lawrence was trying to say something important about the theology of the resurrection.

Here, as elsewhere, Lawrence had a gift for putting his finger on something primitive and important. In his essay, "Resurrection", Lawrence argued that the Churches find it difficult to come to terms with the true resurrection experience: "The Churches, instead of preaching the Risen Lord, go on preaching the Christ-child and Christ crucified." In all his quirkiness, Lawrence could see what the Churches often miss: the beating physical heart of the resurrection.

Jesus's resurrection life is nothing other than life itself, but life understood in its fullness and truth. What Easter opens up is not some other life, but a transfiguration of the life we know.

Easter theology has been stymied in recent decades by debates about the historical realism of the resurrection. But the point of the resurrection narrative — whether understood in realist or non-realist terms — is to direct us to the availability of life now.

This life is not locked away on the far side of death. As the Christian Aid slogan puts it so well: "We believe in life before death." An Easter Church should be utterly committed to our world and its material transformation. There should be a place for all at the resurrection meal.

The embodied Christ of the resurrection invites an incarnational spirituality of the kind we find in Gerard Manley Hopkins, who marvelled at the perfect physical presence of Christ. In his preaching, poetry and diaries, Hopkins tried to find words for "the matchless beauty of Christ's body", which is not "a phantom human body", but a real body "lovely in limbs, and lovely in eyes".

The natural world furnished Hopkins with endless sensations of the incarnate God: from the kestrel in flight to the eggs of a thrush. Hopkins's spirituality was anchored in the created world of physical forms, colours, textures, movements and contours. These are not just metaphors for a disembodied divinity, but concrete manifestations of Christ's physical beauty.

If Hopkins is right, then it is in material beauty and joy that an Easter spirituality should be grounded. This is a spirituality that prays with its eyes open and with all its senses alert. We should not, as the hymn urges, "let sense be dumb".

The Easter event, as the completion of the incarnation, is begging to be seen in the created world in which we live and breathe and have our being. The wonder of this encounter with the incarnate God is not only beautiful, but makes us beautiful. As Hopkins puts it in his wonderfully titled poem "That Nature is a Heraclitean Fire and of the comfort of the Resurrection".

> *In a flash, at a trumpet crash,*
> *I am all at once what Christ is, | since he was what I am, and*
> *This Jack, joke, poor potsherd, | patch, matchwood, immortal diamond,*
> *   Is immortal diamond.*

(2004)

Jesus Christ is risen indeed

The power of Jesus's indestructible life — his bodily resurrection — is critical for our faith, argues **Robin Ward**

The strife is o'er, the battle done;
Now is the Victor's triumph won;
O let the song of praise be sung.
Alleluia!

THE resurrection of Jesus Christ from the dead is the fundamental proclamation of the Christian faith, beginning with the testimony of the apostles in Jerusalem on the day of Pentecost: "This Jesus God raised up, and of that we are witnesses" (Acts 2.32). But why is the bodily resurrection of Jesus so important; and how can something that happened 2000 years ago, however miraculous, affect us now?

The Letter to the Hebrews explains two fundamental truths about the work of Jesus Christ. First, Jesus is made like us, so that he can be a truly obedient priest who takes our sins away: "Therefore he had to become like his brothers and sisters in every respect, so that he might be a merciful and faithful high priest in the service of God, to make a sacrifice of atonement for the sins of the people" (Hebrews 2.17).

Second, what he earns by his obedience is not just for himself, but for all whom he redeems: "For it was fitting that he, for whom and by whom all things exist, in bringing many sons to glory, should make the pioneer of their salvation perfect through suffering" (Hebrews 2.10).

The death of Jesus on the cross earns us our salvation, and it does so in four complementary ways:

- It is a work of *merit*, in which the Son of God, through obedient love, earns us the reward of everlasting life.
- It is a work of *satisfaction*, in which the price is paid for human sin.
- It is a work of *sacrifice*, in which perfect adoration is offered to God by the only one fit to do so.
- It is a work of *redemption*, by which we are freed from enslavement to evil and the dominion of death. But the work of redemption on the cross needs to be accepted, and it needs to be applied; by raising Jesus from the dead, God does both.

133

Resurrection is emphatically something that happens to a body, the body of Jesus in the tomb. The great Anglican theologian Richard Hooker emphasises this continuity between the body that Jesus receives at the incarnation, from his mother, and the body that rises on Easter Day, and is now glorified at the right hand of the Father in heaven: "a body still it continueth, a body consubstantial with our bodies, a body of the same both nature and measure which it had on earth."

Two points are crucial here. First, by divine power, life is restored to what had been dead: as St Paul writes to the Corinthians, "For he was crucified in weakness, but lives by the power of God." Second, the body so raised remains definitively human — the human body of the divine Word, imbued with all the glory of heaven, but still a body like ours, from which we are able to receive the vitality of Christ's risen life.

DEATH is the absolute destruction of what it is to be human, because it destroys the body. There is a chilling moment in C.S. Lewis's novel *Perelandra,* when the diabolical Dr Weston confronts the hero, and tells how he dreamed he had just died and was laid out in the hospital.

Another, more sinister corpse appears at the bottom of the bed, full of hatred for the vestige of the human form that the recently dead man still possesses: "I began like that. We all did. Just wait and see what you come down to in the end."

St Thomas Aquinas says that "if my body is corrupted, I shall proclaim nothing to anyone; I shall be of no use whatever." The resurrection of the Son of God is therefore a resurrection of the body, a work of divine power in which the Christ who obediently glorified the Father on the cross is, in turn, glorified by him, and in the flesh. This is what Peter preaches at Pentecost: "For you will not abandon my soul to Hades, or let your Holy One experience corruption" (Acts 2.27).

When Aquinas thinks about the resurrection, he sees it in just this way: a truth about Jesus, and a truth about us. He calls it a demonstration of God's justice, in which the one who freely humbled himself "even to death on a cross" receives a glorious resurrection. It is a revelation of Christ's godhead, as it definitively confirms what the "deeds of power, wonders, and signs" (Acts 2.22) that accompanied his ministry taught.

It is a sign of hope for us, because the one who is our head has already obtained what we long for: the promise of resurrection. By his rising, our lives receive a new moral orientation, so that, as Paul writes to the Romans, "you also must consider yourselves dead to sin, and alive to God in Christ Jesus" (Romans 6.11).

134

Finally, the work of our salvation is completed, in that as by enduring the suffering of the cross, Christ delivered us from evil, so in rising from the dead, he might advance us to the prospect of sharing in his glory.

THE glory of the risen Lord is preached repeatedly in the New Testament as characteristic of the resurrection: "Through him you have come to trust in God, who raised him from the dead and gave him glory, so that your faith and hope are set on God" (1 Peter 1.21).

But the great Swiss theologian Hans Urs von Balthasar reminds us that the sign of visible glory is noticeably absent from the Gospel accounts of the resurrection. Why is this? Paul writes to the Corinthians that God has "shone in our hearts to give the light of the knowledge of the glory of God in the face of Jesus Christ" (2 Corinthians 4.6). In the Gospel narratives, the reality of the resurrection is demonstrated by clear signs of continuity between the body of the Lord before and after his resurrection. He eats and drinks, sees and hears, talks and reasons. So we learn that he is the same human person. But he also appears in a hidden form to the disciples on the road to Emmaus, only to be revealed in the breaking of bread.

We will know the risen Jesus not by seeing his glory visibly, but by the knowledge of it in our hearts, which comes from the preaching of the mystery of the cross. Like the disciples on the Emmaus road, the "face of Jesus Christ" for us will be his presence revealed in the Scriptures, and given to us as our food in the Eucharist.

The risen and glorified humanity of Jesus Christ is instrumental in bringing about our salvation. Hooker says: "It possesses a presence of force and efficacy throughout all generations of men ... infinite in possibility of application." It was this teaching that so exercised the Church's greatest theologian of the person of Christ, St Cyril of Alexandria, in his controversy with Nestorius in the fifth century: "As God he is by nature Life, and because he has become one with his own flesh he rendered it vitalising."

Hooker describes our participation in the life of the risen Christ as being "partly by imputation", the merit of the cross applied to us for the remission of sins, and "partly by habitual and real infusion" — what St Paul describes when he writes to the Galatians: "It is no longer I who live, but it is Christ who lives in me" (Galatians 2.20).

For Cyril of Alexandria, this real infusion of the life of the living Christ finds its culmination in the Eucharist. He writes to Nestorius: "When we perform in church the unbloody service, we receive not mere flesh (God forbid!) or flesh of a man hallowed by connection with the Word ... but the personal, truly vitalising flesh of God the Word himself." In the sacraments, and in particular in the sacrament of his Body and Blood, Jesus gives us his resurrection life: "But the one who eats this bread will live for ever" (John 6.58).

JESUS'S resurrection causes our salvation, but also shows us how we are to be saved. Christ does not rise alone: Matthew's Gospel reminds us that at the moment of his death on the cross, many saints of the old covenant are raised, and appear in Jerusalem after the resurrection (Matthew 27.52-3). When Dante describes the souls of the blessed in heaven in the *Paradiso* of the *Divine Comedy*, he has them say: "The lustre which already swathes us round Shall be outlustred by the flesh, which long Day after day now moulders underground."

Immortality, survival after death, even the vision of God enjoyed by the souls of the just — these things are not in themselves the consummation of the Christian hope. The Christian hope is one of bodily resurrection, as Paul writes to the Philippians: "He will transform the body of our humiliation, so that it may be conformed to the body of his glory" (Philippians 3.21).

The monastic writer Blessed Columba Marmion compares the linen cloths left in the tomb after the resurrection to our infirmities, which they symbolise: "He comes forth from the sepulchre; his liberty is entire; he is animated with intense, perfect life with which all the fibres of his being vibrate. In him, all that is mortal is absorbed by life."

The spiritual body of which St Paul speaks, and for which we hope, is realised in the resurrection of Christ. The dominion of sin, death, and corruption is defeated, and he who is our head receives "the power of an indestructible life" (Hebrews 7.16).

This indestructible life is our Easter faith and hope. It is indestructible because it is the human life of the Son of God, and it is powerful because it gives to sinful human beings the fruits of the Passion: forgiveness of sins, victory over death, and the promise of eternal life.

> *Come, let us taste the Vine's new fruit,*
> *For heavenly joy preparing;*
> *Today the branches with the Root*
> *In Resurrection sharing:*
> *Whom as true God our hymns adore*
> *For ever and for evermore.*
>
> *St John Damascene*

(2013)

The pinnacle of St Paul's faith

The resurrection is central to Pauline theology,
writes **Paula Gooder**

WEEK by week, in churches up and down the country, people stand and declare their belief in the resurrection.

Depending on which service they are attending, and hence which creed they are reciting, they will declare either that they believe in "the resurrection of the body" (Apostles' Creed) or in "the resurrection of the dead" (Nicene Creed). The interesting question is what people think they mean when they declare this.

Some believe that they are assenting to the resurrection of Jesus; some to their own resurrection. Some aren't assenting to it at all, but simply saying it because it is expected.

Part of the problem is that the statement occurs towards the end of the creeds, with what you might call the miscellaneous fragments of belief. Having dealt with the different persons of the Trinity, we turn our attention to other elements of belief, such as the catholicity of the Church, the communion of saints, baptism, the forgiveness of sins, and life after death. Coming, as it does, right at the end of the creeds, it can feel as though belief in resurrection is somehow more marginal and less central to belief than, for example, the Trinity.

Recent New Testament scholarship, study of the writings of Paul, in particular, has gained significant new insights from our improved under-standing of first-century Judaism. That topic has become an important area of scholarship in its own right, drawing, for instance, on archaeological discoveries of the 19th and 20th centuries. When it comes to resurrection, that means we now have a clearer picture of Jewish beliefs about resurrection in Paul's time. That then helps us to understand what Paul meant by it, and to see how absolutely central the resurrection was for him.

It becomes clear in 1 Corinthians 15 that Paul places belief in resurrection — both Jesus's and our own — at the very heart of Christian belief and proclamation. The Corinthians, in common with many people today, appar-ently struggled to accept the teaching about resurrection ("Now if Christ is proclaimed as raised from the dead, how can some of you say there is no resurrection of the dead?" 1 Corinthians 15.12).

In 1 Corinthians 15 Paul began to demonstrate why, in his view, belief that we will rise bodily is essential. His argument is simply that, if we do not believe in our own resurrection, our own rising in the future, then we are saying that resurrection does not happen. If we say this, then we are saying that Jesus did not rise from the dead (1 Corinthians 15.13).

If we say that Jesus did not rise from the dead, then our sins have not been forgiven (1 Corinthians 15.17 makes it clear that, for Paul, it is Jesus's death *and* resurrection that assure us of salvation). If we say our sins have not been forgiven, then our faith is in vain: the dead are just dead, sin has not been defeated, and we have no good news to proclaim.

In other words, what will happen to us after we die is integrally linked to what happened to Jesus after he died. For Paul, belief in resurrection is not to be viewed as additional extra, but the very central core of belief.

It is clear that the Corinthians struggled with this idea as much as many people do today. Paul does not reveal precisely what their problem was, but it is likely to have flowed from a Greek view of life after death, which understood future existence to involve the soul's leaving the body, not bodily resurrection.

Paul, in common with the Jews of his era who did believe in life after death (the Pharisees, the Essenes), believed that a general bodily resurrection would take place when God intervened to save his people, and to bring in the world to come. This new era would be physical, with a renewed heaven and earth; hence the need for bodies to inhabit it.

This was the glorious future that Paul had in mind, and which he explored in depth in 1 Corinthians 15; an exploration that included a reflection on what our resurrection bodies might be like.

THE challenge for Paul, as for all early Christians, however, was how to make sense of the fact that Jesus had already risen from the dead. Woven throughout much of Paul's writings, we find this emphasis, time and time again. While Paul still awaited God's final intervention in the world, and the resurrection of all those in Christ (see, among other verses, Romans 8.22-23), he believed that the new creation had already arrived (2 Corinthians 5.17). Jesus's resurrection had changed the world, not just by defeating death and sin, but by inaugurating a new era; an era marked by peace, and justice, and the life-giving presence of the Spirit.

The problem was that the new creation had come, but the old creation had not passed away. Paul's message, in his writings, was that those who were in Christ were called to live in the new creation, alive to the Spirit, in harmony with one another and with God, even while they waited for the old creation to pass. This was why Paul became so profoundly upset by the

*New creation:
Paul, 1610–12, by
Peter Paul Rubens
(1577–1640),
Museo del Prado,
Madrid*

many divisions and conflicts in the Christian communities he founded. In them he saw very little of the new creation he had in mind.

They — and we — live in a world marked by both old and new creation, which explains the challenge of Christian existence. We have a vision of the world as it could be, and yet, time and again we are dragged back into the world as it is.

In Paul's mind, therefore, the resurrection is central to the life and faith of a Christian, not just because Jesus rose from the dead, nor just because Paul believed that we will, also. It was central because it provides the motivation and explanation of how we live from day to day as Christians.

We are called to live as though we believe the world to come has already broken into our world, an in-breaking that began with Jesus's resurrection, and will continue until the end times bring about the completion of all things.

For Paul, the declaration of belief in the resurrection of the body, or the resurrection of the dead, would be not an afterthought, but the very pinnacle of the whole of his faith.

(2016)

Our Church is built on joy

The resurrection is for life, not just for Easter,
suggests the **Ecumenical Patriarch, Bartholomew I**

THE Orthodox Church is the Church of the Resurrection. The entire devotional life of Orthodox Christians, as expressed primarily in Sunday matins and the divine liturgy, resonates with the power and the unspeakable joy of the resurrection. The lives of the faithful in the world in all its aspects, the personal adventures of our freedom, our responsibilities in society, in short, our "liturgy after the Liturgy", constitutes a daily Easter.

The life-giving light emanating from the tomb of Christ opens our eyes to the beauty of creation, whose "exceeding goodness" is revealed to us, both in its present and its eschatological truth: "Therefore, if anyone is in Christ, the new creation has come: the old has gone, the new is here" (2 Corinthians 5.17).

For Orthodox Christians, then, the feast of Easter is not simply a commemoration of the Lord's resurrection, but the experience of their own renewal in Christ, and the certainty of their "common resurrection" at the end of time (*Apolytikion* for Lazarus Saturday and Palm Sunday).

The communal dimension is a universal Orthodox experience of exceptional intensity, especially within the liturgical congregation. God is our "common good", and the resurrection of Christ is a revelation and gift of our "common freedom" (Nicholas Kabasilas), and of our "co-sovereignty" — as we hear on Easter Sunday night, in the Catechism Homily of St John Chrysostom.

The life of the Church is the experience of the *eschaton* in the present, and the vision of the present from the *eschata* (last things). In this sense, after the resurrection of Christ, all worldly things are not just "in the world" and "of the world". Instead, all things are moving towards the eschatological perfection of the Kingdom of God, in which the Church already participates.

The world is not only the world of the present, because it remains as yet incomplete. The truth is that the eschatological transformation of the world has already begun in the resurrected Christ. Therefore faith in the resurrection acts as a powerful transformative force in history.

Leaping to life: the Anastasis *fresco in the Kariye*
Museum (St Saviour in Chora), Istanbul

Even if the newer Orthodox theology (during the phase of its so-called pseudomorphosis[*]) sees eschatology as a discourse about the Second Coming of the Lord, the Orthodox life itself actively experiences the presence of the *eschaton*, in the divine liturgy, and in the spirituality and benevolent pastoral ministry of the Church. Orthodoxy has preserved its eschatological ethos intact throughout the entire course of its history.

Eschatology, then, is not just a teaching about the end times, but the principal reason for relating both the end times to present events, and these present events to the end times. It does not mean an escape from history; nor does it lead to a devaluation of life; but it is a positive precondition in the struggle for the transformation of the world.

Of course, the fact that the kingdom of Christ is not "of this world", releases us from the task of transforming the world into an earthly paradise at any price. It also protects us from the cynicism and hardheartedness that results from capitulation to evil and indifference towards human affairs.

But because of the eschatological spirit that permeates the totality of the Church's life, I dare say that the Orthodox believer actually risks becoming over-active, rather than becoming indifferent to history and to the world.

---

[*] Georges Florovsky (1893–1979) used the word "pseudomorphosis" to describe and criticise the effects of a period when Orthodox educational institutions, and their theology, relied largely on Roman Catholic and Protestant sources, rather than the patristic tradition, particularly in the 17th and 18th centuries, the so-called period of "Western captivity" — Editor.

WELL before modernist culture established man as the creator of history, the Church called upon the faithful to be co-workers with God on the journey towards the eschatological Kingdom. In the Orthodox world at least, the danger of the Church's becoming secularised was averted, thanks to her genuine paschal and eschatological orientation. The breath of the resurrection was, in the lives of the Orthodox faithful, the "eschatological antidote" that saved the Church from identifying with the world, and at the same time, preserved her from a dualistic, antiworld spirituality.

All these truths are concentrated in the Eucharist, a foretaste of the eschatological perfection of all creation.

The view that the Eucharist makes us indifferent to history is a colossal misunderstanding. Instead, it invites us to make a eucharistic use of the world, to contribute to making of a more just and peaceful world.

The resurrectional spirit of Orthodoxy also negates the view of Christian morality as being a "morality of the weak". On the contrary, the believer who is renewed in Christ is a person who is all alight, bursting with dynamism and creativity.

I WISH to emphasise the essential connection of the Eucharist with the resurrection and the end times in the life of the Orthodox Church. This is the reason why the eucharistic liturgy of the Orthodox Church is always celebratory, full of light and joy.

The Eucharist does not take us to Golgotha in order to stay there. As the Elder Metropolitan of Pergamon, John Zizioulas, taught, the Eucharist leads us beyond, to the never-ending glory of God's Kingdom.

Redemption in the Orthodox tradition is understood as "deification" or theosis by grace, a term that emphasises the communal and cosmic nature of salvation, and its reference to the eschaton. Through the Eucharist, the Church is revealed as "a community of deification" for humankind, and as the source of renovation of the entire creation.

Karl Barth recognised the Orthodox Eastern Church as having a more highly developed sensitivity towards the resurrection than either Roman Catholicism or Protestantism. In an interview on 15 April 1965, Barth said that, in his *Church Dogmatics*, he described as "embarrassing" for Westerners the fact that the Eastern Church has not ceased to see, and take seriously, that which the "gloomy Westerners" on the whole should have continuously looked upon, and approached, with an ever-new and different outlook.

Barth explained that he meant that, unlike the Western Churches, the Eastern Churches considered the human being in its totality: "Consequently, there is amongst them a more highly developed sensitivity to the resurrection than there is for us. Ultimately, we Westerners have too much of a *theologia crucis* [theology of the cross]. A little more of a *theologia gloriae* [theology of glory] of the Eastern Church would not hurt us at all."

Hans Küng declared that, in the study in his home in Tübingen, Germany, he has not hung a crucifix, which, in his view, unilaterally refers to the Passion, and the suffering that caused the misunderstanding and abuse of this most exalted of Christian symbols. Instead, he has a "Greek" icon of Christ, which, for us Orthodox, like every one of our authentic images, is always an expression of the resurrection and eschatological glory.

THE Orthodox Church today reminds all Christians of the importance of Christ's resurrection, in which the essential meaning of the cross as the core of Christian witness in the world is revealed. The "amazement" of the myrrh-bearers when, "entering the tomb, they saw a young man sitting at the right, wearing a white robe" (Mark 16.5), exemplifies the essence of our faith as an experience of amazement and awe, when we stand before the Holy.

This is a deep reality taking place at the borderline of experience. Humankind is faced with a mystery that deepens all the more as the believer approaches it.

It is no accident that the gospel of the resurrection is the greatest challenge for the modern secular person, who finds it difficult to accept that the denial of this mystery not only does not liberate, but instead diminishes, humanity, and enslaves it to a set of unyielding and unequivocal "certainties".

The feast of Easter, as the victory of life over death, also raises fundamental questions for all those who today preach and commit violence in the name of religion and God.

Nothing in the evangelical narrative of the resurrection appears to limit or annul the freedom of believers. All things are conjoined to our free acceptance of the divine gift. If we were driven to Paradise by force, then this would not be our longed-for homeland, but hell instead. The cornerstone in the life of Orthodox believers is freedom.

Above all, in the light of the resurrection, Orthodoxy is revealed as the Church of freedom. At Easter, the Orthodox faithful experience their ecclesial identity, as a communion with the Risen Christ, who lives in them and among them. The words of the Holy Apostle Paul apply here completely: "If Christ has not been raised, then our preaching is vain, your faith also is vain" (1 Corinthians 15.14).

For all these reasons, when at Easter, "the gates of Paradise have been opened unto us", it is not just a matter of a religious holiday, nor even the biggest celebration of Orthodox people, everywhere. The resurrection is the whole faith, ethos, and culture of Orthodox Christianity.

(2016)

Joy cometh in the morning

For Easter Day, **John Inge** reflects on the closeness of the
relationship between joy and sorrow

FROM the beginning, the resurrection of Jesus has been associated with joy.
There are only two resurrection appearances in Luke and, at the conclusion
of the second, we read that the disciples "worshipped him and returned to
Jerusalem with great joy" (Luke 24.52). Here, as earlier on the road to
Emmaus, when their hearts "burned within them" (Luke 24.32), Jesus "opens
their minds to understand the scriptures", and the disciples' reaction is joy.
At his second and final appearance, we even read, puzzlingly, that "in their
joy they were disbelieving and still wondering" (Luke 24.41).

When the Holy Spirit fell upon the disciples, their joy recorded at the
conclusion of St Luke's Gospel went on to become a hallmark of the Christian
life. We learn in Acts 13.22 that the disciples were "filled with joy and the
Holy Spirit". Paul tells the Romans that "the Kingdom of heaven is righteousness and peace and joy in the Holy Spirit" (Romans 14.17), and prays
that they may be "filled with all joy and hope in believing" (Romans 15.13).

It occurs to me that perhaps, as much as anything else, Christ came to
bring us joy. He speaks to his disciples of God's great love for them so that
"their joy may be complete". It is there at the beginning of his earthly
ministry, as at the end. In *The Brothers Karamazov,* Dostoevsky writes
memorably of Jesus's first miracle at Cana: "Ah yes. I was missing that, and
I don't want to miss it. I love that passage: it's Cana of Galilee, the first
miracle. Ah, that miracle! It was not men's grief but their joy Christ visited.
He worked His first miracle to help men's gladness."

JOY IS surely unique among the fruits of the Spirit listed by Paul
(Galatians 5.22-23). Each of the others implies something active: love, peace,
forbearance, kindness, goodness, faithfulness, gentleness, and self-control
can all be attained by an effort of will — even if it is Spirit-filled effort. Peace
can perhaps be experienced without effort, though we are called to be active
peacemakers.

Joy, however, is different: you can't work at being joyful. It is a glorious
rebuke to the Protestant work ethic. It is a state of being which no amount
of work or concentration will produce. It is gift. It is sheer grace.

I REMEMBER being very struck by a testimony given at a confirmation I conducted by a young woman whose heart was quite clearly bubbling over with joy. She recounted how her colleagues at work couldn't quite work out what was wrong with her. Conversely, Paul asks the Galatians what has happened to all their joy. Doesn't this imply that lack of joy suggests a waning in Christian conviction?

Evelyn Waugh, asked how he reconciled being such a miserable individual with being a Christian, is said to have replied, "Think what I would be like if I were not a Christian." A witty response, but not, to my mind, convincing.

I once read that the reason why it took so long for Cardinal Newman to be beatified was that he had not exhibited enough joy in his life. I don't know whether that's true, but I do know that the Christians who have impressed me most are those who have clearly been filled with a deep-down joy, even in adversity. Archbishop Desmond Tutu seems always to be full of joy and laughter. Surely this is a sign that he has been able to keep a Godly perspective on things, rather than being weighed down with the terrible situations which he has had to confront.

Laughter is associated with happiness, which is different from joy, although they are not unconnected. Like joy, laughter enables us to rise above things and see them from a different perspective — to perceive them in proportion, perhaps.

IT MIGHT reasonably be asked how we can possibly be filled with joy in the face of some of the terrible things that life throws at us, and joy certainly cannot be the only thing we experience as Christians. It is no accident that the joy of the disciples came after the desolation of the Passion.

The Passion and resurrection witnessed by the disciples were two exceptional experiences, but we find echoes of them in our own human experience, since death and resurrection are the pattern of things as we understand them as Christians.

That being the case, joy and sorrow are bound to be mingled in our life. As William Blake memorably wrote in *Auguries of Innocence*:

Man was made for Joy & Woe
And when this we rightly know
Thro' the World we safely go
Joy & Woe are woven fine
A Clothing for the soul divine
Under every grief & pine
Runs a joy with silken twine

JOY and woe have been much on my mind since my wife, Denise, died on Easter Day three years ago, leaving me and my two daughters (then aged eight and 14) bereft. I recently watched the BBC1 documentary *Rio Ferdinand: Being Mum and Dad*. It spoke to me deeply. He has experienced the depths since the death of his young wife, as I have since Denise's death, acting as both mother and father.

For most of the time, even as Christians, we prefer to pretend that death does not exist. That is foolish; for, as Denise wrote in her remarkable book *A Tour of Bones*, published posthumously, "questions about the limits of life and the limits of love go right to the heart of how we understand ourselves as human beings. Much of the time, we pretend that death isn't a part of life. Yet, death is a crucial part of the human condition; when we avoid talking about death we avoid talking about life."

In the face of death, Denise suggested that we need tears and laughter as well as talk: "How else can any of us face mortality? The unexpected joys of life, the grim brutalities of death? Tears and laughter and friends. How grateful I am for these tears and laughter."

Tears and laughter, sorrow and joy. Since her death, sorrow has often prevailed, but joy has crept up on me unawares, as it can do even in times of desperate sadness. It did so especially when, last year, my 17-year-old daughter herself gave birth to a baby daughter. It was not what she had planned or I had expected, but Lily, now one year old, has brought untold joy and laughter in the midst of sadness. It is indeed true that "under every grief and pine runs a joy with silken twine".

Flashes of joy are intimations of the profound truth that, though joy and woe are "woven fine, a clothing for the soul divine" in this world, it will not be so in God's future. The Christian hope — resurrection hope — tells us that "neither death, nor life, nor angels, nor principalities, nor things present, nor things to come, nor height, nor depth, nor anything else in all creation, will be able to separate us from the love of God in Christ Jesus our Lord" (Romans 8.38-39).

Love will prevail. God will prevail. Joy will prevail.

(2017)

Walking away from the garden

Easter Day: **Simon Jones** on the new dawn

*"But suddenly, at the edge of her mind, Religion appeared, poor little
talkative Christianity, and she knew that all its divine words from
'Let there be light' to 'It is finished' only amounted to 'boum'."*

SO REFLECTS Mrs Moore in E. M. Forster's *A Passage to India*. A lifelong
Christian, whose faith and the comfort it brings her have become increasingly
cold with the passing of the years, Mrs Moore has come to India seeking
new meaning, new purpose, new significance in her life. During a trip to
the Marabar caves, Mrs Moore's life and beliefs are turned upside down by
an unexpected and disturbing experience. Standing in one of these cavernous
spaces, she realises that her ears are filled by the haunting sound of a
persistent, incomprehensible echo. No matter which words leave her lips,
however pious or well meant, the sound comes back the same — an empty,
meaningless echo.

And from this unsettling experience, Mrs Moore reflects on the faith
that has sustained her throughout her life, and concludes that from God's
first words in creation to Christ's final words on the cross, it is no more than
"poor little talkative Christianity".

On Easter Day, I suspect that many of us approach the tomb of Christ
with some of the same hopes and aspirations with which Mrs Moore travelled
to the Marabar caves. As Christians, we believe that all human history
converges upon the saving events of the death and resurrection of Jesus;
and, unlike the three women who, in Mark's Gospel, bought spices in order
to anoint the lifeless body of the one whose brutal execution they had
witnessed, our early-morning journey to the tomb is not filled with the
same heart-broken grief and heavy sorrow.

Our advantage over those first disciples is that we have already heard
the message proclaimed inside the tomb: "He has been raised; he is not
here," and so our expectations are high. We may be confident that retracing
steps along which countless disciples have travelled for 2000 years will lead
us to joy and fulfilment when we see the place where they laid him.

Yet in none of the Gospel accounts do those who come to the tomb
remain there for very long. The Easter experience is not complete unless,

having entered the tomb to see for ourselves, we then leave with a message for others. For us, who have heard and seen it all before, and whose response to the resurrection may have become dulled by familiarity, there is a danger that, in growing weary of the challenge of stepping back into the garden to discover what it means to be a disciple of the Risen One, we have become content to remain in the tomb, filling its emptiness with "Alleluias" that are not heard by those outside, but return to our ears as a confused, meaningless echo — "poor little talkative Christianity".

If our Easter faith has got stuck inside an empty, echoing tomb, then perhaps we need to find other images of the resurrection that speak more realistically to our experience. For me, one such image stands in the great 12th-century Abbey Church of St Mary the Virgin in Tewkesbury, Gloucestershire. Over its history, at different times and in varying circumstances, the worshipping community has expressed particular aspects of its faith in Christ through images of his mother. Of all these, none is more striking than *Our Lady, Queen of Peace*, the work of the contemporary sculptor, Anthony Robinson, given to the Abbey in 1992

Standing in front of the image, the eye is drawn first to the base of the statue, which appears to be no more than a pile of scrap metal, rusted and misshapen. In his Pilgrim Guide to the Abbey, Michael Tavinor describes

how some have seen within its contorted features instruments of torture or the wreckage of a car crash. In more recent years, it has been identified with the Ground Zero of 11 September. This ugly pile of twisted metal speaks powerfully of the pain of a disordered world of chaos and despair — of a world and its people disfigured by the effects of earthquake, flood and famine; of terrorism and military conflict; of religious and racial intolerance.

Our Lady, Queen of Peace,
Statue by Anthony Robinson,
Tewkesbury Abbey

But from this chaotic base rises the image of Mary. Made from shining stainless steel, its most striking feature is that Mary is completely hollow, holding her hands out in a gesture of prayer which is both open to God and to those who are drawn towards her. With its two parts, the statue speaks of the movement from death to life, from crucifixion to resurrection.

This is no sentimental Christmas-card representation of the sort of mother who cradles her child in her arms in order to protect him from the painful reality of what is happening beneath them. Rather, the twisted metal is an integral part of the statue. Without it, the image is incomplete and would topple over.

By making scrap metal the foundation for stainless steel, Anthony Robinson expresses the Christian truth that the resurrection of Jesus Christ does not obliterate his Good Friday experience; it does not remove the intense Passion of its pain, or its darkness, or its God-forsakenness. Without the cross, Easter is no more than a theatrical sleight of hand, a meaningless charade. Without the resurrection, the crucifixion has no more significance than any other Roman execution.

At one level, Tewkesbury's Mary may appear to be an unlikely icon of resurrection life. The New Testament contains no evidence to suggest that the Mother of Jesus was among those who went to the tomb early on the first day of the week. And yet, the juxtaposition of the two parts of this image reflects an important reality of our own post-resurrection lives. We, who were also absent on the first Easter morning, find ourselves, for much of the time, not basking in the gleaming, reflective, and ecstatic splendour of resurrection glory, but struggling to find our way in that often sharp and ambiguous place of what often appears to be a spiritual wilderness or no man's land, where twisted metal and shining stainless steel meet.

Comparing the Evangelists' accounts of the resurrection, it is interesting that they present subtly different pictures of how light or dark it was when the women journeyed to the tomb. In Matthew, they arrive "as the first day of the week was dawning"; in Mark, it is "very early … when the sun had risen"; and Luke describes the scene "at early dawn", whereas in John it is still dark.

Responding to this ambiguity, as well as to our own experience of living in the light of the risen Christ, Tewkesbury's Mary helps us to come to terms with the reality that, for much of the time, our lives are lived in the dawning half-light of Easter morning, very early, in that often confused and uncertain place that is neither light nor dark, where we must wait to discover the full reality of what it means for the bloodstained wood of the cross and the transforming glory of Easter to embrace and clothe each other in eternal significance.

Such a place is described by Elizabeth Jennings in these four verses from her poem "Dawn Not Yet":

Dawn not yet and the night still holding sleepers
Closed in dreams, clams in shelter, a hiding
Of half the world and men turned back into

Primeval matter. A closed world only tides
Ruminate over. Here men could be fossils
Embedded in strata, all to be discovered

By morning, skilful archaeologist
Cutting down carefully, drawing up debris
Of centuries but also precious gems,

Ivory figurines, kings' hoards.
We are shown Riches the sun at last gives shape and glint to
Sun the explorer, sun the diver, too.

As those who inhabit a world that frustratingly feels all too often as if it is "dawn not yet", our Easter response to the resurrection of Christ is not so different from that of Jennings's skilful archaeologist, who makes careful use of the rays of the sun to give shape and glint to riches embedded in strata, all to be discovered.

This Easter, may our early-morning pilgrimage on the first day of the week not reach its final destination in an empty tomb where faith in Christ's resurrection echoes meaninglessly around our heads. May it rather empower us to rejoice in the ultimate defeat of sin and death in a world still painfully scarred by their reality. As we continue our Easter journey by walking away from the garden, may our eyes be opened to recognise in the half-light of the new dawn the transforming light of the risen Christ, shining upon the twisted, misshapen, and rusted disorder, to form us into his own likeness and to bring to birth a new creation.

(2006)

Finding your way in the dark

The moon and a black, underground Mary speak to
Barbara Brown Taylor of the spiritual treasures of darkness

WHEN I was a parish priest, I learned to use the table in the back of the [American] Book of Common Prayer to find the date for Easter every year. That table may well contain the only hard science in the book, but the rule that accompanies it sounds distinctly Druid:

"Easter Day is always the Sunday after the full moon that occurs on or after the spring equinox on March 21, a date which is fixed in accordance with an ancient ecclesiastical computation, and which does not always correspond to the astronomical equinox."

Yet even a child who came upon the page during a particularly long sermon could not help but notice this: Easter comes on a different day every year. Like Passover, it is tethered to the spring equinox, but on that relatively long leash it may occur anywhere from 22 March to 25 April, never falling on the same day two years in a row.

If Christians look to creation for wisdom about the spiritual life, seeing resurrection in springtime, divine promise in a rainbow, or the flight of the Spirit in a dove, why don't we look to the moon for wisdom about our relationship to God? But there is a whole dark night of spiritual treasure to explore.

ALTHOUGH I am not a Roman Catholic, I am devoted to Mary. Part of it is that she is a she; the other part is that she is entirely human. Most of the time, I think she understands me better than her son does, since she has a whole DNA spiral and a body that operates on a lunar cycle – or did.

Even if she has left that part of her life behind now, as I have, she remembers what it was like to fill like the moon every month, and then to empty. She knows what it is like to go through this routine diminishment without ever getting used to it, the same way one never quite gets used to a night with no moon.

In 2009, I visited the Cathedral of Notre-Dame in Chartres for the first time. It had been on my radar for years, and I wanted to see the flying buttresses, the carvings over the doors, the stained glass windows, and above all the labyrinth.

151

The rose window that dominates the façade of the church and the labyrinth on the floor inside are both 40 feet in diameter – perfect twins in size and placement. If you could lower the front wall of the church gently to the floor, the window that channels the light would fit right over the labyrinth that covers the darkness. The number of stones in the labyrinth is the number of days a full-term baby spends in its mother's womb.

In these ways and more, Chartres Cathedral is a microcosm of both the human journey from life to death, and the journey of the earth around the sun, offering a concrete corrective to anyone who thinks of the physical and the spiritual as two separate things.

The labyrinth was spectacular, but I expected that. What I did not expect was the church beneath the church – the vast crypt that was undamaged by the fire of 1194, and became the footprint for the new Gothic cathedral to rise above.

The crypt is one long mall of chapels: seven plain Romanesque ones along the sides, and the Chapel of Notre-Dame de Sous-Terre at the end – Our Lady of the Underground – a low, dark cavern, lined with dark wood pews.

Above the altar is a small wooden statue of a Madonna and child, carved to replace the more ancient one destroyed during the French Revolution. Mother and child are both so dark that it is difficult to see them from a distance.

It is only when I walk behind the altar for a closer look that I clearly see the face of the stiff woman sitting on her throne with her stiff baby on her lap. Her eyes are closed. Her son's are wide open. Neither of them is lovely, and yet they are arresting, if only because they require such careful looking to see.

Statue of Madonna and child in the Chapel of Notre-Dame de Sous-Terre, Chartres Cathedral

Art historians count the statue among the many *Vierges noires* in France – black Virgins – so called not because their features are African, or because they have got covered up with candle soot, but because their skin is dark. One theory favours the identification of Mary with indigenous people. The darker she is, the more she resembles those who serve, instead of those who rule.

As I continue looking at her, another possibility occurs to me. The darkness is not meant to convey anything about Mary; it is meant to convey something about those of us who look at her.

We see through a glass darkly. She does not care how curious we are. We can rest a flashlight right on her nose if we want, and still she will not open her eyes. No amount of light can make her give up her mystery.

Earlier, in the gift shop, I saw a silver medal with her image on it and her mantra on the back. "All must come through me in order to live in the light," it read. She might as well have signed it *Our Lady of the Cave.*

There is no moonlight down here, but that is clearly her kind of light. If I want something more brightly lit, I can go upstairs and look at one of the white Virgins in the main cathedral. That is where all the tourists are anyway. Almost no one comes down here to visit Our Lady of the Underground, either because they have bad knees or because they have heard it is a crypt.

"What's down there?" I hear someone at the top of the steps ask a woman ahead of me on the way out.

"Nothing," she says. "It's dark and incredibly gloomy."

LATER, after dark, I go back to see *Chartres en Lumières.* The whole city is lit up, with elaborate coloured designs projected onto the cathedral and other buildings. The largest crowd stands on the plaza in front of the cathedral, gaping at the huge Virgin covering the western façade of the church.

This Mary is an exact replica of the *Belle Verrière* window inside – a vividly coloured version of Our Lady of the Underground. Then I see the real moon, hanging over Chartres with such pale white light that it is barely visible above all the hot colours below.

Looking back and forth between the two light shows in front of me, I understand the choice I am being offered: do I want the kind of light that shines *on* things, or the kind that shines *from* them?

The next morning, I stop by the cathedral gift shop to buy the silver medal with Our Lady of the Underground on it. *All must come through me in order to live in the light.* She has been talking to me ever since.

Our Lady of the Underground never asks me to choose between day and night. If I want to flourish, I need the ever-changing light of darkness as much as I need the full light of day. *Give your heart to them both*, she says.

When I complain that I cannot see as well at night as I can during the day, she tells me this is a good thing. *Maybe it will slow you down*. When I tell her that I cannot get as much done at night because darkness makes me sleepy, she says yes, that is the plan. *Maybe you will get some rest*.

When I point out that slowing down just makes me think about things I would rather not think about, she laughs. *Do you think that not thinking about them will make them go away?*

She is always right.

What do you want from me? I ask her. *Nothing*, she says.

At first, I think she means that she does not want anything from me, but that is not what she means. She means that she wants nothing *for* me, because she knows how scared I am of it – of being nothing, doing nothing, believing nothing, being good for nothing, ending up nothing. *Nada*.

She seems to think there is more to it than that, which is why she wants it for me. If I could lean into it a little more, she says, I might be surprised. I tell her I will take it under consideration.

"The soul does not grow by addition but by subtraction," wrote the 14th-century mystic Meister Eckhart:

Leave place, leave time,
Avoid even image!
Go forth without a way
On the narrow path,
Then you will find the desert rack.

ACCORDING to the Gospels, Jesus knew that track well. He made a habit of sleeping outdoors under the stars – on a mountain, if he could find one. The fact that this is reported, more than once, without any further detail, suggests that he went alone.

When he took people with him, they usually had plenty to say about it afterwards, but no one has anything to say about what Jesus did on those nights alone. Even his famous forty days and nights in the wilderness pass without comment until they are over, which is when he and the devil sort out who works for whom.

When you put this together with the fact that God speaks to Jesus only once in the entire New Testament – shortly after he is baptised by John – it seems clear that this father and this son were not in constant public conversation. Their conversation was almost entirely private, when Jesus went out on the mountain to spend the night with God in prayer.

If Jesus was truly human, as Christians insist he was, his sleep architecture was like anyone else's. He stayed awake awhile. He slept awhile. He woke awhile later, rested a few hours, then slept some more.

When he opened his eyes, he saw the night sky. When he closed them again, the sky stayed right there. The only witnesses to his most intimate moments with God were the moon and the stars – and it was all prayer.

Outside my window, the full moon has risen high in the sky, casting such strong light on the pasture that there seem to be twice as many trees as usual – the trees plus their shadows. *All must come through me to live in the light*, the lady in the moon says, and I believe her.

WHEN I wake in the morning, I will give thanks for all the bright gifts that spill forth from the *nada* of God: sunshine, warmth, and work; faith, hope, and love.

What I now know for certain – perhaps the only thing I know for certain – is that while these gifts may arrive by day, they come burnished by darkness, like shoes left outside our doors for polishing while we sleep. Or better yet, like dazzling stones we have brought back from our shallow caves in the darkness of our pockets.

If they do not dazzle in daylight, then what better reminder could we have? The light was never in the stone. It was in our eyes all along.

My Lord God, I have no idea where I am going. I do not see the road ahead of me. I cannot know for certain where it will end. Nor do I really know myself, and the fact that I think I am following your will does not mean that I am actually doing so.

But I believe that the desire to please you does in fact please you. And I hope I have that desire in all that I am doing. I hope that I will never do anything apart from that desire. And I know that if I do this you will lead me by the right road, though I may know nothing about it. Therefore I will trust you always though I may seem to be lost and in the shadow of death. I will not fear, for you are ever with me, and you will never leave me to face my perils alone.

Thomas Merton, from *Thoughts in Solitude*

(2014)

Revealed: a New Testament pioneer

Mary Magdalene is a victim of mistaken identity, argues **Marie-Elsa Bragg**. She is not the penitent prostitute of popular myth, but strong, and of independent faith

THROUGHOUT Holy Week, the presence of Mary Magdalene guides me, drawn from all four Gospels: she is near Jesus while he walks the Via Dolorosa; stands with the other women at the foot of the cross; hears his last words; watches Joseph of Arimathaea take him down from the cross and carry him to the tomb; and then observes the sabbath, before returning early the next morning to anoint the body with sacred oils, as demanded by custom.

I am always aware that to walk with her still includes the need to sweep her mistaken identity aside. I remember how she may have been seen as a strong figure for the first few hundred years of the Christian faith, but, since Pope Gregory's homily in 591, she was merged with Mary, the woman from the city who was a sinner, and who washed Jesus's feet with her tears; and with Mary of Bethany, even though they are separate in the text.

From then on, Mary Magdalene has been the example of a redeemed prostitute. There are beautiful paintings from the Renaissance of her naked with only long hair to cover her, which are partly the influence of another Mary again, Mary of Egypt, a repentant prostitute from about AD 400.

Mary Magdalene grieving as Jesus is taken down from the cross in the Deposition of Christ, *a panel painting by Rogier van der Weyden, c.1435, Museo del Prado*

As I ask who she really was, I am aware that this question is one that women have been through alongside her. We ask who we are, once we have been freed from oppression and mistaken identity — a subject still vigorously discussed today in books such as *The Beauty Myth* by Naomi Woolf (1990), and Natasha Walter's *Living Dolls: The return of sexism* (2010).

When I was a teenager, before I found out that there was no mention of her as a prostitute in the Gospels, I always admired the strength that she showed in her ability to stand as a known redeemed sinner, and yet remain central to the teachings of Christ — especially as she stood in isolation, without a male equivalent, who could have been seen to have strayed in sexual abuse or prostitution and then redeemed.

When I discovered that her story had been fabricated, and came instead from our history of difficulties with women, I was for a moment sad to lose the image of her unique strength. But the sadness of what we have done to women over the

The Penitent Magdalene *(c.1635), an old-school depiction of Mary Magdalene, by Guido Reni, Walters Art Museum, Maryland, USA*

ages was stronger, and, like her, I decided not to run away. I looked deeper into who she was, to find support and to discover how she remained firmly at the centre of the Gospels, when times were so hard for women.

MARY MAGDALENE was certainly a woman who served Christ with honour. She was regularly named first when there was a group of women, and so was possibly a leader. Many scholars have wondered whether she was one of the women mentioned in Acts who supported Jesus and the disciples financially, possibly a widow.

If this were the case, she would have had an extraordinary pioneering spirit to live as a single woman and equal disciple of Christ, travelling the country, sitting at the feet of Jesus, alongside Mary, the sister of Lazarus, and the other disciples, listening to his teaching.

If that was her life, then I have often wondered what social opposition she weathered, and how she kept strong while living a life she knew to be true, but one that the society around her was not yet able to accept.

The Gnostic Gospels have made me consider her place in the group, and, of course, we have seen the public fervour arising about her from *The Da Vinci Code* by Dan Brown, which is based loosely on the Gospel of Mary and Philip.

People are clearly relieved to find a way of seeing Mary as central to the teachings of Jesus. They argue that, if she was Jesus's wife, then sexuality has a much-needed redeemed and sacred place in our lives. They also infer that, if she was accepted as the partner of a man such as Jesus, then she would have been wise, and played an important part in his life and the work after his death.

Over time, I have come to respect the questioning that we do with such small evidence; I see it as a reaction to the false identity she was given for so long, and a search for her true strength.

But the more I have looked into the texts that we have, the more I am convinced that we do not need her to be a wife, or indeed a provider, to see that she was central. Whatever her position was with Jesus and within the group, she was certainly a pioneer, following a rabbi who brought radical new spiritual teachings.

MORE importantly, however, the Gospels are not devoid of information about her — far from it. Over the years, I have come to see that her real strength is in her actions, and her consistent presence. The very fact that she is noted in the Gospels at such significant times in the life, death, and resurrection of Christ adds weight and truth to her character.

Even though the texts were written years after the event, in a culture where a woman's word was not taken in law unless supported by two men; and when it would have made proselytising easier if the first to see Christ had been a man, there she is — so central to the true message that she had to be written in.

From what we know, her ability to inspire such loyalty must have come with wisdom born from experience. We know that she was healed by Jesus from seven demons, which is hard to understand in modern times, but may have been a type of breakdown — perhaps after her husband died, perhaps having made mistakes, or while trying to become an individual in a difficult world.

Whatever it was, it means that she was someone who had been through inner darkness, and had come out on the other side. There is no record that she betrayed Christ after his death, as others did; she stayed at the cross, no matter how hard it was to watch.

We also know that she had the courage and skills to face death, as she returned early after the sabbath, with sacred oils to anoint Jesus's body; and, again, she stayed at the tomb after she saw that it was empty. She is a consistent and courageous guide in dark times.

Mother Emily Ayckbowm, who founded the Anglican Sisters of the Community of the Church in 1870, described Mary at the empty tomb as not able to "tear herself away from the sacred spot".

This is a strength of devotion that many, including Mother Emily, have needed as a guide, while they set up schools, orphanages, and other projects in deprived areas.

MARY was also seen in a group of women, clearly being part of a community. I have often wondered what that final sabbath was like — how supportive their community was, and how they managed to continue their rituals and the prayers.

I wonder whether they kept to the traditional liturgy, or developed something with the new teachings that Jesus had brought. But the fact that Mary turned up early the next morning with sacred oils to anoint Jesus's body shows that she still observed the traditional rituals.

This, coupled with her sabbath observance, and the fact that, in every Gospel, she, or she along with other women, is spoken to by angels at the tomb, suggests that she lived a devotional life supported by her tradition and renewed spiritual practice. This is a resource that is much needed for the fullness of a soulful life, and for the integration of such profound spiritual experience.

When Mary was outside the tomb, she did not at first recognise the man whom she thought was the gardener, and I have often asked why Jesus called her by name. He did not do that with Cleopas and the other disciple on the road to Emmaus. He did not do that when he later appeared to all the disciples.

Why did he call her name straight away? How extraordinary it was that this simple action woke her to the truth. Here, I find the opposite to what she has endured through history. Rather than being merged with other women, she is asked to see Christ, called as an individual and mature woman.

I imagine that she felt like falling at his feet, but she was asked not to touch him. I cannot help but hear the words that Jesus later spoke to Thomas, who needed to see and touch Jesus's wounds to make sure that he was Christ: "Blessed are they that have not seen, and yet have believed."

Mary did not stop to look for his wounds, or need to touch them for proof. Jesus knew that she did not need to: her faith was strong. Then he affirmed a true vocation within her, and called her to serve him and spread the news.

THIS calling as a strong individual, as a woman of faith, and as someone with a true vocation is why she remained central to the gospel. Her consistent presence, her strength and wisdom, even in the darkest of times, brings grace and guidance that is truly transformative.

This is why she has weathered the difficult history that we have come through, while we discerned how to be men and women serving together. And this is what also makes her an invaluable mentor in our much-needed review of what it is to stand together, women and men, both sacred in the eyes of god, both capable of falling, and both capable of serving together with faith and integrity in the future.

(2013)

Come back, Eostre, all is forgiven

For many, Easter means chocolate and very little else.
But all can glimpse the resurrection message in nature reborn
and the return of light, says **Terence Handley MacMath**

YESTERDAY I did my egg trick for the local primary school's Easter assembly. You have to, don't you? Easter is about eggs, now. The Easter miracle we're called upon to perform nowadays is to explain how all those mini-eggs relate to the astonishing gospel.

"All you need for a Happy Easter," proclaims Tesco's confidently. No, not over its shrink-wrapped trays of slaughtered lambs or bags of ready-washed bitter herbs, but the mountains of bright cardboard and cheap chocolate piled at the end of every row and check-out line. Chocolate is definitely where Easter is at.

Interestingly, a quick visit to Clinton's card shop yielded a surprising choice of Christian cards: at least half a dozen. If you must exchange Easter greetings by pasteboard (and charities are hoping to profit by this urge), you can send "love and prayers", "blessings", or even a cross with chicks and bunnies on it, to go with any amount of secular fluffy good wishes.

"Do they know it's Easter?" asks the Spire Trust's latest booklet for RE in secondary schools. They ought to: they get a holiday out of it, because we do still organise our school terms round the major Christian festivals. Those two precious weeks are still called "Easter holidays" — though not for much longer, if the exam boards get their way, and the school year gets carved up into six equal terms. Then Easter will pale into a long weekend; even (and here one recalls the great rift in Christendom over the holy dating of Easter) a fixed date in the calendar, to suit life's organisers.

Worldly wise children might also notice the commercial opportunities. Any shop that can cash in on it is now awash with displays of lilac, pale green or dazzling yellow. Point number one, then, is that Easter is very noticeable. This is positive — though, when you look more closely, you see that Easter is a package: DIY, spring fashion and confectionery.

Naturally, anyone who can get away with stocking Easter eggs does. But the colour-coding means that everyone can join in. The Bradford & Bingley Building Society in my High Street has a window display of yellow balloons; and even our Holy Week council-issue dustbin bags come in Lenten purple on which the dates and times of the Easter collection are efficiently printed.

Point number two is that chocolate is everywhere. This isn't new: my childhood in the 1960s was certainly sweetened by Easter eggs, though you were lucky to be given three or four, then. For a time I grew up in the USA, so I assumed that everyone hunted for little Easter eggs left in the garden by the Easter Bunny. But Rosie, who returned from the States about ten years ago, tells me that this was still an idea new to her English friends. Her American church gave all the children little baskets so they could hunt for eggs in the churchyard on Easter Day.

Gradually, though, British children have learned to see if the Easter Bunny has been on Easter morning. Just as the Church has had to accommodate Santa Claus, so expect the Easter Bunny to be worked into family-service liturgy.

I don't know where the egg hunt originated, although its apotheosis is the annual egg-hunt on the White House lawns. The odd thing is that every Jewish child will be hunting for the *afikomen* at their Seders just a few days before. The origin and significance of the *afikomen,* part of the unleavened bread broken and shared, also seems to be a mystery. It could symbolise all sorts of things, including the hidden Messiah. Still, Jewish or Christian, those who wanted to communicate the mystery and joyfulness of God to children knew a thing or two.

There is no question about what came first, though, the chocolate or the egg. For me, coveted though the chocolate was —especially after the renunciation of sweets in Lent — the Easter Day highlight was my atheist father's pleasure in making pace eggs, a relic of his Westmoreland childhood. He made them properly, tying up each egg (they were largely white, in those days) in primrose leaves and onion skins. East Anglia isn't Westmoreland, and we couldn't roll them down hills, but we duly bashed each other's eggs to smithereens and ate the remains for lunch.

Those were the days when Good Friday was truly good. All work stopped; all shops shut, except the bakers, to sell hot cross buns. Incidentally, the death of the hot cross bun has been exaggerated. The opposite seems to be true: they are on sale in many bakers' shops and supermarkets all the year round.

Deep memories remain of my father explaining about hot cross buns and Good Friday ("Why *Good* Friday, Daddy?") when I was about five. Growing up in a non-churchgoing family, I was impressed by his solemnity and by the fact that the world would, in some sense, stop on that day. A sort of super-Sabbath without the rejoicing, for these post-Christians.

THE PUBLIC observance of Easter depends, as with other religious and cultural events, on how far you live from London. Before moving to a city just outside the capital, we lived in a Suffolk coastal town, where, when our oldest children were small, the day still had its solemn character. Good Friday was marked by a procession through the town behind a large wooden cross, ending up on a green near the sea with an ecumenical open-air service. All was quiet and sombre.

The last time we were there, however, the procession had become ever so slightly competitive. The change came when the police stopped blocking off the high street: when pilgrims jostle with holiday traffic, a procession of witness takes on a depressingly reproachful air. Tourists and churchgoers watch each other with incomprehension.

Nevertheless, the lucky children of that town still have an unusually rich Easter: a procession and hot cross buns at church on Good Friday; the blazing joy of Easter Day at a sunrise service on the beach, sometimes with the sun in attendance. And in between, the purposeful business of Easter Saturday, when garden flowers are brought into church, and children arrange them round the font and create a tiny Easter garden.

In our more cosmopolitan town, things are a little different. Tesco's, the remaining supermarket in the town centre, will be closed on Easter Day; but Good Friday is now a day of shopping for the feasts ahead. It is easy to get a false impression by talking just to churchgoers, but most people I spoke to plan to spend at least part of Easter with family or friends. Sunday lunch (and for many it's always lamb) is still important. The Italian delicatessen offers special cakes and sweets; the restaurants are already advertising special Sunday lunches.

Christians here celebrate with an ecumenical service, but it is held at night, in the cathedral. The Maundy Thursday services are not, by and large, packed: Thursday is a working day, and the commuters return late. The Three Hours on Good Friday is respectably attended, though many people tell me they will be away then, seeing family. This affects Easter Day congregations as well.

But there has been an interesting development: the Camphill Village Trust shop, run by a German woman, is full this year of exquisite German wooden eggs, chicks, flowers, lights, candles. The smart women of the town are lapping these up.

The German connection reminds me of another strand to add to the northern European Easter of *Kinder, Küche,* and occasionally *Kirche.* An Easter I spent as a child in Germany was more familiar than the one I spent in Spain, where the drama of the crucifixion hits the streets and has to force its way through the casually pious crowds. The German family I stayed with didn't go to church; but we walked, rejoicing in von Trapp fashion, over flower-studded hills. We visited relations on a farm where I could pick up the newborn lambs (and silently register their butchery arrangements: a bleeding tree stump by the back door, with the axe left handily balanced in its own cleft).

In British non-Christians, Easter seems to bring out a residual longing for the countryside. Stately homes and tourist attractions all open for Easter. The M25 tarmac will be hot.

For the British, who work long hours in a poor climate, Easter means a few precious leisure hours to do what we want. Harry is going to the bike track at Herne Hill; George is going fishing; Nelson Gabriel's old beauties and pals will plant their potatoes on Good Friday; garden centres everywhere will bloom.

IF THERE is a common thread in British Easters past and present, town and country, I think it is in our usual way of turning inwards to celebrate home and family — whether it's giving way to the DIY bug, or the traditional Sunday lunch with as many of the family as possible gathered together.

Make no mistake: this is wonderful. But without the public and shared religious observance, without shops closed and churches full, family lives lose the transcendent dimension that keeps them sweet and meaningful.

Easter is at a crossroads. It could go the way of Christmas, when the Church colludes with folk sentiment and commercial forces to create something (mainly) life-affirming. Or it could become as flat as an August bank holiday. And this is why: people in Britain work too hard, and so, on bank holidays, too many just want to rest. We have lost the art of celebrating together, because it takes too much time to organise and too much effort to carry off. Or if we do celebrate, we are uncertain about what it is we're supposed to proclaim.

Perhaps the passion for the countryside is our best reminder of the reality of the gospel. "The world itself keeps Easter Day" begins one neglected Easter carol. It reminds us that, in this hemisphere, nature itself is our most reliable witness to Easter. Society may have lost the plot, but we still find, in the spring and in the returning light, a symbol of resurrection — just as Christmas communicates some of its spiritual power through the contrasts of darkness and light, cold and warmth. The Christian story is made intelligible to neo-pagans through the sacramentals of the natural world.

If my children can make those connections, I shall not much mind which Easter traditions they pass on to their children. If they see God in the joyful rush of blossom and green buds, they will still want to sing Easter alleluias, and will still ask the right questions. They will discover for themselves that life is a poor bare thing without the sap of Christ's resurrection life flowing through it.

(2003)

Poet's corner: Death be not proud

April is proving a cruel month, but Easter brings us hope,
says **Malcolm Guite**

APRIL has indeed become the cruellest month. Even as life blossoms in our gardens, death stalks our streets and hospitals. As Henry Scott Holland, Canon of St Paul's, lamented a century ago, in the passage from his sermon that nobody quotes: "But how often death smites, without discrimination, as if it had no law! It makes its horrible breach in our gladness with careless and inhuman disregard of us."

And now we must fight on through grief, resisting an enemy that seems to have defeated our friends, while the indifferent April sun shines on. And shall we keep Easter in spite of the grief, in spite of churches locked and empty, in spite of packed hospitals, exhausted doctors and nurses, clergy and carers pushed past their limits?

Yes, we shall keep Easter, and not in spite of these things, but because of them. For it was into the cruellest of Aprils that Christ came to find and save us. He came to take on death at its worst, to experience for us, with us, and in us that hideous combination of exposure and isolation, which was his cross. To know with us what it feels like to perish within reach, and yet beyond the reach of the ones we love.

But if he shares our Good Friday, and especially this dark one that we are all sharing now, it is so that we can share his Easter. On this strange Easter Day, we will discover that he is not lost somewhere in our locked churches, any more than he was sealed in the sepulchre. He is up and out and risen, long before us. He is as much at work in the world as the spring is at work in the blossoms. On this Easter Day, the Risen Christ, who might have been a wafer in the hands of the priest, will be strength in the hands of the nurse, a blessing in the hands of the carer. He goes with them to their work as surely as he came to us in our church.

Victory over this virus is some way off, but victory over death is already achieved. It was because he knew that in Christ "death is swallowed up in victory" that Canon Scott Holland was finally able to say that "Death is nothing at all."

A Dean of St Paul's who lived through just such times as ours had said that before, with even greater power. John Donne saw more than his fair

*A 2012 bust by Nigel Boonham of the Church of England minister and poet
John Donne (1572–1631), with St Paul's Cathedral, London, in the background*

share of "poison, war, and sickness", but he could still fling this great defiance
into the face of death. It is Christ's defiance, and, this Easter, it is ours:

Sonnet X

Death, be not proud, though some have called thee
Mighty and dreadful, for thou art not so;
For those whom thou think'st thou dost overthrow
Die not, poor Death, nor yet canst thou kill me.
From rest and sleep, which but thy pictures be,
Much pleasure; then from thee much more must flow,
And soonest our best men with thee do go,
Rest of their bones, and soul's delivery.
Thou art slave to fate, chance, kings, and desperate men,
And dost with poison, war, and sickness dwell,
And poppy or charms can make us sleep as well
And better than thy stroke; why swell'st thou then?
One short sleep past, we wake eternally
And death shall be no more; Death, thou shalt die.

(2020)

Lost in the shadows at Easter

Personal experience has taught **Katharine Smith** that
many people will identify with Doubting Thomas at Easter —
feeling left out and alone

IT IS a perfect Easter morning: the sun is shining, and the air is clear. A light breeze reminds us that it is not summer yet. The blossom is unfolding: "Jesus Christ is risen today. Alleluia!" We hear good news of redemption and resurrection. Who could help but be uplifted, joyful, and filled with new energy?

With Mary Magdalene and the other Mary we go to the garden, where an angel shows us the empty tomb. With them we see our risen Lord, and worship him with wonder, fear, and excitement. Death has lost its sting and the grave its victory, and we celebrate again this wonderful festival of life.

All sorts of special occasions, such as Christmas and anniversaries, can be especially poignant for some, and Easter is no exception. Without in any way diminishing our celebration, perhaps we can also show sensitivity to those for whom the joy of Easter resurrection may seem distant — may seem impossible to imagine, let alone experience.

I have been plagued by bouts of clinical depression, and, sometimes, being in church on Easter Day has been a lonely and painful experience. There will be in our congregations those who are bereaved (not necessarily recently), traumatised, afraid, or grieving over a broken relationship — people who struggle in their own valley of shadows, whose pain and inner emptiness cannot be healed by hymns of joy or flowers on the cross of suffering.

If we are grieving like this, we may have found that throughout Lent, our liturgies and readings resonated with our Good Friday experience. Perhaps we felt in closer fellowship with other people in church, as together we followed the way of the cross.

The mood around us changed as Easter Day dawned, and we were left behind, once again alone in Gethsemane or at Golgotha, praying for deliverance and feeling utterly forsaken.

Having come through some dark times into an experience of resurrection in my own life, I am concerned about how we, as a Church, respond to people who on Easter Day feel that they have been left behind, alone and isolated. There is much that we can do to care for people who, for now, are living in the valley of shadows.

IT MIGHT be helpful to consider how we would support Thomas through his week of agonised doubting after the crucifixion of Jesus. On Low Sunday, we read Thomas's story and how he comes to believe that Jesus is risen from the dead because he sees Jesus for himself and acknowledges him as "My Lord and my God."

The first thing I would want to say about this is that Thomas cannot be criticised for his inability or refusal to believe in an experience that he has not shared in. He is very honest about how he feels, and if we are to be alongside people in pain, we need to give them time and space to be honest about that pain. It can be disrespectful to say something like: "Well, never mind, you'll feel better soon," or "You shouldn't feel like that, Jesus died for you," or to deny or minimise the other's suffering.

The experience of Thomas might sound familiar to people today who are troubled in mind and spirit. Like all close followers of Jesus, Thomas has been bereaved. He has lost someone he loved very much, and he is in the early days of grieving. He may be traumatised by events in the garden of Gethsemane, and what he has heard about the trial and crucifixion of Jesus. Today, he might be identified as someone at risk of developing post-traumatic stress disorder, with disturbing flashbacks, dreams, and feelings of guilt, shame, and self-hatred.

Thomas needs to tell his story. He needs to be heard, believed, and understood, and so, too, do people today who are grieving or traumatised. We need to hear their stories, to believe them, and show compassion. We must not try to hurry this process, which, if allowed to unfold naturally, will take as long as it needs to, before giving way to a more peaceful state of mind.

Thomas misses the appearance of Jesus to the other disciples. The effect of this on him is catastrophic. "Why did Jesus appear just then, when I wasn't there? He must have done it deliberately to exclude me; he doesn't love me. It's so unfair. The others saw him, and now they're all joyful and trying to make me be the same. Well, I can't, and I won't.

Show and tell: part of The incredulity of St Thomas *(1601–2), by Caravaggio*

"God, you've punished me for something, and you're going to have to come up with something really special to make me come back."

We can hear so much of Thomas's hurt in today's voices. "Why me?" "Why did an innocent child die?" "Why isn't God here when I really need him?"

Once again, painful as it is, we need to stay alongside people during these times of hurt, anger, and doubt. We need to show by our compassion that what they are going through is not God's will for them: it is not meant to be like this, and it is unfair. Any other approach risks adding yet more guilt or shame to the burden of one who already feels rejected by God.

Of course, when someone is deeply regretting something they said or did, or did not say or do, we also need to allow space for the expression of that regret, and to offer reassurance of God's forgiveness. Again, this is a process that needs to be allowed to unfold at its own rate. We might, for example, remember Peter's walk with Jesus on the beach after a breakfast barbecue.

There is always a balance to be found between offering reassurance of faith in God's goodness, and walking beside someone who cannot yet believe in or choose that road for themselves. We cannot walk beside someone if we are also pulling them somewhere that they cannot go, or do not want to go.

We could offer opportunities within our Easter liturgies for the expression of pain, anger, regret, and grief. At a simple level, we can include in our public intercessions prayers for people who find Easter a difficult time. Such an open acknowledgment of a darker side to the day or season may invite someone to talk for the first time about how they feel, as they realise that perhaps they are not as alone as they thought.

We might use a place in the church for prayer candles to be lit — a place where people can say quietly what is on their mind, perhaps to God, or to someone who has died leaving unresolved tensions behind.

At the Easter vigil, we could emphasise that place between death and resurrection, when everything, as it were, holds its breath and waits.

We might want to offer prayer for healing after someone has taken communion, or perhaps hold an evening service on Easter Day when emotions are less heightened and there may be space for deeper reflection and prayer.

Ministry to people in pain is always costly, and can be scary, but, from my experience, I would say that God in his love always reaches out somehow to those who suffer. If we offer to be part of that reaching out, we might make all the difference to another's pain and loneliness, especially if they feel they have been left behind at Easter.

(2011)

Easter and the invitation to be fully human

Rachel Mann explores the limits of compassion

I HAVE always been moved by that story from the Great War in which a war-weary Tommy, on his way up to the front line, spots a shell-blasted Calvary, or wayside crucifix of Jesus, and says, "Who was he, anyway? I bet I've suffered more than he ever did."

This past year of pandemic has, of course, been rather different from wartime conditions, but I cannot be alone in feeling worn thin and exhausted. So many of us are traumatised.

Not least among the deleterious effects of pandemic, for me, is a kind of compassion fatigue. I have been overwhelmed by the sheer scale of death, the level of human need, and the limitations imposed on life. The lockdowns have pushed me inwards, leading me to focus, a little to my shame, on my own sense of suffering and distress. To cope, there have been days when I've sealed up my compassionate heart.

God calls us out of ourselves into compassionate service, however, and surely the death and resurrection of Jesus Christ is the very icon of divine compassion; for this is the God who demonstrates his abundant compassion by laying down his life for the sake of the world.

Herein lies one of the joys of Easter: that, in the midst of the torture and death of Good Friday, and the absence of God on Holy Saturday, Jesus Christ comes forth from the tomb to offer us the promise of reconciliation. In crucifixion, Jesus suffers death and trauma; in resurrection, he does not seek revenge for what we have done to him, but offers us friendship and renewed love.

AS MANY people know, at its root, "compassion" means "suffer with". Through his suffering with and alongside us, Jesus invites us to grow into his likeness: to shape our lives according to the way of self-offering, giving, and compassion.

That is the theory, and it is an impressive one. What seems possible for God, however, is problematic for us. If God is infinite compassion, we humans clearly are not. I cannot be alone in feeling that this past year has found my compassion wanting.

If being compassionate is, in part, a matter of suffering with and alongside, too often I've found myself "switching off". In this era of 24-hour rolling news and instant access to endless data, I have often felt overwhelmed. Just to stay sane, I have sometimes had to switch off access to the incessant groans of a world in need.

Critics of religion might take such a response as yet another token of the falseness of faith: if I, a "mature" Christian, have struggled to remain compassionate, what hope is there for the rest of us?

Perhaps the Dutch theologian and writer Henri Nouwen can help us to diagnose both the blockages to compassion and the routes back towards re-engaging with its demands.

Nouwen suggests that compassion is nothing more nor less than the "full immersion in the condition of being human". Nouwen reminds us, then, that compassion takes us to the deepest and profoundest reality of our human embodiment. When we are compassionate, we are caught up in our fullest humanity.

If he is right, and I think he is, then compassion surely implies that to be human is all about relationship and connection; for without relationship I can't see how it is possible to "suffer with" and alongside other humans.

WHEN we, as people, fail to be compassionate or good or loving, it has become something of a modern refrain to say, "Well, we're only human." Here's the rub, though: that is precisely what we're not.

We struggle to be human. Indeed, I have come to believe that there is a liberating beauty and challenge in acknowledging that there has only ever been one human being, Jesus Christ. The rest of us are approximations. We are sketches. If we were in a movie, we'd be the badly rendered CGI.

We are not human, yet. In so far as we are unable to be compassionate, it is not that we are being "all too human" but not yet human.

For me, part of the power of the Easter Triduum — as it takes us from Maundy Thursday through to Easter Day — is the permission that it gives us to come to terms with our failure to be compassionate, and how much we struggle, thereby, to be human.

Part of the power of the Passion narrative lies, then, in the way in which it holds the drama of life: it reveals how the most significant friendships and relationships can end up in the wreckage of betrayal, failure, denial, and cowardice.

The behaviour of Judas, Peter, and the rest earths the cosmic drama of redemption in recognisable failure. Our failures in friendship and love, which reflect our retreat from the call to compassion, find a place in God's story.

Fool of God (Christ in the Garden) *by Mark Cazalet (1993)*
from the Methodist Modern Art Collection (used with permission)

The Passion reveals yet more. At its locus is the torture and execution of the Son of God. Perhaps torture and state-authorised execution are the very acme of the capacity of our species to suspend and limit compassion and empathy. Ethicists such as Jeremy Wisnewski and R.D. Emerick have suggested that, in torturing his victim, the perpetrator renders himself less than human.

In short, if the torturers immersed themselves in their full humanity, they could not do their job. In so far as we, on Good Friday, make Jesus our victim, we reiterate only our capacity to circumvent compassion. The Passion reveals us for what we are: the species that can suspend its capacity to "suffer with".

THE death and resurrection of Jesus Christ reveal that bodies matter. The work of God's love at Easter is undertaken through the body of Jesus Christ, and we are invited to become part of that body.

To become a Christian is always, ultimately, a bodily matter: that is why baptism is essential. Equally, it should not surprise us that the central sustaining liturgical act of the Christian faith, the Eucharist, is profoundly bodily. To share in the feast of Christ involves feeding on Christ's body and blood.

The fact that so many of us have struggled with being denied that feeding in the past year underlines just how embodied we are. In Eucharist, God gives us a ritual to treat "compassion fatigue"; in feeding on Christ's body and blood, we are restored and renewed. We are made ready to be sent out into the world for service as human beings.

I have long adored the fact that compassion in both Hebrew and Greek has a bodily significance. The Hebrew word for compassion is *rachuwm*, taken from the root word *rechem*, which means "womb". When I became aware of the connection between womb and compassion, I felt I had encountered something of the structure of God's first language. This is the God who feels for us in her womb. Equally, the ancient Greek for "guts" is *splagchnizomai*. One of its implications is "being moved to one's bowels", which itself means "moved to compassion"; for, in classical culture, the bowels were the seat of compassion and pity.

These etymological connections underline how in baptism, as we are born again in Christ, we encounter the compassion of God who feels for us in her womb. They underline how, in Eucharist, we are sustained and renewed as we take God into our guts. To be members of the Body of Christ means that we are people of compassion — of gut and of womb. '

THE life of compassion to which God invites us is a costly, embodied one. It is never simply an idea, or reducible to good intentions. It entails coming to terms with the violence and cruelty seemingly sealed into our species' DNA, as well as being prepared to live in resistance to such violence.

The life of compassion entails daring to be caught up in this world without simply being crushed by it. The novelist Milan Kundera suggests that "there is nothing heavier than compassion. Not even one's own pain weighs so heavy as the pain one feels with someone, for someone, a pain intensified by the imagination and prolonged by a hundred echoes" (*The Unbearable Lightness of Being*, 1984).

To live the life of compassion is a costly vocation. Jesus Christ shows us that. When I feel that such a vocation is too much for my frail flesh, I remember that Christ shows me otherwise. To become more compassionate is to become more human, and, therefore, more divine. In my own power, that is unfeasible; in Christ, however, nothing is impossible.

(2021)

Waters of death and rebirth

Easter and baptism have been linked closely since the earliest days of the Church. **Cally Hammond** reflects on the theology, history, and practice

WHEN Christianity was a young religion, it had not yet developed all the complex rituals and festivals that we know today. Baptism and the *pascha* (Easter), though, were fundamental from the beginning.

It is not always easy to get answers to our questions about them, because they were both regarded as holy mysteries, only for initiates (those who had themselves been baptised). Christians were cautious about committing such sacred mysteries to writing.

Baptism and Easter were both outworkings of the "Christ-event" that shapes the New Testament, but, as with much else, the first Christians quarried the Old Testament for parallels and clues to the meaning of both. They found the main key in Exodus 12 (the Lord's *pesach*, or Passover); 13 (the exodus-journey); and 14 (the crossing of the Red Sea and emergence into freedom). This is one reason that baptism and Easter are so closely associated in Christian thinking right from the start.

The sacrament of baptism and the celebration of Easter are, in one key way, alike. Each is first an event and then a process. Easter is the once-for-all moment of the Lord's resurrection; baptism is the once-for-always moment of incorporation into the body of Christ.

But Easter is also the lived, repeated experience of generations of Christians. They follow the ministry, Passion, crucifixion, and resurrection with their imaginations, with their prayers — and, sometimes, with their lives. And baptism marks the beginning of a process of sanctification (in one view), or resisting sin (in another); it is a preparation as well as a conclusion, for those who make a commitment to "fighting the good fight".

THIS, you might say, is the theological angle on how baptism and Easter go together. It is how we find meaning in the once-for-all events, and in the repeated processes. But, because Christianity is a historical faith, theological interpretation has to grow out of historical events.

And that is another way of saying that we understand the meaning in things only because those things first happened. And that, in turn, is a convoluted way of saying that religion is not something that happens in our minds or our imaginations: it is real. Baptism makes a real difference to our lives and deaths; and Easter makes a real difference to the whole human race, because, as the writer of 1 Timothy 4.10 puts it, "We have our hope set on the living God, who is the Saviour of all people, especially of those who believe."

This understanding helps us to avoid two extreme positions which are characteristic of certain Christian groups. The first says that everything depends on what we believe and think about baptism, or about Easter. The water is a mere token: it is there to help the simple to understand its real meaning, which is internal, and spiritual. Easter is something that God brought about to prove his power and authenticate his Son's lordship, but only to be appropriated by those on the inside, the believers.

The second position treats baptism as a magic rite, in which the proper use of physical materials (what a Harry Potter reader might think of as potion ingredients), with the correct use of a verbal formula ("In the name of the Father, and of the Son, and of the Holy Spirit" being equivalent, more or less, to *expelliarmus*) can effect a change in reality.

Such a change will happen — indeed, it must happen — regardless of the attendant circumstances, or the character of the person concerned. So Easter transforms human destiny, regardless of whether human individuals know or care. These two extremes frame a range of more moderate understandings, but they are characteristic of many other aspects of Christianity, too.

SO WE set baptism and Easter side by side, because Christians have always linked them together like this, from earliest times. In the century or so after Jesus died, baptism is already fully formed, theologically speaking, as it features in early Christian writings. There are four aspects to the meaning of the rite which are present from the beginning, and remain central: remission of sins, redemption from death, new birth, receiving of the Holy Spirit.

All four of these elements still depend on the use of water and the threefold name of God. All four are linked, for their efficacy, to the physical act of washing, but also to the Passion and resurrection of Jesus.

The earliest writer to explore this in detail was a lawyer from North Africa, Tertullian (c.160–240). He used the baptism of John to make sense of Christian baptism; for him it was unimportant that Jesus did not himself baptise, because what set Christian baptism apart from the baptism of John was the fact of the Passion and resurrection:

"His disciples used to wash people ... with a baptism like John's ... the only other kind is Christ's, which came later: and the disciples certainly could not have practised it then, because our Lord's glory was not yet fulfilled, nor was the efficacy of the washing yet established by his Passion and resurrection. Our death could only be annulled by our Lord's Passion; and our life could only be restored by his resurrection." (*On Baptism* 11)

For Tertullian, the consequence is obvious. Easter is the proper time for baptism because, at Easter, the Passion of Christ found its fulfilment in resurrection, thus giving meaning to the "mystic grave" that the baptised share with Christ.

His view was expanded by a Greek writer of the fourth century, St Basil of Caesarea, who shifted the focus from Passion to resurrection. He argued that, because Easter is a memorial of the resurrection, and baptism is a "power for resurrection," we should receive the grace of the resurrection on the day of resurrection.

But both had enough realism about their thinking not to let theology dominate practicality. Tertullian went on to say that Pentecost was also a good time for baptism, because both mark the reception of the Holy Spirit. Basil emphasised that there was no wrong time for being baptised: "Every time is the right time for the salvation of baptism — every night, every day, every hour, every moment, however fleeting."

So the four key elements of baptism are tied to events in the life of Christ: redemption from death, and new birth, are both tied to his resurrection; receiving the Holy Spirit to Pentecost; and remission of sins to the atonement. But these events form a single nexus, and, similarly, the four aspects of baptism cannot be separated from one another.

NOT that Christians haven't tried to. Some emphasise the inherent power of the other elements, in a way that refuses to engage with the part played by Christian nurture and formation in making baptism effective in the life of a growing Christian.

Others emphasise the remission of sins, excluding all else (which reduces Christian baptism to little more than the baptism of John). This results in a theology which empties the baptismal washing of power, and puts the focus on individual moral choice.

Remission of sins is the first thing that most Christians think of today when asked what baptism is for, or what it does. It is also problematic, because baptism has come to be associated with infants, and it feels counter-intuitive to claim that such infants, helpless, entirely without moral responsibility, have any need for such remission of sins.

It is as if Christian baptism had become the architect of its own obfuscation: seeking to act on the highest sacramental view of baptism, early Christians began to baptise infants to ensure their salvation, and protect them from limbo or damnation, regardless of their choices or intentions.

This functional view of baptism opened the rite up to criticism that it was a meaningless ritual. It also separated the sacrament of baptism from its proper setting at Easter; so vulnerable were the newborn that baptism must be immediate, lest it come too late.

But there is a way to reclaim the true understanding of baptismal remission of sins: strengthen the association of baptism with the whole of the Easter season, from Easter Day itself right up to Pentecost.

Making the Easter season into the baptism season opens up the mystical death which leads to new birth. It shows how remission of sins can be separated from the narrower realm of personal and intentional wrongdoing, and reach out to encompass the global wrongs in which humankind is helplessly complicit, and which, by reason of the very magnitude of the challenges, makes Christians feel powerless to do good.

Such global pressures and guilts (pollution, global warming, endemic violence, sexual exploitation and inequality, economic injustices, and the like) rank high in the subject-matter of Christian intercessions, but low in the scale of reasonable expectations of resolution. They trouble Christian consciences because, too often, and for too many, "sin" means only "personal sin," and so has nothing to say to such global wrongs.

TO TAKE this reclaiming of past wisdom a stage further, we could also draw on St Ambrose, the bishop who baptised St Augustine. Like Tertullian and Basil, he understood baptism and Easter in the light of the Passion, and interpreted it through the lens of the Exodus.

But he reflected on the example of the Blessed Virgin Mary, too. He concluded that the new life wrought in her by the descent of the Holy Spirit was prefigured by the Spirit's brooding over the face of the waters before creation began; and he found an echo of it in the descent of the Spirit on the baptismal font, bringing about a new birth in the baptised.

This interpretation forms a parallel to "Christ yesterday, today, and for ever" (Hebrews 13.8) for the Holy Spirit; a valuable corrective to comparative neglect of the third person of the Trinity.

But Ambrose turned to another Old Testament book — the Song of Songs — to do justice to the aspect of both these Christian mysteries which perhaps matters most to any Christian who enters upon them. The relationship between Christ and the believer should be a relationship of passionate love, in which Christ, who suffered, died, and rose again for us, looks on the believer and exclaims, "You are beautiful, my love, behold, you are beautiful! Your eyes are doves behind your veil" (Song of Songs 4.1; Ambrose, *On the Mysteries* 7.37).

(2019)

Uncovering Easter

Knowledge of Christ's death and resurrection depends on the Gospels. Can archaeology help to authenticate their account? **Peter Head** considers the evidence

RECENT ARCHAEOLOGICAL discoveries have added a little to our understanding of the events of Jesus's death and burial, but have added practically nothing to our grasp of the meaning given to Jesus's death and resurrection within early Christianity.

The primary resource for understanding the significance of Jesus's death and resurrection within the New Testament and for Christians today remains the apostolic witness as the New Testament presents it. But, to aid reading the Bible, and to gain a complementary angle on the Easter events, it is worth considering the contribution of archaeological discoveries concerning Jesus's trials, crucifixion, burial, and resurrection.

Popular thought in this area has never really outgrown the Schliemann school of archaeology — the search for individually spectacular pieces whose beauty and importance can transcend their point of origin, such as the golden treasures of Troy, which Schliemann smuggled out of Turkey.

In some periods, Christians have pursued relics — of the apostles or of other saints and martyrs — as a means of constructing a tangible link between the past and the present. For some people (pandered to by Israel's tourism or pilgrimage industry, and aided by headline-hungry journalists), archaeology can provide such a connection with the past, a kind of "Fifth Gospel", witnessing to Jesus in a special way.

For example, in 1986 a first-century boat was discovered in the Sea of Galilee, between Gennosar and Magdala, an area with which Jesus was certainly familiar. This discovery, important to scholars for increasing our understanding of the construction of boats in the first century, was immediately dubbed "the Jesus boat", despite there being no evidence of any association with Jesus. Some have even dubbed this one of the ten most important archaeological discoveries of the 20th century. It can help to remind us that boats were important for Jesus and the first disciples (travelling in boats is mentioned dozens of times in the Gospels), but its importance is indirect.

Much the same can be said about archaeological finds relating to Jesus's death and resurrection. They are important; they contribute to our knowledge of the origins of Christianity in various ways; and they can be drawn into a discussion with the New Testament evidence and other historical sources.

SOME OF the difficulties and potentialities of archaeological evidence can be illustrated with reference to the two prime characters involved in the decision to crucify Jesus — Pilate and Caiaphas.

In terms of political responsibility, the Nicene Creed has it right in its rare expression of historical context: "he was crucified under Pontius Pilate" (cf. 1 Timothy 6.13; Tacitus, Annals 15.44). In 1962, an inscription was found in Caesarea Maritima which included part of his name: " ... NTIUS PILATUS" and part of his job description " ... ECTUS IUDA[ ]E".

No one knows what the inscription said originally, and no one has ever doubted the historical existence of Pontius Pilate (who is referred to in Josephus and in Philo, as well as the four Gospels, Acts, and 1 Timothy). But this inscription is significant because it confirms Pilate's job description as "prefect of Judaea", and thus as the person with judicial rights to pronounce a death sentence (as was the case with Jesus).

In 1990, a first-century burial cave was discovered near Jerusalem in which there were 12 ossuaries, one of which was large and richly decorated. It had (in two places) a rough inscription with the name "*yehosef bar Qapha*" and "*yehosef bar Qayyapha*". The ossuary contained bones from six people, including a 60-year-old male.

It has been widely, although not unanimously, thought that the inscription refers to "Joseph son of [or perhaps "of the family of"] Caiaphas", which would connect this burial site to Caiaphas, the high priest named in the Gospels (Matthew 26.57, John 18.13ff), as the one who charged Jesus with blasphemy, before handing him over to Pilate (Josephus supplies his additional name, "Joseph").

If the positive interpretation of this evidence is accepted, then we have archaeological materials relating to the two key named authority figures who were in charge of the trials and crucifixion of Jesus. The archaeological evidence would, in this view, confirm the existence of Jesus's two key

Ossuary of the high priest, Joseph Caiaphas, found in Jerusalem in 1990, now in The Israel Museum, Jerusalem

protagonists of the Passion narrative. But, in the nature of the case, the situation is not that simple.

With the so-called "Caiaphas ossuary", problems remain in the identification of "*Qapha*" with the Caiaphas mentioned in the New Testament. The ossuary does not refer to his position as high priest, nor is the tomb as grand as we might expect. The shorter form of the name on the ossuary ("*Qapha*") is difficult to reconcile with the longer name "Caiaphas". Nor is it clear how "Joseph, son of Caiaphas" can easily be equivalent to "Joseph, surnamed Caiaphas" (as Josephus names him). Archaeology produces only one piece of the ancient jigsaw, a piece that needs careful evaluation, in dialogue with other evidence — particularly that from the New Testament and Josephus.

IN THE BURIAL of Jesus, which remains central to the New Testament witness to the Easter event (Acts 2; 1 Corinthians 15.3-4; Romans 6), we could note that recent interest in ossuaries has focused attention on the practice of secondary burial among first-century Jews.

This was prompted partly by an ossuary with the forged inscription "James, the brother of Jesus". In 2002, the media were full of the news of this ossuary box, which seemed to confirm the existence of James and Jesus in the combined inscription. The news that the owner of the ossuary is currently on trial, charged with forging antiquities to sell to collectors, has not been so widely publicised.

While the box looks genuine, the inscription on it is certainly a forgery. This is one of the hazards of so-called "biblical archaeology", but many hundreds of genuine ossuaries have been discovered, often in situ in rockcut tombs. They have contributed to our knowledge of first-century burial practices and beliefs.

The normal practice, which seems to be reflected in the Gospel narratives, was of a burial in a tomb, followed some time later by a reburial of the bones in an ossuary box, perhaps in a family tomb. Both the linen cloths and the herbs and spices associated with Jesus's burial are fully compatible with this understanding of what was planned for Jesus.

One important archaeological discovery in this area was the ossuary box of Jehohanan, found in 1968 among 15 ossuaries containing the bones of about 35 people, many of whom had experienced a violent death. Jehohanan, too, died violently — by crucifixion. A large iron nail remained where it had been driven through his heel; the marks of a nail had left a groove in the bones of his forearm; his shinbones, both right and left, had been fractured, even shattered, at the time of his death.

The evidence of Jehohanan has been very helpful, when used in conjunction with other literary evidence, for our perception of the practice of crucifixion. It certainly helps us understand a little more about Jesus's crucifixion, suggesting that it was likely that he was nailed through the forearms or wrists (and almost certainly not the soft tissue of the palm of the hand), and through the feet.

In Jesus's case, of course, his bones were not broken (John 19), and some doubts about the posture of a typical crucifixion remain. Jehohanan's secondary burial in an ossuary also shows that it was possible for convicted criminals, sentenced to the shameful public death of crucifixion, still to receive a careful burial among family and friends.

THE CONTRIBUTION of archaeology in relation to the resurrection is even more limited than in relation to Jesus's death. There is nothing comparable with Jesus's resurrection. In addition, the empty tomb, while central to all of the canonical Gospel accounts, and an important element of the early apostolic preaching (for example, Acts 2.29-32; 13.29-31; 1 Corinthians 15.4), had limited significance on its own. The empty tomb produced mainly confusion: only when supplemented by the appearance of the risen Jesus and the testimony of those who had seen him could its significance be understood.

Of course, we don't have any archaeologically authenticated "empty" tomb. In the Church of the Holy Sepulchre, we have an example of fourth-century Christian political archaeology: the newly Christian empire sponsoring excavations to provide evidence that might provide a focus for Christian unity.

Yet the stubborn fact remains that ancient Christian memory led Helena to a site that, for all its mythic and romantic associations, is rather likely to be the site of Jesus's burial. First-century tombs are in the area, and although within a generation it was enclosed within the city walls, good evidence confirms that it stood outside the walls at the time of Jesus, thus making it less likely to be a site marked out only by pious imagination. Properly controlled archaeological excavations have not been possible there, however.

All this archaeological material suggests that the New Testament accounts remain anchored in first-century realities, in a way that later accounts, such as the apocryphal *Gospel of Judas*, do not. This Gnostic text has little to do with Jesus, though it sheds light on the Cainite sect from which it came.

Furthermore, what has been discovered reminds us of the sheer physicality of the New Testament accounts of Jesus's death — a bloody and shameful death; burial in a rock-cut tomb; and bodily resurrection, which, of course, transcends pure physicality.

(2006)

Caught up in the drama

Holy Week can be a busy time for the laity as well as the clergy.
Caroline Chartres charts a personal pathway through the
opportunities to be holy

HOW do you put the "holy" into Holy Week — the holiest days in the
Christian calendar? The extensive smörgåsbord of services on offer reinforces
the secular view that "This must be your busy time, Vicar" (as if the clergy
do nothing between Easter and Christmas, apart from the occasional
Sunday service).

Holy Week starts with Palm Sunday and the favourite ecclesiastical
audio-visual aid: not just palm branches and palm crosses, but live donkeys.
These are usually imported on the grounds that they engage children's
interest — which they do, although the interest tends to be chiefly in whether
the donkey will leave a steaming deposit on the church floor, and the Palm
Sunday procession is frequently followed by a character (not readily identifiable from the Gospels) bearing a large shovel.

Evidence from the *Church Times* suggests a decreasing number of adver-
tisements for Holy Week and Easter services, but no fewer services, and
certainly no smaller congregations. St Paul's is not the only cathedral to
experience a steady increase in worshippers, with the huge attendance at
some of the Easter services rivalling Advent, and even Christmas.

Nor is there any shortage of options, from "high" churches offering the
more traditional ritual observances to Evangelical Good Friday services
that include "commissioned video, various multimedia elements, and opportunity for prayer".

Among our sister Churches, Westminster Cathedral warns prospective
penitents that "the queue for confessions will be closed up to 30 minutes
before the end of the times listed ... Please arrive at the Cathedral in good
time to avoid disappointment."

By no means all the offerings are liturgical: musical settings of the Passion,
Pergolesi's *Stabat Mater*, come-and-sing *Messiahs*, and carefully chosen
offerings of words and music ... With so much variety on offer, where do
you start?

I TEND to drop in and out earlier in the week, reserving my feeble spiritual
energies for the Triduum, the time between Maundy Thursday and Easter
Day once known as "the still days". On Maundy Thursday, the memorial of

the Last Supper increasingly now includes foot-washing. It is a great idea: the trouble is that we are so — well, Anglican about it.

You can imagine the shock and embarrassment on the face of someone who came to church unbriefed and unknowing, and was suddenly selected as a victim of foot-washing. So it is not the blind leading the blind, but the clean washing the clean: we have to tip people off in advance, so that — like tidying up before the cleaner arrives — they can wash and powder their feet, and adopt clean footwear, in order to take it off in church and have their feet washed again.

It may be only symbolic, but the inauthenticity can make it uncomfortable to watch, as well as to participate. Once, the youngest of our regular gentlemen-of-the-road turned up at our vicarage, proudly and unaccustomedly smart in a shiny new suit, its too-short trousers flapping above his ankles, and grey leather shoes a size too small crippling his feet. As I rummaged for a towel, and knelt to soak his blisters in a washing-up bowl full of cold water, I heard clearly the echo in my head: "Do this in remembrance of me."

How often we fully understand something only with the benefit of hindsight, only belatedly grasp the deeper meaning behind the words. Some churches hold a vigil on Maundy Thursday, the Watch of the Passion, remembering Jesus's watch in the Garden of Gethsemane the night before his execution.

A RECENT experience of elective surgery gave me a different sense of what it might mean to go voluntarily into suffering in cold blood: I knew what it was to be bowel-churningly afraid — and that was facing the prospect of potentially life-saving surgery in clinical conditions, anaesthetised, and with all the advantages of post-operative pain relief.

How do you go willingly into an excruciating and humiliating experience that you know will end only with your death? How do you remain loving and only mildly reproachful to your unknowing friends, slumbering beside you as you struggle to prepare yourself for the ordeal ahead?

The Bible recounts the great dramas in words that have inspired great music and great poetry, but our own attempts to emulate them too often sound like something out of *Private Eye*'s Rocky Horror Service Book. Words can shape our worship, but they can also diminish our sense of the sacred.

It is a hard thing to lead a three-hour service on Good Friday, and the best tend to allow plenty of space for meditation; but attending a three-hour service can be a challenge also, when too often it feels like death by words — as the 18th-century parson and wit Sydney Smith memorably put it, being "preached to death by mad curates".

Each year the Wintershall Passion takes place in Trafalgar Square in London

I feel that I should be excited at the prospect of churchgoing at this time rather than daunted by the prospect of a three-hour service. (I know that I will feel guilty if I leave before the end.) Better, perhaps, to turn out earlier in the day for the litany, and spend a free-range three hours walking the dog (which tends to be my best prayer-time, anyway).

PUBLIC re-enactments of the Passion are increasingly popular: the Wintershall Passion fills Trafalgar Square, and there are reportedly 15 or so other performances of the Passion around the UK, plus unnumbered (often ecumenical) Walks of Witness. Like Palm Sunday, Good Friday is an event perhaps best understood and experienced as a member of the crowd of onlookers, caught up in the drama and the spectacle.

By Holy Saturday, the mood has changed as we look forward to Easter Day, although "vigil" is sometimes a euphemism for what actually happens on Easter Eve. One of the difficulties with Easter is that so much depends on when it falls in the calendar (especially whether or not the clocks have gone forward).

Kindling the first light of Easter with half a litre of barbecue fuel is less convincing in broad daylight, just as the Exsultet can feel less like an outpouring of praise than a verbose way of delaying the gratification of a glass of Prosecco with our paschal lamb.

183

To be an early Christian on Easter Eve meant being plunged into the waters of death to be baptised, gasping and spluttering, to new life; it meant watching through the night until the sun's rays finally irradiated the chilly dawn.

Anyone who has taken a night flight eastwards and flown in along the dawn will know that extraordinary moment when the sun pours in over the edge of the world. Struggling to recapture that moment of dazzling, transforming glory is enough to make you long for commissioned video and multimedia elements.

Perhaps it is easier to do darkness. It is hard not to be moved by Tenebrae, the extended meditation on Christ's suffering. The lights are extinguished, but the Christ candle holds out the promise not merely of hope, but of victory.

Easter observances are too easily characterised by guilt: not the guilt that Jesus died to save us from, but the guilt of boredom, of well-intentioned lip service, of failing to be engaged by the commemoration of the greatest drama in the history of the world.

AT ST PAUL'S, the dawn Eucharist on Easter Day used to be celebrated on the steps in front of the cathedral. (One year, a shades-wearing reveller leaned out of the darkened windows of a stretch limo to yell "Spawn of Satan" at the assembled worshippers as he sped past.) Now, the service starts inside, around the font, which feels more reminiscent of a stone sepulchre; and we emerge into the light of the new day.

Good Friday is the answer to the perennial question "Where was God in the tsunami/the mudslide/the atrocities in Syria, in South Sudan?" The strength of our Holy Week observances depends on how far and how effectively we carry those experiences into our everyday life.

My father was buried in Holy Week. Two days later, my sister and I went to a Good Friday performance of Bach's *St John Passion*, and experienced its pain and its hope as never before.

Just as Jesus died on the cross on our behalf, I realise that my most powerful Easter experiences have been when I have let go, and been transported beyond my own experience by others.

While that is almost certainly a comment on my own spiritual shortcomings, perhaps it is also one of the lessons of Good Friday. Or perhaps the drama of that first Easter is simply so astonishing that anything we do to try to emulate it will seem pale by comparison.

(2014)

Word from Wormingford

Three hours have shrunk to one,
notes **Ronald Blythe**

GOOD FRIDAY, then. The little early-morning town barely awake when they sent us off to fetch the hot cross buns. Other erranding children boasting how many they were going to eat. Bakers' vans like Arks of the Covenant on wheels, being trundled through the empty streets. Home with our bags full, and just one each before breakfast proper.

The sad day was half mourning, half play. There was the Three Hours and there was the Boat Club and strident football. On Good Friday, the Boat Club rowed about four miles down river to eat hot cross buns and drink bitter at the Henny Swan. Should it be atrocious weather, which it often was, it was an honour to arrive at the Stour-side pub in an equally atrocious state, soaked through, but grinning bravely. Should it be lovely spring weather, which it frequently was, it was the thing to arrive glamorously with naked legs and trailing scarves.

Centuries before, the youthful Rector of Little Henny, Samuel Crossman, had written *The Young Man's Meditation,* a collection of poems that included "My song is love unknown". Crossman had been reading George Herbert's "Love Unknown", and Herbert had been reading Psalm 51. For this is what happens with divine love: it streams through the consciousness of poets, making a rhyme here and there. Knowing nothing of this, the Boat Club would row its beery way home.

If it was an early Easter, it could be snowing; if late, the sticky buds would be forming on Miss Baker's huge horse-chestnut, and swallows could be whirling round St Peter's green steeple. But, whether early or late, the Three Hours would pass in ice-box conditions. The wan Rector would fidget in the medieval miserere seat that was his stall, and the old ladies scattered about in the nave would thank God for their fur coats. Mourning worshippers came and went. The truly saintly saw the Three Hours out to the bitter end.

Every quarter of an hour, or so it seemed to a boy, Mark the organist would play a verse of "O Sacred Head", and we would sing, "Thy beauty, long desired, Hath vanished from our sight" Although with me it hadn't. It was all too cruelly present, which was heart-breaking. And, all around, Suffolk voices were pleading, " I pray thee, Jesus, own me." The sun or the

storm, or just Good Friday's greyness, would batter at the glass, as the flower-arrangers eyed the font and counted lilies in their heads.

Good Friday now is ante-communion for two or three, and one hour for the many. I can just about make out Henny from the hilltop behind the house. It rises in the greening distance. There are bees on the rosemary, and some far-flung shouts from the playing-field.

I look up hot cross buns in the *Universal Cookery Book,* a very pre-Delia effort, and see that I need cassia, three tablespoonfuls of yeast, mace, and much else. They must be "brushed over with warm milk and baked a nice brown". I make toast instead.

At 2 p.m. we have a service called "Lift High the Cross", which is tragic, but not severe. The immensity of the day is taken on board — to use a rivery image — but privately.

(2002)

Night to outshine all others

What is sleep compared with this?
Michael Perham argues that Easter celebrations
should start in the dark

LATE on the evening of Easter Eve, or very early in the morning of Easter Day, a minority of Church of England people will celebrate what they have found to be the most powerful and life-enhancing liturgy of the year, at the very core of their life and spirituality.

The majority of members of the C of E do not even know such a service exists, or will not find it available to them, or will have decided it is not for them. What a blessing it would be if that could change.

Those who know about it will call it the "Easter liturgy", and that is what *Common Worship: Times and Seasons* calls it. Some may know it as the "Easter vigil", which is a description of part of it. Some may refer to it as the "Easter ceremonies", which somehow suggests something esoteric or peripheral.

My own experience of it was as the last of these, on a Saturday night with a faithful few and an uncertainty about whether Easter had or had not begun. This was until my first year at theological college, when I encountered the Easter liturgy in the village church, presided over by the bishop, as something exciting, glorious, and transformative. Every year since, with one community or another, I have tried to celebrate it like that. After 30 years, it still never fails to thrill me and renew me.

It will be important to explore when this liturgy is best celebrated, if it is to be a gathering of the whole community to mark the transition from death to resurrection. But, before that, I must describe its shape and content. We need to know the what before the when.

IN ITS fullest form, this is a liturgy that has four stages. The first is a Service of Light. The community gathers around a "new fire", which ideally means that the liturgy begins in the open air, and from it is lit the Paschal candle, which, both in this liturgy and throughout the Easter season until Pentecost, becomes the primary symbol of the Risen Christ.

The candle, traditionally marked with a cross, with an alpha and omega and the year, and often with nails representing the wounds of Christ, is carried into the darkened church, and other lights are lit from it. "The light of Christ," sings the deacon or another minister three times, holding the candle high.

Then, by the light of the candle, the deacon sings an ancient song of praise, the Exsultet, which celebrates the mighty act of God in the Passover experience of the Israelite people, rejoices in the significance of Easter night, and blesses the candle.

THE SECOND STAGE is a vigil (from which the whole service sometimes takes its name) by the light of the Paschal candle. In its fullest, richest form, this vigil continues for some hours, telling the salvation history of the Old Testament in a series of stories, beginning with the creation from Genesis 1, and always including Exodus 14 with its account of the escape from Egypt

Monks of the Order of Saint Benedict preparing to light the Christ candle prior to Easter Vigil mass

of the Israelite people — God's mighty act of deliverance in the Old Testament, prefiguring his even greater act of deliverance in the death and resurrection of Jesus Christ.

There may follow other sagas, whether water stories, such as Jonah, as a preparation for the baptismal liturgy that will follow, or fire stories, such as that of the burning fiery furnace, which resonate with the fire and light theme.

These great biblical stories (*Common Worship* provides a choice of 22) may be treated in a number of different ways, whether read by a skilled storyteller or acted out dramatically. Between them come silence and psalmody or other singing, each section concluding with a collect.

The vigil has something of the character of recapitulation, because already, in the Service of Light, the truth of resurrection has been gently proclaimed.

In the vigil, the account of God's saving activity is rehearsed, until the moment is reached where the good news of the resurrection strikes again, this time without restraint. This is the moment for the Easter acclamation, the first time we hear the words that will be heard in every Eucharist until Pentecost: "Alleluia. Christ is risen," with its response: "He is risen indeed. Alleluia."

It may be said three times at this point, first in a whisper, in the way wonderful news might first be shared, then louder, and then in a great shout. Immediately the organ thunders, every instrument of music is employed, lights fill the building, and sometimes the people stamp on the floor. There can even be football rattles.

All this gives way to the Gloria. Easter has fully arrived. The vigil, which has been an extended Liturgy of the Word, gives way to the reading from chapter 6 of Paul's letter to the Romans, with its talk of being baptised into Christ's death and rising to newness of life, and to the Gospel account of the empty tomb.

It needs to be said that there is an equally old tradition, which reverses the Service of Light and the vigil. Here the community gathers for the vigil, perhaps in a place other than the church in which the later part of the liturgy will be celebrated, with minimal lighting, but not the Paschal candle. At the end of the vigil, the community moves outside to the fire and the candle-lighting, and, once again in the church, moves speedily from the song, the Exsultet, to the Gloria.

Both orders have their own logic, and local decisions have to be made about which will be the more effective in each place.

THE THIRD STAGE is the Liturgy of Initiation. The whole community moves to the font, or if space does not allow that, turns towards it. At the very least, there will be a blessing of water and the renewal of baptismal vows. As the president says: "As we celebrate the resurrection of our Lord Jesus Christ from the dead, we remember that through the paschal mystery we have died and been buried with him in baptism."

The renewal of baptismal vows will, of course, be a more telling experience, and connections more easily made, when at this moment there are candidates for baptism, especially adult candidates who have been preparing through Lent for this moment.

In a few places, when the bishop can be present, there may also be confirmation, here at the font, of those baptised. Almost certainly there will be the sprinkling of the congregation with water from the font to help them remember their own baptism.

THE FINAL STAGE of the Easter liturgy is the Eucharist, and inevitably people will here feel themselves to be on more familiar ground. There may be more alleluias and Easter forms of the prayer over the gifts, the preface, and the invitation to communion, but, in the familiarity of the Eucharist, it would be possible to miss the truth that something extraordinarily important is happening here.

Those who have celebrated the mighty acts of God, culminating in the raising of Jesus from the dead in the dark of the night, are now reunited with their Risen Lord, recognising him, as did disciples on the first Easter Day, "in the breaking of the bread".

After communion, there is little more to add, but to go in the peace of the Risen Christ, possibly to the sound of the bells and the sight of fireworks overhead, or, if you are lucky, a glass of something sparkling to continue the celebration in a less liturgical way. The Lenten fast is over. The Great 50 Days of Easter have begun.

AFTER THIS description, we have to go back to the question of timing. When should the Easter liturgy be celebrated? In its fullest, richest form, it begins in the darkness of Saturday evening, and, through a long vigil of scripture, silence, and song, reaches the Eucharist as dawn breaks on Sunday morning. That way, the Christian meets the Risen Lord early in the morning, as Mary Magdalene did.

To be honest, the places where it can be like that are few and far between. Anglicans do not often do eight-hour liturgies, especially in the middle of the night, though it would be wonderful if more of them would. It is better to aim for something shorter, even if it involves some compromise; for, if the Easter liturgy is exciting and important, it must be for the whole community, not just the very keen and the very well instructed.

There are four possible timings of a shorter liturgy. An obvious one is to celebrate the liturgy at midnight, just as at Christmas. Although there is something appealing about reaching the climax as daylight breaks, this is essentially a liturgy of the night, celebrating the victory of light over darkness, around the Paschal candle. God's mighty act that rolled back the stone and brought the Son back to life was an activity in the deep darkness of the night. Midnight is an appropriate time, if people will come.

Where they will not, there is nothing wrong with moving the Easter liturgy to an earlier stage in the evening, as long as it is dark, which means a start not earlier than 8.30 p.m. The argument that it cannot be Easter until after midnight is unnecessarily narrow, not least because the Jewish day began at dusk. On the evening of Easter Eve, "the third day" on which he rose again has begun. If that is when the people will come, that is the time to celebrate the liturgy.

There is also, of course, the dawn possibility. The community gathers at four or five in the morning for the parts of the service that need to be when it is dark, and continue through beyond dawn to share in the Easter Eucharist, and perhaps some breakfast after.

Finally, there is the community where, realistically, nothing will work but Sunday mid-morning. Inevitably, much of the power and vitality of the Easter liturgy has to be sacrificed if that is the case, but those who plan the celebration need to rescue as much as makes sense to create an Easter morning service that captures as much as possible of the richness of the night celebration.

This means: the lighting of the candle, the three-times-repeated Easter acclamation, baptism, and the renewal of vows at the font, and perhaps more. The aim has to be to expose as many people as possible to the most powerful liturgical experience of the year.

Common Worship: Times and Seasons puts it like this: "From earliest times Christians have gathered through the night of Easter to recall the story of God's saving work, from creation through to the death and resurrection of our Lord Jesus Christ. However, the Easter Liturgy is not merely a presentation of God's work. It is meant to be a real experience of new life for the worshipper, a passing from darkness to light which offers hope to all the faithful."

The Easter liturgy is a powerful setting to experience the new life that comes from the Risen Christ who burst from the tomb in the darkness of Easter night. How much we need to rediscover its power and potential!

(2009)

Poet's corner: George Herbert's "Easter"

Malcolm Guite finds in the words of George Herbert the strength to cajole himself out of bed for the pre-dawn Easter vigil

I AM glad that there are now so many early-morning Easter services: pre-dawn vigils and fires, gatherings of Christians to greet the rising sun in the light of the Risen Son.

At least, in theory I'm glad. In practice, I find that I am not such an early riser as I would theoretically like to be, and that my drowsy and gradual coming-to, all my yawning and stretching, seem to take more effort, and, together with that essential first cup of tea in bed, seem to take longer than they used to.

But perhaps I am in good company. Many of us will read George Herbert's glorious poem "Easter" on Easter Day. One way of reading the poem is to see it as Herbert's long, metrically intricate way of cajoling himself to get out of bed.

Easter day would have started for Herbert like every day, with early morning matins, and his poem "Mattins" opens with the line "I cannot ope mine eyes". I know how he feels. Though, of course, Herbert goes on in the following lines to change the sense of the first line, because of Christ's transforming presence with him:

I cannot ope mine eyes,
But thou art ready there to catch
My morning-soul and sacrifice:
Then we must needs for that day make a match.

"Ah, you're already there in church ahead of me, I'd better get going and catch up," he seems to be saying. But, as he crossed the little lane in Bemerton from the rectory to the church, still wiping the sleep from his eyes, and stumbled through Psalm 57, one of the proper psalms on an early Easter Day matins, Herbert might well have recited verse 9 with feeling: as a quite literal "wake-up call":

Awake up, my glory, awake, lute and harp: I myself will awake right early

Certainly, it was that line which became the inspiration and starting point for "Easter", whose first verse opens:

Rise heart; thy Lord is risen. Sing his praise
Without delays,

And whose second verse echoes that with a call to his Lute:

Awake, my lute, and struggle for thy part
With all thy art.

But this Easter wake-up call differs from his poem "Mattins", in which we sense an effort to catch up with Christ, who is "ready there", an effort all packed into those two words "must needs". But, in "Easter", it is the Risen Christ himself who graciously comes to Herbert where he lies abed and actually helps him rise:

Rise heart; thy Lord is risen. Sing his praise
Without delays,
Who takes thee by the hand, that thou likewise
With him mayst rise.

We are not far off that moment when, in his masterpiece "Love (III)", Herbert will sum all this up in the simple phrase "Love took my hand".

So I intend to get up early this Easter Morning. Like Herbert's lute, I might "struggle for my part", but I also know that, when I stumble into church to celebrate an early Easter communion, Love will have risen before me and be ready to greet me, and I will say to him, as Herbert does in "Easter":

I got me flowers to straw thy way;
I got me boughs off many a tree:
But thou wast up by break of day,
And brought'st thy sweets along with thee.

(2018)

At the Easter Vigil, God zooms in

At Easter, the Church sings of the ordinary become extraordinary,
says **Edward Dowler**

Rejoice, heavenly powers! Sing, choirs of angels!
O Universe, dance around God's throne!
Jesus Christ, our King, is risen!
Sound the victorious trumpet of salvation!
Rejoice, O earth, in glory, revealing the splendour of your creation
radiant in the brightness of your triumphant King!
Christ has conquered! Now his life and glory fill you!
Darkness vanishes for ever!
Rejoice, O Mother Church! Exult in glory!
The risen Saviour, our Lord of life, shines upon you!
Let all God's people sing and shout for joy.

Introduction to the Exsultet
Common Worship: Times and Seasons

I WAS recently introduced by a friend to the website Google Earth. You type in the name of any single place in the world, and wait as, in a dizzying experience, the earth spins on its axis, and you zoom in to an aerial view of the exact location that you have selected.

The Exsultet, an ancient (c. fifth-century) hymn in praise of the Easter candle, is sung by the deacon at the Easter vigil on the eve of Easter Day, immediately after the candle has been brought into church before the Liturgy of the Word.

Singing the Exsultet is one of the most terrifying tasks in the first year of ordained ministry, not only because of the comparative musical complexity of the piece, but also because of the enormous scope of what it describes. As with Google Earth, the opening verses begin with the widest possible picture: "Rejoice, heavenly powers! Sing choirs of angels!", but quickly zoom in further: "Rejoice, O earth, in glory ...!", and further: "Rejoice, O Mother Church!"

Sadly, the various versions found in *Times and Seasons*, and the predecessor version in *Lent, Holy Week and Easter*, all omit the final verse from the Roman rite, which focuses in even further on the gathered community in a particular time and place:

My dearest friends, standing with me in this holy light,
join me in asking God for mercy,
that he may give his unworthy minister
grace to sing his Easter praises.

With the addition of this, we are taken, in four short verses, from the macro-level — the widest view of a universe rejoicing on Easter Day — down to the micro-level of Christians celebrating together the resurrection of Christ in countless individual communities.

What the opening verses do geographically, the continuing verses do historically. As Benedicta Ward notes in her meditations on Holy Week (*In Company with Christ*, SPCK, 2005), the recurrent phrase of the Exsultet "This is the night" ("This is the night when first you saved our fathers"; "This is the night when Jesus Christ broke the chains of death") centres all time in the events of this one night.

The Old Testament readings that immediately follow the Exsultet echo its words by placing the resurrection within the broadest historical context, as they make explicit the links between Easter Day and the great deeds of God in creation and redemption.

Ascribing universal or cosmic significance to events that are local and particular is not, of course, without its problems. How could the events that happened at a particular location and date have universal significance in the way that Christians say they do? Celsus, the second-century critic of Christianity, excoriated Christians for worshipping "to an extravagant degree this man who appeared recently".

His complaint was that those who claim to be monotheists, worshipping one God who is, by definition, immeasurably greater than we can ever imagine, undercut their claim by paying attention to a single human life, which, however exceptional, took place in a particular location and time in history.

This was sometimes referred to by theologians of the previous century, in a phrase that now sounds a little quaint, as the "scandal of particularity". It is summed up by Karl Barth: "The Word did not simply become any 'flesh', any man humbled and suffering. It became Jewish flesh ... [Christ's] universality is revealed in this particularity." The Exsultet bears eloquent witness to the fact that, in Jesus's resurrection, the particular breaks through to the universal in just the way that critics of Christianity have found so hard to stomach.

THE DOMINICAN writer Herbert McCabe pointed out in the 1960s that the threat of nuclear war (to which we might now add a variety of other possible catastrophes) has made it rather easier for us to imagine that events that seem to be local and particular might have cosmic consequences. Fr McCabe writes that:

> A generation ago it was quite generally felt amongst educated people that one of the things that really disqualified Christianity as a serious account of man was the ridiculously provincial idea that the events of a few hours on a hill outside Jerusalem could be of significance for the whole of human history. Let us by all means admit that Jesus of Nazareth played a startlingly large part in history, but the Christians make an absurdly larger claim. I think our present generation cannot feel quite the same, for we know that the events of a few hours on a slope outside Washington, where the Pentagon is, could undoubtedly have this total significance.
>
> *Law, Love, Language* (Continuum, 1968, 2003)

Moreover, if events that take place at local level might lead, as Fr McCabe suggests, to some large-scale problems, the local might also be the source of some of the solutions. For, on one assessment of the possible future that we face — environmental degradation, or the threat of war — we may, contrary to expectations, be led to a society that is increasingly parochial, freed from the delusions of globalisation. As American author J.H. Kunstler predicts: "Life will become intensely and increasingly local" (*The Long Emergency*, 2005).

Luckily, as the Exsultet and the entire Easter vigil remind us, we have a God who loves to work with the small-scale, the local, and the particular. His greatness shows itself not only in the rejoicing of heavenly powers, but in the celebrations of each and every small Christian community celebrating the resurrection. His light originates in a single spark (struck traditionally in Jerusalem from the rock of the cave-tomb), but one that comes to illuminate hundreds of candles. His power is made manifest in the single night when Christ rises from the dead, for "this is the night" when the whole earth really is made to spin on its axis.

(2007)

"All the resources of the Church ..."

Jo Spreadbury on the resurrection in worship

"ALL the resources of the church — music, flowers, bells, colours — are used to celebrate Christ's resurrection ... The Easter Gospel is proclaimed with all the joy and splendour that the church can find." Thus the *Common Worship* introduction to the Easter Liturgy in *Times and Seasons*.

Christ's mighty resurrection is emphasised as a dominant note throughout the Great Fifty Days of Easter: "The tone of joy created at the Easter Vigil is sustained through the following seven weeks, and the Church celebrates the gloriously risen Christ."

The resurrection, for which there can never be adequate words in liturgy and prayer, thus gives something of a challenge for more reticent Anglicans who wish to sustain the season of celebration, and to do justice liturgically to this cornerstone of our faith. Cranmer, one suspects, shared this reticence: his Collect for Easter Day, emphasising moral rather than cosmic significance, is a masterpiece of modified rapture:

> Almighty God, who through thine only-begotten Son Jesus Christ hast overcome death, and opened unto us the gate of everlasting life: We humbly beseech thee, that as by thy special grace preventing us thou dost put into our minds good desires, so by thy continual help we may bring the same to good effect ...

Happily, there are centuries of resources. The Exsultet or Easter Proclamation dates back at least to the seventh century, and celebrates the light of Christ's resurrection triumphing over the darkness of death, as the Paschal candle is lit:

> *This is the night when Jesus Christ vanquished hell,*
> *broke the chains of death and rose triumphant from the grave ...*
>
> *This is the night that gave us back what we had lost;*
> *beyond our deepest dreams; you made even our sin a happy fault.*

In a fourth-century hymn, *"Aurora lucis rutilat"*, even Hell responds as the risen Christ appears to his followers:

> *The glad earth shouts her triumph high,*
> *and groaning hell makes wild reply: Alleluia.*

Charles Wesley's 12-verse hymn "All ye that seek the Lord who died" depicts something of what occurred within the tomb:

The bands of death are torn away,
The yawning tomb gives back its prey …
The body breathes, and lifts His head,
The keepers sink, and fall as dead.

In another Wesley hymn, "Love's redeeming work is done", Jesus himself is greeted as the Resurrection (John 11.25).

One of John of Damascus's Easter hymns celebrates "The Day of Resurrection" as "the Passover of gladness, the Passover of God"; another with a succession of titles:

Now the queen of seasons, bright
with the day of splendour,
with the royal feast of feasts
comes its joy to render.

In the Orthodox tradition, Easter Week is called "Bright Week", and the holy doors of the iconostasis are kept open for the whole week, representing the open tomb with the stone rolled away, and with the *epitaphion*, or shroud, visible inside.

The Resurrection exceeds our praise. As Stuart Townend's "See what a morning" has it:

And we are raised with Him:
Death is dead, love has won,
Christ has conquered.
And we shall reign with Him,
For he lives, Christ is risen from the dead!

(2016)

Absorbing Easter hope takes effort

Angela Tilby explains why

THE latest liturgical publications urge us not to let Easter end on Easter Day. Easter is the beginning of the Great Fifty Days, "a single festival period in which the tone of joy created at the Easter Vigil is sustained through the following seven weeks". At least, that is the theory according to *Common Worship: Times and Seasons*. It is not so easy in practice, though, especially with the immediate Bank Holiday, the Vicar "off" on Low Sunday, and — depending on the date of Easter, one school term ending, holidays, and a new term starting to interrupt the period.

All of this might lead us to conclude that Easter is a terrible time to celebrate Easter. But I suppose that is part of the point. Our time is always "ordinary", and God's time interrupts it. It remains a challenge, though, to keep the Paschal flavour of the fifty days right through to Pentecost, in spite of much repeating of the "A" word that I am not allowed to write, let alone say, as I am writing this for publication before the end of Passiontide.

Easter, in the 1662 Prayer Book, is a sombre business — more an invitation to a reformed life than an outburst of new hope. There are few liturgical changes to mark the Paschal season: a proper preface is provided at communion, and the Venite is replaced by the Easter Anthems on Easter Day.

Although the Prayer Book has five Sundays after Easter, and special readings for the Monday and Tuesday in Easter Week, it drops nearly all reference to the resurrection of Christ by the Second Sunday. The theology is downbeat: Christ is raised for our justification, and the gate of everlasting life is open, but we enter it only after death. So much for seven weeks of Eastertide. Ascension Day and Whit Sunday are separate festivals, not part of the whole.

There is good sense, as well as ancient practice, in extending the Easter period, and ensuring that the season of joy is longer even than Lent. But I expect that many of us are still, at heart, Prayer Book people, all too ready to revert to "normal" once the Easter lilies have faded.

It takes effort to absorb joy and hope. All those readings from Acts through Eastertide don't help. All that gospel excitement and mission make our pathetic efforts seem tawdry. But Acts is not our only biblical resource for the Easter period. This is where we need to dig deeply into the St John's Gospel and St Paul's epistles in anticipation of the gift of the Holy Spirit. The Easter Anthems, said daily, as *Common Worship* Morning Prayer allows, provide an antidote to the ordinary and encourage our rejoicing.

(2017)

Carols are not just for Christmas

Carols have a historical resonance with Easter, too,
as can be seen on BBC television, says **Stephen Cleobury**

EASTER and Christmas fall outside Cambridge University full terms, but at King's College the great seasonal liturgies are celebrated in words and music.

A Festival of Nine Lessons and Carols has been held annually on Christmas Eve since 1918, and has been broadcast since 1928. More recently, *Carols from King's*, recorded for television, has become a fixture.

The Holy Week and Easter services are equally popular with our congregations. For many years, these have included a Eucharist and stripping of the altar on Maundy Thursday, evensong on Good Friday, and, on Easter Day, a Eucharist (usually Mozart with strings, as on Christmas morning) and evensong. Holy Saturday would see alternately a performance of Bach's *St Matthew* or *St John Passion*.

Since 2005, the Festival Easter at King's, featuring those services and the Bach Passion, as well as performances from the choir of King's College and other leading artists, orchestras, and choirs, has meant that the chapel has been a focus both for liturgy and for sacred music during the whole of Holy Week through to Easter Monday.

So, when the BBC approached King's with the suggestion that we record a televised Easter service in 2010 as a companion piece to *Carols from King's* on BBC2, it presented a natural addition to our existing pattern.

Like *Carols from King's*, but unlike the Festival of Nine Lessons and Carols, *Easter from King's* uses poetry as well as scripture readings, upon which the musical items are "hung".

THE richness of Passiontide and Easter music has meant that we are faced with an *embarras de richesse* as far as repertoire is concerned, and, as with our Christmas programmes, we are not bound by the title "carols" in limiting our musical performances to that particular genre.

In fact, since the early days of the Festival of Nine Lessons and Carols, there have been musical departures from carols per se; my predecessor Boris Ord introduced an extract from Bach's *Christmas Oratorio* ("And there were shepherds ...") in 1947, and *Wachet auf* is a constant item in the televised service. But carols, of course, are the staple fare of our Christmas services, and have made King's College Choir famous throughout the world.

Modern audiences tend to be hazy about what constitutes a carol; so we have never had any complaints about the non-carols in our Christmas programmes. Nowadays, after all, the word "carol" is frequently applied to anything from the Coventry Carol to "Rudolph the Red-nosed Reindeer".

It would not be right to confine this genre to religious music, because this would be an artificial constraint on a style of music-making which developed outside the confines of the Church, arising from the need felt by ordinary people to express simple ideas and emotions that were not addressed by the more solemn church music.

Carols tended to be joyful and direct. Often, they told stories — some Christian, some pre-Christian, and some entirely non-religious. And their universal accessibility has helped to ensure their survival through centuries of historical turmoil, broad swings of fashion, and even religious prohibition.

WE DO not know whether the noun or the verb ("to carol") came first. In its Breton and Romance forms, it seems that the original vowel was "o" rather than "a", which seems to indicate a derivation from the Greek-Latin "chorus". There may well be links with *coraulare* (to tread or dance) and the Latin *corolla* (little crown, coronet, or garland), perhaps indicating dancing in a ring.

Indeed, in France, from where the tradition passed into England, a *carole* in the 14th century was a song accompanying a dance in the round, frequently characterised by the lively triple-metre so familiar in medieval carols.

TODAY, a number of carols retain verses or titles that celebrate dancing as an appropriate manifestation of faith, the obvious example being "Tomorrow shall be my dancing day", a carol equally at home in the context of Christmas or Easter.

The origins in dance meant that carols generally had a joyful feel to them. Thus, in 1625, Bacon could contrast them with more serious-sounding music, noting that "Euen in the Old Testament, if you listen to Dauids Harpe, you shall heare as many Herselike Ayres, as Carols."

And yet so many medieval Christmas carols contain dark hints at the events of Holy Week. The Fayrfax Carol, the words of which Thomas Adès, the composer from King's, chose to set for the Festival of Nine Lessons and Carols in 1997, has the child Jesus telling his mother of the "Derision Gret passion", and Jesus foreseeing "Many a wownd Suffyr shall I. On Calvery … Ther shall I be, Man to restore, Naylid full sore Vppon a tre."

For many years, carols thrived outside the Church, and were sung by the populace in all sorts of contexts and at all sorts of times. The reference to carols in Shakespeare's song "It was a lover and his lass" ("This carol they began that houre, With a hey, and a ho, and a hay nonino") is but one indication that carols found their way into entirely secular, slightly risqué, contexts, and that in 1600 they were associated with springtime as much as Christmas.

In fact, New Year, Easter, saints' days, and planting and harvesting time all generated their own carols. It was only in the late-19th century that carol-singing become almost exclusively associated with Christmas.

AS WITH many other secular traditions, carols came to be seen by the Church as useful didactic tools. It is probable that some existing carols were given new words, and that, at some point in the 15th century, those Christian carols that had thrived at secular venues, from the village inn to wealthy homes, were simply brought into liturgical use, perhaps as processionals.

After Parliament abolished Christmas and other festivals in 1647, no carol was published in England for a further 150 years. Nevertheless, popular tunes continued to be passed from one generation to the next, and some, such as that of "O come, all ye faithful", were strong enough to become Christmas "standards". Others, however, disappeared, and, unless they happened to have been written down and preserved in manuscript, were lost altogether.

Those that survived were rescued by Victorian collectors, who scoured the country searching for people who could summon up musical memories from their youth. Two Cornishmen, William Sandys and Davies Gilbert, published collections of "ancient" Christmas carols in the 1820s and 1830s (just as another Cornishman, David Willcocks, through his *Oxford Book of Carols*, had such a huge effect on the Christmas carols we have sung since the 1960s).

CAROL-singing became an important part of the Victorian Christmas. Cathedrals, which had hitherto neglected carols as a genre, began to include them in their choirs' Christmas repertoires from the 1870s.

Many more old texts, and the traditional tunes associated with them, preserved only in the memories of a handful of country people, or in a few forgotten manuscripts, began to be unearthed and recorded around the turn of the century by Ralph Vaughan Williams, Cecil Sharp, and others.

In 1880, Truro Cathedral led the way with Dean Benson's creation of a Festival of Nine Lessons and Carols, which was adapted and introduced at King's by Dean Eric Milner-White immediately after the First World War.

Arguably, the BBC's broadcasting of *A Festival of Nine Lessons* and *Carols from King's* from 1928 has done more to confirm the position of carols within our own experience of Christmas than anything else. But the redis-

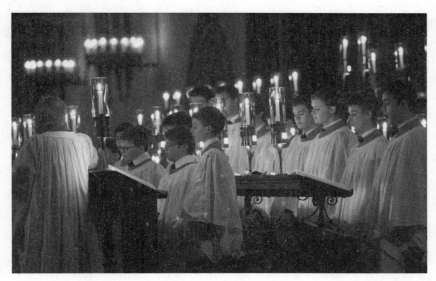

The Choir of King's College Cambridge, rehearsing under the direction of Stephen Cleobury

covery and resurgence of carols has been, almost exclusively, focused on those that are appropriate for Christmastide.

Even those that are appropriate to Eastertide were classified by Victorian collectors as "Christmas carols". "This have I done for my true love" ("Tomorrow shall be my dancing day"), so memorably set by Gustav Holst, was a traditional Cornish carol printed by William Sandys in his *Christmas Carols, Ancient and Modern* of 1833.

MANY medieval and indeed later carols contain references to Christ's death: the 15th-century "Jesu, thou the Virgin-born", also by Gustav Holst, like many a medieval carol, refers to the blood Jesus shed when he "died on the rood".

"Joys Seven", which I arranged in 1984, derives from popular devotion on the events of the life of the Virgin Mary, but it is interesting that it is rarely, if at all, heard in the context of Holy Week, despite Mary's "sixth good joy ... to see her own son Jesus upon the crucifix".

Tom Adès's Fayrfax Carol, which I mentioned above, is full of references to the Passion of Christ, yet is firmly fixed in nativity repertoire. The 17th-century "Rocking Carol" by George Withers, which Vaughan Williams set and published in *The Oxford Book of Carols*, which he co-edited in 1928, also refers to Christ's "torments and his pain". (Vaughan Williams's setting was first performed at King's only in 2009.)

Any of these could be sung during Holy Week, as well as at Christmas. It seems, however, that we prefer to confine all references to the nativity and to the Christ-child to Christmas, or, at the very latest, to Candlemas, while references to the Cross punctuate the Christian year, and are quite permissible within the context of Christmas carols.

Indeed, the way in which so many medieval Christmas lyrics point towards the events of Holy Week renders such carols not only surpassingly poignant, but also theologically profound, in that they express a holistic understanding of Christ's incarnation and death. Such an understanding is rarely replicated in modern carols.

A further consideration must be that there is no opportunity to express Passiontide events in the carol genre, since carolling during Lent, let alone Holy Week, seems so inappropriate.

ONE of the carols to be broadcast on Easter Day is unusual in that its tune, at any rate, is associated with both periods of the Christian year: the 15th-century French tune *Noël nouvelet* is derived from the first five notes of the Marian hymn *Ave Maris stella*.

At King's, we have performed it regularly since 1985 at Nine Lessons and Carols in Stephen Jackson's arrangement. Its original French words are said to be associated with New Year. The lyrics "Now the green blade riseth", however, written by John MacLeod Campbell Crum (1872–1958), have in a very short time made this tune equally associated with Eastertide. Indeed, Crum skilfully preserves a hint of Christmas in his refrain "Love is come again like wheat that springeth green", with overtones of Christina Rossetti's 1885 poem "Love came down at Christmas".

There is no hint of darkness in Charles Wood's exuberant arrangement of the 17th-century Dutch psalm melody *This joyful Eastertide*, surely the most famous of Easter carols, to which words were added in 1894 by George Ratcliffe Woodward.

In common with many cathedrals and churches, we find ourselves singing this carol as an "opener" on Easter morning almost annually. (Woodward's words seem to lend themselves to opening carols; his "Up! good Christen folk and listen" sets the tone so well for Christmas services — literally "telling the story" — that it is difficult to resist scheduling it every year at the beginning of carol services.) "This joyful Eastertide" makes its appearance in the broadcast from King's this year, although not, this time, as an opener.

OUR BRIEF from the BBC was to make an *Easter from King's* service that also covered the events of Holy Week. So, after the opening hymn "Jesus Christ is risen today", the service moves, as if in cinematic flashback, back

The magnificent interior of the Chapel of King's College Cambridge

to Palm Sunday, and traces its way through the events of Maundy Thursday and Good Friday through to Easter morning.

Every year, at Christmas, the BBC skilfully weaves images of the great works of art of King's Chapel into our musical performances, marrying words and music, and particularly finding scenes in the magnificent 16th-century stained glass which reflect on the words the choir is singing.

Because so many medieval Christmas carols point towards the crucifixion, shots of the crucifixion have been shown by the BBC before, but *Easter at King's* has afforded rich new opportunities for the windows of King's — not least the magnificent east window — to cast their brilliant light on the events of Holy Week and Easter.

The hope is that viewers will perceive and experience, as our musicians and our congregation in the chapel do, something of the existential depth and significance of the biblical story illuminated through this music (carols and non-carols alike), poetry, and stained glass, in their sublime architectural setting.

As philosophers and theologians down the ages have insisted, the beautiful can, and ought to, be a window into the true and the eternal. This insight is something we hope *Easter from King's* will enable us to share.

(2010)

Considering Bach's ways and means

Edward Wickham had sung the *St John Passion* often.
But when he studied it as a conductor, he found the work
yielded unexpected, even disquieting, riches for reflection

MANY a fine tenor has come to grief singing Bach's aria *"Erwäge"*. It is the longest and surely the most exhausting movement in the *St John Passion*, requiring a voice that can sit on top G for what seems an eternity, and then negotiate lines that dart around the register with relentless energy.

I remember a student performance some years ago at which one could almost hear groans of horror, mingled with gasps of amazement from the audience, as the tenor, having died once, turned back to the beginning for the *da capo*. "He's going to try it *all over again?*" they seemed to whisper.

Whether causing the soloist actual physical pain was part of Bach's expressive intent is not clear, though it would be entirely appropriate for an aria that sets one of the most disturbing, indeed nauseating, texts in the Passion.

Jesus has just been flogged, and we are asked to imagine his back, beaten not just black and blue, but all the colours of the rainbow. It is as if the clouds of our sin have been dispersed, and this is a sign of our redemption (*"Der allerschönste Regenbogen Als Gottes Gnadenzeichen steht"*).

The poetry of the German Passion tradition is full of strongly visual conceits such as this. At least as bizarre as the text of *"Erwäge"*, if not quite so gory, is that of the bass aria *"Mein teurer Heiland"*, which follows directly on from Christ's bowing his head and giving up the spirit. The soloist asks of the crucified Christ whether the sinner is now free of death, and takes Christ's bowed head as a nod in the affirmative (*"Doch neigest du das Haupt Und sprichst stillschweigend: ja."*)

WHEN I started work on Bach's *St John Passion* with a view to conducting it, I confess that many of these details were revelations to me, despite the fact that I have sung the piece at least once every year of my adult life, and the *St Matthew Passion* oftener still. It is easy, as a listener and a performer, to be lulled into a sense of false but fond familiarity by those aspects of the Passion settings that are most immediately dramatic and appealing: the cries of *"Barrabam"* and *"Kreuzige"*, the chorales with infectiously singable melodies and subtly shifting harmonies, and the grandeur of the opening and closing choruses.

For me, it has taken something like a process of deprogramming to appreciate how eccentric, extraordinary and challenging Bach's *St John Passion* is.

This is not to say that the work reveals itself only after years of scrutiny. Bach clearly had a fine sense of the dramatic, and his taut pacing of the action eases off only towards the end of the *St John*. Nor did he let textual fidelity get in the way of his compositional ambitions: he inserted into St John's narrative two important passages from St Matthew which provide the composer with opportunities for dramatic word-painting: Peter weeping bitterly after the revelation of his betrayal, and the chaos that follows hard upon Jesus's death.

But in many other parts of the work, performer and listener are confronted with material whose mood and motive is highly ambiguous.

The first chorus is a case in point. Over a rhythmic bass, which pounds out quavers unceasingly, we hear an angular, chromatic figure played by two oboes that seem to enjoy conflict more than its resolution. The struggle continues when the chorus enters. Without properly understanding the words, I had always assumed that this opening was intended to sound threatening and anxious.

The translation of the opening text, however, is laudatory: "Lord, our master, whose glory fills the whole earth..." Perversely, when in this opening chorus the text actually refers to the Passion, the music is transformed into a sunny major key.

We read much about the way Baroque music concerned itself with the expression of "the Affections", but here, as in other passages in the work, a reliance upon instinctive and literal translations of sound into emotion proves inadequate.

THE AMBIGUITY of tone that this first chorus demonstrates is not the only puzzling aspect of a work that defies any one, all-embracing interpretation. For there is a contradiction to be found in the religious culture that nurtured the Passion tradition. The poem from which most of the aria texts is drawn was published by Barthold Heinrich Brockes in 1712. *"Der für die Sünde der Welt gemarterte und sterbende Jesus"* ("Jesus tortured and dying for the sins of the world") is in the spirit of much 17th-century Lutheran religious writing, which stresses the importance of an intense, personal relationship between the believer and God.

Characterised as a mystical style of belief, the Pietist movement nevertheless retained a respect for the acts and forms of worship, and its sacramental basis. The most influential work in this tradition, Johann Arndt's

Source material: Barthold Heinrich Brockes (left) wrote the intense, disturbing, and strongly visual poem, published in 1712, from which many of the aria texts of the St John Passion *are taken*

Wahres Christentum of 1605, was so popular that it enjoyed fresh editions in the 18th century.

On the face of it, one would assume that a religious poetry that valued personal contemplation as a means of achieving union with God would not have much in common with such public expressions of communal faith as a Passion play with hymns. And it has been argued that the awkwardness that some of Bach's employers felt about the *St John* when it was first performed (an awkwardness that led to some substantial revisions for the second performance) might have been because of the peculiar composite nature of the work: part act of worship, part opera, with texts drawn from traditional hymns, scripture, and personal poetic expression.

But there is no reason to suppose that Bach did not intend us to feel awkward, both as performers and as listeners, as we move from the (overly) familiar story to the intimate confessions of the Christian soul.

While these juxtapositions of tone challenge the musicians to structure a performance with the right combination of vigour and repose, rhetoric and intimacy, the chorales provide another kind of interpretational challenge.

With their varying and often complex harmonisations, these hymns characterise the contrasting sentiments of the texts in a manner so subtle that it is with great reluctance that a conductor relinquishes responsibility for their performance to a congregation.

This is not to denigrate the power and importance of congregational hymn-singing: but in Bach's Passion chorales, harmonies require space, melodies must be supported, and the quickly shifting mood of the text and music needs to be appreciated. These are not requirements that are readily met by the average congregational choir; and I was somewhat relieved that, for our performance of the *St John,* the choir shelved the idea of inviting the audience to participate in the chorales.

Again, it is the text that lies at the root of the problem. The pattern that many of Bach's chorale texts adopt is one of commentary followed by inner reflection. In *"Petrus, der nicht denkt zurück",* for example, the poet comments first on the action we have just witnessed — Peter's betrayal — before turning inwards to meditate on how Jesus might touch our consciences when we do wrong.

The point at which this shift of emphasis occurs demands, in my opinion, a change of mood in the performance — a gesture that is far easier to effect with a chamber choir than with a congregation of several hundred. A chorale such as *"O grosse Lieb"* is beautifully characterised at the words *"Ich lebte mit der Welt in Lust und Freuden"* with sensuous, hedonistic clashes between the upper voices on *"Lust* and *"Freuden".* But that is a harmonisation whose subtlety is best communicated by small performing forces.

IF WE experience a certain disquiet about so elitist an attitude to the performance of an apparently democratic musical genre such as the hymn, then, again, I believe we are experiencing some of the disquiet that the early performances of the Bach Passions must have entailed.

The conflict of the personal and confessional with the public and rhetorical is one that is hardly unique to these works — it is, after all, an enduring theme in the history of sacred music — but the creative potential inherent in this tension is rarely as dramatically exploited as in Bach's sacred operas.

Nevertheless, plenty of people will disagree with me about the performance of the chorales, and no doubt about many other points of interpretation. Few works in the standard choral repertoire are so open to different styles of performance as the Bach Passions: from grandiose Bach Choir productions to the informal, jazz-cafe approach taken by Jonathan Miller in his televised version of the *St Matthew* in 1994. It is not something we can just stand and gawp at, paralysed by admiration for a work that will never be fully contained within one performance: Nor is it a piece whose problems, complexities and pitfalls should deter us.

Rather than muttering and tutting, we should be cheering on our tenor as he approaches yet another top G.

(2002)

Word from Wormingford

Ronald Blythe sings hymns that
tell of Christ's Passion

NEVER such an April. Perpetual sunshine, some of it hot; today's not so, although brilliant all the same. It lines the birds' wings and gilds the pear blossom. Yesterday, the merest feathering of rain on my face. The ancient farm track is Saharan with pale dust. And such pear blossom! The little valley orchard is on tiptoes, drawn up in its longing for light, or its need to see what is going on in Little Horkesley, to amazing limits. This will be fruit that cannot be picked, but must fall.

Preaching on Passion Sunday, I mention the Socratic nature of "If it be thy will, let this cup pass from me." This said by the one who only hours before had instituted the Cup of Life. Those who had drunk from it were a few yards away in the night air, worn out, while he, the giver, sweated blood at the thought of the prospect before him.

Right from the start, the Church has done its level best to walk closely with Christ because of this natural inability to do so in the darkening olive orchard. At this moment, the main characters in the awful drama were taking up their positions: the pain-blunted soldiers in the flogging room; the Jewish high priest in the Temple; the complex Pilate; the alarmed mother and women friends; the distinguished Joseph from Arimathaea.

There were elements of hurry, of swift dispatch, of getting the wretched business over. The Passover was about to begin, and dead bodies must be out of sight. They defiled the feast. We sang "We may not know, we cannot tell, What pains he had to bear," and the lovely spring day lit the Victorian glass. My dear friend Nell's funeral had taken place this week, and it was all death and life, life and death, wherever I looked. Blackness and brightness.

Once, the young teacher who was the Christ had asked a woman for a cup of water from, for him, a forbidden well. They had a lively exchange — she was used to men. He said he could give her a cup from which she would be able to drink life itself. What a gift, she thought. Never to have to walk all this way to the well every day!

It was Jacob's well, but the Samaritans had seized it long ago. It was, in fact, natural water in the desert, and nobody's well. Lost cups, similar to the one that he had shared with his friends at their Passover meal, would no doubt be lying in it, their clay splitting. Poetically, he had held out a similar cup to the bemused woman — "Drink from this, and you will never thirst again."

All these pre-Easter days he offers those who live by his teachings the terrible refreshment of his own blood. All around in the glorious East Anglian churches they are singing Bach's Passion music. A sea of cars islands the concert-goers. Light refreshments during the interval. We sing Isaac Watts's peerless "When I survey the wondrous cross" — he had set Paul's words to the Galatians — and they leave me drained, as usual. Others, too, no doubt.

Both Henry, the Vicar, and I brush against a crucifix whenever we climb the pulpit. It ceases to horrify us. We — all of us — are used to it: the naked tortured God, the defiled man. It is part of the fittings. Watts draws our attention to it: "See from his head, his hands, his feet, Sorrow and love flow mingled down."

(2011)

Handel's glad tidings of good things

Handel is not a composer generally associated with Holy Week, but the Cross is central to his outlook, argues **Michael Lloyd**

HANDEL was a composer and theologian, first and foremost, of the Cross. That may sound a strange claim, given that his only setting of the Passion is one of the least inspired of his works, and that *Messiah*, one of the most inspired, is more associated in our minds with Christmas and Easter than with Good Friday. (It is Bach who has almost a monopoly there.)

The sheer confidence of his music may also sit uneasily with such a statement. As the Canadian poet Elizabeth Smart puts it: "Sometimes Handel is loud, triumphant, insistent. I wanted to say Shut up! Can anything really be that successful and sure?" (from "A Musical Note").

Yet the themes to which he keeps returning are truths that are anchored in the failure and uncertainty of the Cross, as befits a Lutheran.

First, Handel proclaims (because the Cross reveals) the messiness of history as the theatre of divine action. In an age when Deism was forcing God out of history and restricting him to the act of creation and to personal experience, Handel chose to focus on the (sometimes perplexing) ways in which God was at work in history: *Israel in Egypt, Saul, Solomon, Belshazzar, Judas Maccabaeus*. For Handel, as for the Orthodox theologian John Zizioulas: "History is a real bearer of the ultimate, of the very life of God" (*Being As Communion*, SVS Press, 1985).

Second, he points to the person of Christ as the fulfilment of that history, the focal point of God's work in human time and space. Many contemporary theologians were attacking the whole concept of Christ as the fulfilment of Old Testament prophecy: Jennens's text of *Messiah* confronts that head on.

Jesus is God returning at last to his people after the exile. Jesus is the glory of the Lord that all flesh shall see, and that is risen upon us. Jesus is the Son that the Virgin conceived — Emmanuel, God with us. He is the One who will feed his flock like a shepherd, the Suffering Servant of Isaiah.

Handel is aware that these Old Testament passages spoke first — and particularly — into their own times. But he insists, by the very structure of *Messiah*, that they do not say all that they have within them to say, until they say it in relation to Jesus Christ. Equally, he found that he could not tell the story of Jesus without drawing on these passages.

Third, Handel underlines the fact that the Cross directs us to what is otherwise overlooked. He had taken profoundly into himself the crucial lesson that God defines himself by dying the degrading death of a slave. He had learnt the message of the Cross that God has chosen the lowly and despised things of this world, before the celebrated things (1 Corinthians 1.27-8).

Although Handel is generally known for the "muscularly triumphant" nature of his music, the opera critic Robert Thicknesse rightly describes him as "one whose best work treats with fathomless, appalled sympathy the wretched of the world: the traduced in love, the bereaved, the victimised, the dispossessed".

Louis-François Roubiliac's 1762 monument to Handel in Westminster Abbey

In *Aci, Galatea e Polifemo*, for example, he gives the best music not to the lovers, but to the spurned monster. Knowing that his Lord was despised and rejected of men, Handel directs our attention to all who are despised and rejected, that we do not miss something of Christ in them.

Fourth, Handel operates with a model of the Cross that is more than substitutionary — but not less. "Surely he hath borne our griefs, and carried our sorrows! He was wounded for our transgressions; He was bruised for our iniquities; the chastisement of our peace was upon him. And with his stripes we are healed."

That is what Handel sees in the Cross, and what he most admires in human beings is some small reflection of that love that gives itself for others — be it Didymus sacrificing himself for Theodora, or Alcestis for Admeto. Such impressive human representations go some way towards defusing the arguments of those who see substitution as immoral.

Fifth, for Handel, the Cross shows us how to live harmoniously with one another. His opera *Berenice* is typically tortuous in its romantic and political machinations. It is one of those "A loves B, B loves C, C loves A but has been promised to D" plots. Add to that the fact that A is Queen of Egypt, and Rome wants her to marry some Roman bigwig to cement an alliance against Rome's current enemy, Pontus, and what you end up with is romantic, political, and diplomatic gridlock.

All the characters have their own goals, their own fears, and their own agendas, which are mutually contradictory and totally irreconcilable. Things seem to be heading inexorably towards war, until one relatively minor character, Arsace, renounces his claim on the Queen's sister, despite having been promised her by the Queen.

This act of relinquishing his power and giving up his rights breaks the whole log-jam, and slowly the knot unties as others relinquish their rights, too. In the final scene, valid claims are waived, deceptions are forgiven, and harmony is restored.

The same thing happens in *Solomon*, in the famous story of the two prostitutes (1 Kings 3.16-28), where the one who is the true mother gives up her right to the child in order to protect her baby's life — and it is that which leads to understanding, to justice, and to right prevailing. So often is that the message of Handel's narratives that we may feel reasonably confident that here we are somewhere near the heart of Handel's view of life.

The ethicist Professor Nigel Biggar says that the lesson we must learn "about the just exercise of political power, about the use of power to heal and build relationships, is that nothing quite becomes it so much as the giving it up ... So, if we would exercise power justly, in such a way as to promote the flourishing of human community, then we must practise the art of surrendering it" (from a sermon on John 10).

The Cross tells us that God himself surrendered his rights, sat loose to his status, and gave up the joys of heaven to become a man of sorrows, when he became a human being in Jesus of Nazareth, lived a human life, and died a human death. Therefore, when we give up our power and our rights to preserve or repair relationships, we are acting in a way that is not humiliating, but human: not degrading, but divine.

Last, for Handel, the Cross guarantees that God is no dictator, no infinite imposer, no cosmic controller. Messiah ends with a vision of a slaughtered Lamb upon the throne — not a lion. God, as we meet him in Jesus, is the One who suffers violence — not the One who metes it out.

Postmodernism has been summed up by the slogan: "All ideology reeks of the death camps." Our generation understandably fears that if you believe anything too strongly, you will end up imposing it on others. But a worldview that is based on the Cross defuses that fear.

Christ went to the Cross precisely because he would not impose his views or his vision on others. On the contrary, he allowed others to impose their agenda violently on him. He was no Samson, no Joshua, no Judas Maccabaeus, but the Lamb who was slain. Only with him on the throne may we be triumphant without being triumphalist.

(2009)

The drama is in the detail

We need to look behind the central event of *The Procession to Calvary* by Pieter Bruegel the Elder, to find the universal truths it contains, says **George Pattison**

Look beyond: The Procession to Calvary *(1564) by Bruegel, Kunsthistorisches Museum, Vienna*

BEFORE us is a dramatic and crowded panorama of the road from Jerusalem to Calvary. To the left, the city, secure behind the glowing stone of its ramparts and dominated by the great dome of the Temple, is still emerging from the blue haze of a lovely spring morning.

From its gates, the road winds to a flat low hill on the right, where two crosses have already been erected, attracting a constantly growing crowd of spectators who are forming an expectant circle around the place of execution. Above them, the sky is already dark with the gathering storm, and the wind-blown crows add a further ominous note.

It is a picture full of incident, some of it taken from the biblical narrative, some from the artist's own keen observation of the life of crowds. As well as the central action, we see old men debating the events as they unfold, families seemingly treating it as a good day out, and young people playing, fighting, being chased by dogs, or arm-in-arm and deep in conversation.

A couple of dozen red-coated cavalrymen are spread out along the road, providing a vivid visual link between the various moments of the drama.

We could spend many minutes poring over such details, but what of those whose story this is? The one being taken to his death is situated at the very centre of the picture, although otherwise not marked out from the multitude.

Near by, some soldiers are dragging Simon of Cyrene away from his family and friends. His wife desperately tries to fight them off, despite the threatening pikeman, but she gets little help from the crowd, who react with the usual mix of shock, fear, indifference, and "not wanting to get involved". Some protest, some flee, some just look.

JUST ahead of Christ in the procession are the two thieves, seated in a tumbrel and anachronistically being given spiritual counsel by two friars, a Franciscan and a Dominican. Both the condemned men are shocked and pale, but, while one clutches a cross and seems to be attentive to the urgings of his confessor, the other gazes up to heaven with an expression of despairing wretchedness. The accompanying mob looks on with a mixture of malice, dread, and dumb pity.

Prominent to the right of the picture are Mary, John, and other of the women who are following the way of the cross with them. Mary's back is turned to where her son struggles forward on his last mortal journey, and John and the women are looking solicitously at her rather than at Jesus.

These figures are altogether and strangely detached from the rest of the scene. While those in the crowd are dressed in their everyday clothes, these are attired in fine, almost courtly robes. While the crowd conveys a sense of seething motion, these are portrayed in the kind of formal, monumental poses that we might see in a sculptured reredos. They seem to belong to a world of hieratic, sacred art that is alien to the earthy realism that is Bruegel's

trademark and that is so evident in his portrayal of the other figures in this great canvas.

Yet it would be a mistake to think that their formality rendered their response irrelevant. On the contrary, it is almost as if the artist is reminding us that it is not the outward appearance that matters here: the mob circling Calvary — ghoulish or merely curious as the case may be — has an eye for the spectacle, but not for what it means.

Mary, however, treasures in her heart the angel's message, and because she knows who it is who is going to his death, she also knows the full horror of all that is being done on this day. She knows that it is a day when, as the Muslim writer M. Kamel Hussein put it, men are choosing to put conscience itself to death.

Mary's grief is not just for her own child's suffering, but for a world that is refusing the love he came to bring. Turned towards us rather than towards the long, slow procession making its way to Calvary, it is as if her anguished face is asking us: "Do you not see, do you not feel, do you not understand?"

What are we to understand? Above where Christ has fallen to the ground, a precipitous and jagged splinter of rock rises sharply from the ground. Improbably, and perhaps impossibly perched on its summit is a windmill, a symbol to Bruegel and his contemporaries that the good grain of Christ's word has to be ground in the mill of suffering before it could be given to us as the bread of life.

Here, then, is a terrible scene in which the very worst of human nature is on full display: its cruelty, its indifference, its cowardice, its voyeurism. But, although Christ may have fallen beneath this weight of sin, we are being reminded that the good seed must fall to the ground and be buried, if his love is to rise up and bear fruit "an hundredfold".

Finally, one small detail: at the extreme right of the picture, and only half in it, we see the profile of a bearded man. Art historians have identified this as a self-portrait of the artist, and his presence raises an interesting question, not only for our interpretation of this picture, but for our approach to sacred art as a whole.

To paint such a scene, the artist must detach himself and observe it with a cool, clinical eye, noting every detail and nuance. We, too, must train ourselves to look carefully, if we are to see all there is to see. But does this mean we must become indifferent to what is happening, mere observers?

By no means, but we must learn to look, as he has looked, beyond the external display, beyond the surface, and see for ourselves and judge for ourselves and respond for ourselves to the eternal truth that this drama reveals.

(2011)

217

Frozen to the spot by eyes that have seen it all

The Resurrection by Piero della Francesca is well known.
But is it well read? – asks **John Drury**

IT nearly got blown to bits. In 1944, the Allies were advancing northwards through Italy, driving the retreating Germans before them. The advance was led by the Royal Horse Artillery's fast-moving guns. They came up to the country town of Borgo San Sepolcro (town or "bury" of the Holy Sepulchre), which stands in the flat valley of the river Tiber below a range of wooded hills.

Since it had some strategic importance and was likely to hold a German garrison, the soldiers had orders to bombard it. The guns were drawn up. The commanding officer ordered a ranging shot to be fired. It fell 200 metres short of the town centre. Scrutinising his map to correct his aim, the name of the town rang a bell in the officer's mind.

He had read somewhere that the best picture in the world was in this town. He decided that he had better look into it before going any further. Reconnaissance revealed that there was not a German soldier to be found. "The best picture in the world", a representation of Christ rising from his sepulchre, was saved.

The phrase — pretty childish art-criticism, it must be said — came from an essay written by Aldous Huxley in 1925, "The Best Picture", in a collection, *Along the Road*. Huxley made much of the difficulty of getting to Borgo San Sepolcro in order to make still more of the moment of his seeing the picture.

> The best picture in the world is painted in fresco on the wall of a room
> in the town hall … Its clear, yet subtly sober colours shine out from
> the wall with scarcely impaired freshness … It stands there before us
> in entire and actual splendour, the greatest picture in the world.

Remarkably, the picture is not in a church, but dominates the anteroom of a secular town hall, a place of business and justice. Huxley's essay then wanders off into speculative dogma: "There does exist an absolute standard of artistic merit. And it is a standard which is in the last resort a moral one."

On the basis of that (much disputed) assertion, he decided, following the lead of the great Victorian moralist-critic John Ruskin, that "the man who painted it was genuinely noble as well as talented". That man was

Invisible fishing net: The Resurrection *(1465) by Piero della Francesca,*
in the town hall in Borgo san Sepolcro

Piero della Francesca. We have not the faintest idea how noble a man he
was, but the nobility of his work is obvious and secure.

THE work is the thing, and form is the thing in the work. That is meant to
be a bossy remark. It is intended to correct our natural inclination to go
first for the content: "What is this of? Christ's resurrection. There he is with
his victory flag, and there are the sleeping guards. What next? The guide
book says there are more pictures to see in the next room."

First, and very much to the point, this sort of reaction is not true of
people confronting this picture. It stops them in their tracks.

Bernard Williams, that most completely atheist philosopher, told me
that he felt himself addressed with an authority that left him, for once,

speechless. (He was not, of course, converted, but that power of the Christian picture over the secularist is a problem of intense interest and delicacy — I hope this article will help with it.)

Second, going head-on for the content and then going away deprives us of great riches of meaning which, if attended to, will send us away well fed in our spirits. So let's forget what it is of, and see what it is.

Scanning across the picture from left to right is assisted by horizontal bands of pale stone-colour: at the top, at the bottom, and the ledge of the sepulchre at a judiciously gauged level between. We glide along them between fluted columns at either edge.

They are echoed by the verticals of the trees, set between them against the hillside. On the left are the columnar trunks of two bare trees. On the right are the spindlier trunks of younger trees in leaf. We have moved from winter to summer. The axis of that natural revolution is supernatural: the Easter Christ rising from his sepulchre into the dawn sky of the great spring festival.

The lower part of the picture is different. It is all lassitude. Instead of distinct verticals, there are the recumbent forms of sleeping soldiers, all knotted together in one tangled group, heavy and dark. Two of them interrupt the lines of the ledge of the sepulchre. But, apart from that connection, how do they relate to the wide-awake world above them?

The clue is the soldier on the right with the green helmet. He is a problem. Piero liked to place his figures firmly and steadily on the ground. He respected gravity. But this man leans out into space, our space, with no visible means of support. And he seems to float.

But just imagine that there is a great invisible net, heavy with fish, drawn up from the depths by some mighty fisherman. In the picture, it would be gathered and held by Christ's left hand at the very centre of it all. The pole in his right hand, planted on the sleepers' ground, supports and steadies his lifting pull.

That imaginary net would solve our problem. It would contain and support the floating soldier on the right. On the left, it would go around the curved back of his opposite number, the soldier with a brown helmet. Christ has caught them in his net, and, rising, draws them up from the murky depths into his world of day.

There is not, actually, a net in the picture. It was suggested to me by Christ's pink robe, the most spectacular colour in the picture. Piero does nothing without a reason. Christ's left hand, supported by his knee, gathers his robe into strongly marked folds. Project these downwards, and they become the lines of force that draw up the human freight, pulling it up as he himself rises from his tomb.

IN THE famous prologue of St John's Gospel, which we hear on Christmas Day, Christ is the divine light "which lighteth every man". The light was revealed in a body, "made flesh". Piero understood this, and put the two together in his picture's central revelation: the unequalled light of Christ's body. The revelation is given to us by the luminous torso, the head with those riveting eyes, the flag — and (not least) the ample pink robe, the picture's colour-climax, falling but pulled up.

There is also strength. The torso confronting us is muscular — very much more so than Christ's smooth body in Piero's Baptism in the National Gallery in London. This muscularity impressed Huxley. "The body is perfectly developed, like that of a Greek athlete; so formidably strong that the wound in its muscular flank seems somehow an irrelevance."

An incautious Italian critic called it "bovine". English admirers are more polite. Kenneth Clark noted the "earthy, peasant quality" of "this country god". But his friend Roger Fry put it best:

> Nothing can exceed the impressiveness of this figure which rises from the tomb with the slow and irresistible movement, the imperturbable gravity of a statue endowed with life. In a sense it (the picture) becomes miraculous from its very insistence on the material properties of the figure.

There are strong notes of pagan classicism in those quotations. In Piero's time, the imagination of educated Christians like him had been formed as much by classical as Christian literature. They were at home in both, pleased by their resemblances, and not unduly troubled by their tensions.

Piero's classicism speaks from this picture, and whispers to the classically aware the name of Hercules. Piero did a fresco of him on a wall of his house in Borgo san Sepolcro. Isabella Stewart Gardner bought it and had it installed in her house in Boston, Massachusetts, where it remains.

Hercules, like Christ, was born of a human mother and a divine father. He was a human hero who became a God, much worshipped in Rome. He was worthy of worship because his whole life was a series of labours for the benefit of humankind and the defeat of its monstrous enemies. He brought a dead woman back to life. He died in torment and was taken up into heaven. His nature, works, and destiny were so close to Christ's that a touch of him here could be part of the picture's power.

ANOTHER part of Piero's world, this time his world as a painter, was the newly developed art of perspective. He was deeply interested in it, and a grand master of it. Previously, the size of depicted figures had been determined by their importance: huge Madonnas with tiny donors at their feet, and so on. Now it was decided by precise, objective calculation of their exact positions in space.

But a master is free. He can play with the rules he knows inside out, and make them serve his imagination. Piero does it here. There is double perspective, two points of view, one mortal and the other immortal. They are divided along the line of the sepulchre's edge, on which Christ's foot rests, perfectly drawn with the foreshortening required by scientific perspective.

It is our eye-level for the bottom of the picture; so we can see the ground on which the sleepers lie. But, in the upper part, we and our eye-level have been raised to the level of Christ's commanding gaze. "If ye then be risen with Christ, seek those things which are above" (Colossians 3.1).

So we are back where we started, frozen to the spot by those eyes. Eyes seized our attention as babies, before we could speak, or even distinguish bodies. We learned to read them for the laughter, love, or trouble that they conveyed.

With the utmost care, Piero has given them their relentless stare by showing the white beneath their irises. The eyes that meet ours from the town-hall wall have the authority of complete knowledge. They are the eyes of one who knows it all: the bright world lost by suffering, death, and hell, and now restored as the kingdom over which he rules for ever.

(2012)

Easter's two-eyed vision

Richard Harries looks at the changing ideas seen in images of
the resurrection over two millennia in East and West

ALTHOUGH the first Christians shared something of the Jewish suspicion
of figurative art as a form of idolatry — and they were certainly hostile to
the Roman statues of gods and goddesses — simple illustrations of basic
Christian beliefs began to appear from about the middle of the third century.
These were designed to express and encourage Christian faith in a
difficult period.

In time, both theology and art became more sophisticated, developing
in relation to one another. Theologians kept an eye on what artists produced
to ensure it conformed to what they thought was orthodox; and works of
art, whether in ivory, mosaic, or paint, expressed what the Church at the
time thought was most important about the faith.

So we can look at Christian works of art and gain different insights into
our faith, depending on the time and culture from which they emanated.
I want to look at the somewhat different emphasis that exists in Eastern and
Western understandings of the resurrection of Christ, as reflected in some
dominant images.

In Western Christianity, especially since the late-medieval period, there
has been a tendency to focus on the cross of Christ. This is true both of
Catholicism and Protestantism. In the East, however, although the cross
has not been neglected, there has been a much stronger sense of the resurrection underpinning and suffusing all things.

In the earliest Christian art, this polarity is avoided. If there is one theme
that unites paintings in the catacombs in Rome, where Christian art from
the third century is located, it is of Christ the great deliverer. There are also
themes from the Hebrew scriptures, such as the crossing of the Red Sea,
Daniel in the lions' den, and the three youths in the fiery furnace. For these
early Christians, Christ is the one who delivers us from persecution, sin,
and especially death, for the catacombs were, of course, where many of
them were buried.

Neither the crucifixion nor the resurrection of Christ is depicted. But
two images in particular focused their minds on the resurrection: the raising
of Lazarus, and the Jonah story. The first reminded them of the wonderful
verse in John's Gospel: "I am the resurrection and the life," and assured

them that Christ had not only raised Lazarus from the dead, but would raise them, too.

The Jonah cycle, depicted here in paintings and elsewhere on sarcophagi, reminded them of the words of St Matthew 12.40: "Just as Jonah was in the sea-monster's belly for three days and three nights, so the Son of Man will be three days and three nights in the bowels of the earth."

The last scene in the Jonah cycle shows him reclining luxuriously under a tree, indicating the paradise that Christians, too, hoped to enjoy when Christ raised them from the dead.

THE RESURRECTION theme is more explicit in a wall-painting dated about 250 in a house-church at Dura-Europos, a small town on the frontier between the Roman and Persian empires. This seems to show three women approaching a tomb. It was this that became the dominant image for both East and West at that time.

What is noticeable about the image is its reticence. There is no attempt to show Christ rising from the tomb. What happened between the burial on Good Friday and Christ's resurrection on the third day is left as a profound mystery, around which Christian artists tiptoed.

It was this image of the women visiting the tomb which held the Christian imagination for centuries, and there are many fine examples in many different media: mosaic, as in Ravenna from the fifth and sixth centuries; and in ivory, as in a plaque now in the British Museum dating from 420.

Women at the tomb of Christ: wall mosaic decoration in the Basilica of Saint Apollinaire Nuovo, Ravenna

THE next development led to one of the greatest achievements of the Christian imagination. It seems to have been connected to the disputes that shook the Church for centuries over the humanity and divinity of Christ, and how they were to be held together.

If the problem was severe for theologians, it was acute for those who sought to depict Christian doctrine in a pictorial form. How do you paint Jesus in a way that does justice to both his humanity and his divinity? In particular, how do you show Christ dead on the cross in such a way that you also proclaim his resurrection?

The difficulty over this issue appears to have been the reason why depictions of Christ dead on the cross, not awake and triumphant, were comparatively late in arriving, and were not properly accepted until about the tenth century.

The way in which the issue was eventually resolved in pictorial form was to depict Christ in two separate images: one dead on the cross; and the other trampling Satan under his feet and releasing the dead from hell.

It was this latter image, the *Anastasis* ("resurrection" in Greek), that became, and still is, the canonical image for the resurrection of Christ in the Orthodox Church.

Details of this icon developed over the centuries, and they vary, but at the centre is Christ plunging his cross through a Satan sprawling on the floor of hell, while all around the broken bars and locks are scattered. To the left of the image are often depicted Kings Solomon and David (the latter with a beard, as the elder), indicating the human descent of Christ, together with John the Baptist, pointing at Christ the way.

On the right are various Old Testament figures, beginning with Abel with his shepherd's crook, the first person to be murdered, and whose blood cried out to God for vengeance. He is one of the first to be raised from the dead. Christ with one hand pulls out Adam, and with the other, Eve. In my favourite depiction (shown on page 141 of this book), at the church of the Chora in Istanbul (which does not have a cross plunged through Satan, but instead shows Christ in a mandorla of light), both of them are almost lifted into a Matisse-like flying dance.

THE biblical basis of the *Anastasis* is 1 Peter 3.19-20, where it is said that Christ went and made his proclamation to the imprisoned spirits. The iconography may be based in part on the medals of Roman emperors liberating a city, but the details of the scene are based mainly on the circa fifth-century Gospel of Nicodemus.

This describes how, because the Jewish authorities disbelieved in the resurrection of Christ, Joseph of Arimathaea summoned the two sons of

Simeon, who had been raised by Christ, to give witness to what they saw in hell. There was a great light, and Psalm 24 was sung exultantly:

> *Lift up your heads, O ye Gates, and be ye lift up ye everlasting doors:*
> *and the king of glory shall come in.*
>
> *Who is the king of Glory? It is the Lord strong and mighty,*
> *even the Lord mighty in battle.*

He then describes how the gates of hell are smashed, Satan is bound, and the dead are raised. Although this scene of the *Anastasis* appears early in Rome, and is present in the West later, Western iconography developed in a different direction. The early reticence about showing Christ rising from the dead was put aside, and Jesus is shown rising from the tomb.

The image most familiar to us shows him striding triumphantly out with a flag. Sometimes, however, he is shown in a circle of light floating above the grave, as in the vividly coloured scene to one side of the famous crucifixion altarpiece at Isenheim. At other times, he is shown actually emerging from the tomb, as in Piero della Francesca's depiction at San Sepolcro in Italy, reproduced on page 219 of this book. This is a haunting picture: the eyes, in particular, look at you as of one come from the dead. Aldous Huxley, who was no believer, thought it was the greatest painting of all time.

Personally, although I can admire the technical mastery of such paintings, and sense something of their vitality, I see in them no sign that Jesus has been raised out of this life into another dimension altogether. They are so real, in a human way, that they fail to convey what is fundamental to the New Testament view — that Christ was raised, as St Paul put it, in a spiritual body. The risen Jesus is not just a resuscitated corpse, but the eternal Son, whose being is now shown to be united for ever with the Father.

IN MY view, these Western depictions of Jesus emerging from, striding out of, or hovering above the tomb, fail to do justice to the nature of the resurrection. Yet Western art had its own triumphs — above all, in the scene known as *Noli me tangere*.

This is based on the deeply moving encounter of Mary Magdalene with the risen Christ in the garden, as recorded in John 20. It catches the scene where he says to her: "Do not cling to me, for I have not yet ascended to the Father. But go to my brothers and tell them that I am ascending to my Father and your Father, to my God and your God."

Commentators down the ages have speculated about why Jesus should have been so emphatic in telling Mary not to cling to him, but I have always found the explanation of the late Raymond Brown, the distinguished Roman

Noli me tangere: *Giotto's fresco in the Scrovegni Chapel, Padua, c.1303–5*

Catholic biblical scholar, the most helpful. He pointed out that, in John's Gospel, Jesus had told his disciples that, in the future, he would be with them in a way nothing could destroy. They would have a joy that no one could take from them, and a peace that nothing could destroy.

Mary misunderstands this, however, and thinks that his appearance to her is that permanent presence. So, in the garden, Jesus has to tell Mary that this appearance to her now is not what he has promised, yet: that will be when he has ascended to the Father and he is present with his followers through the Spirit.

That is why the translation "cling to" is more satisfactory than the traditional "touch". It is not simply a question of Mary's not touching him. It is a matter of not holding on to him now, in the mistaken view that this is his unshakeable spiritual presence with her.

My favourite depiction of this scene is by Giotto, in the Scrovegni (Arena) Chapel in Padua. Giotto, like other painters of the early Renaissance, still manages to convey something of the numinous. This is because a Byzantine feel for things still suffuses their newly discovered techniques of perspective.

There is a sense of "the other", as well as a gentleness in the way that Mary and Jesus look at one another. It is captured in the *contraposto* of the body of Jesus, defined as "leaning towards her, he also withdraws". This well conveys the closeness, with distance, of the risen divine presence.

WHAT has not been depicted in art (and, though it may be impossible to do so, this is still a pity) is the theological profundity of the words that Jesus says to Mary after telling her not to cling on to him in his present form. First, he calls his followers "brothers" (and "sisters"). Then he describes his God as their God, his Father as their Father. His ascension into heaven lifts them into the same relationship with his heavenly Father that he himself eternally enjoys. In short, we are taken into the heart of Godhead, the very life of the Trinity.

There is one modern work I like that does in some way hint at this, and that is the scene depicted in a sculpture by David Wynne, which is outside the chapel in the garden of Magdalen College, Oxford. It shows Jesus with his arms and hands gracefully lifted heavenwards, and his face looking up.

It is as though he and Mary and the disciples are already being taken into that reality. Mary is not clinging, but is already coming to recognise, in the figure before her, a beloved in transition from the material to the immaterial; an immaterial in which she, too, will be caught up.

IF ONE of the strengths of the Western tradition is captured in the intense, moving relationship of Mary Magdalene and Jesus — a relationship that even death cannot sunder — the strength of the Eastern approach is its sense of the cosmic dimension to the Passion and the resurrection.

Noli me tangere:
the David Wynne statue in
Magdalen College, Oxford.
There is also another, larger
version in Ely Cathedral.

In the West, the theme of the rescue of the dead from hell — the harrowing of hell, as it was called — was expressed in the poetry of William Langland in *Piers Plowman*. He recounts the scene in hell in a way that recalls the apocryphal Gospel of Nicodemus, and says he has heard secret words that it is not granted to a human being to utter.

"My righteousness and justice shall rule over hell, and my mercy over all mankind before me in heaven. I should be an inhuman king if I refused to help my own brethren."

The theme is also present in the writing of Julian of Norwich, who describes Christ descending into hell; and "then he raised up the great root out of the deep darkness which rightfully was knit to him in high heaven".

The Mystery plays were another context in which this idea found powerful expression. I remember seeing a wonderful production at the National Theatre a few years ago, in which hell was depicted as a vast rubbish truck with its metal claws drawing everything in and grinding it up.

In modern times, it has been central to the theology of Hans Urs von Balthasar, often regarded as the outstanding Roman Catholic theologian of the 20th century. For him, the phrase "He descended into hell" in the creed is fundamental to the meaning of redemption and atonement; for it means that Christ has entered into and taken upon himself our deepest darkness.

That said, visually and liturgically, it is the East that most powerfully conveys the sense that the whole of creation is altered by the Anastasis: the sense of some fundamental shift in the foundation of things which grounds it in a descent to utter darkness and which, through the resurrection, has united even the most estranged of creatures with God now and for ever.

I do not find it in the least surprising that, in recent years, the icon of the *Anastasis* has found increasing favour with Western Christians. This is part of the growing popularity of icons in general, but there are two more fundamental points.

First, this icon avoids what can seem the crude literalism of pictures of Jesus stepping out of his tomb, for it is clearly symbolic.

Second, it must be the most hopeful symbol ever produced by a human being. Not only does it say that death is conquered, and that we can die with a sense of trust and hope, but, even more important, evil itself has been overcome. Moreover, this is not just for a few chosen individuals, but, in principle, for all human beings of all time and indeed of all creation. There is a universal dimension and a cosmic sweep that is awe-inspiring.

As the matins of Holy Saturday in the Byzantine rite puts it:

Uplifted on the Cross, thou hast uplifted to thyself all living men; and then descending beneath the earth thou raisest up all that lie buried there.

The whole creation was altered by thy Passion; for all things suffered with thee, knowing, O Lord, that thou holdest all in unity.

(2008)

229

Raised by the Gardener to a lively estate

Mary Magdalene's Easter 'mistake' about the risen Lord's
identity inspired a whole tradition in Christian art,
says **Pamela Tudor-Craig**

IT IS NOT really surprising that two of the most significant comments on a
phrase in the account of the appearance of the Risen Christ to Mary
Magdalene (John 20.11-18), "She, supposing him to have been the gardener,
said unto him, Sir, if thou have borne him hence, tell me where thou hast
laid him ..." — Lancelot Andrewes's sermon and Rembrandt's painting and
attendant studies — should have been made with 18 years of one another.

There is no actual connection, but both stem from contexts with a passion
for gardens, and therefore a high esteem for great gardeners.

John Gerard's *Herball* had been first published in 1597. The taste for
elaborately designed flowerbeds, laid out in designs that go back to Leonardo's
patterns, was in train. Such planting can be properly appreciated only from
above, which meant from the upper windows of stately homes. We can still
savour the effect at Hampton Court or Kirby Hall.

No chapter of garden history depended more on artifice, on prodigious
expenditure of labour, or on daring expeditions in search of novel plants.
John Tradescant the elder was the most intrepid. He went to Archangel, in
a ship of Sir Dudley Digges, to bring back the first account of Russian plants.
He travelled in Flanders, the Low Countries, and Paris, in search of rare
plants for Robert Cecil, who, in 1611, was building Hatfield House, and
laying out ambitious gardens.

Tradescant would enter the service of the Duke of Buckingham in 1623,
and Charles I in the 1630s. In 1620, he again risked his life on the seas to
join an expedition of Sir Samuel Argall against Algiers, whence he brought
back, among other novelties, the "Algier Apricot". In the same spring, Lancelot
Andrewes preached the Easter sermon before James I at Whitehall on "Christ
the Gardener".

In February 1637, the astonishing two-year bubble of Tulipomania broke.
A year later, the young Rembrandt, prosperous, happy, and in collecting
mode, bought in Amsterdam a set of Albrecht Dürer's woodcuts, *The Little
Passion*, of 1511. Among the four resurrection images in that cycle, Dürer
departed from the traditional formula for the *Noli me tangere*, where Christ
carries the banner of the red cross on a white ground. Dürer's Christ carries
in its place a large spade. He also wears a hat with a wide brim, the kind

Christ with spade: Albrecht Dürer's Christ Appearing to Mary Magdalene *(c.1510), from the* Small Passion

often worn by medieval pilgrims on the long road to Compostela to protect them from the sun. The Easter sun rises immediately behind the Gardener.

Had Dürer entirely invented this novel iconography? I don't think so. One of the jewels of the National Gallery is Titian's small painting, *Noli me tangere*, where the scene is set in a pastoral landscape. It is undated, but always placed among his first pictures. His date of birth is unknown, but he was working alongside his contemporary Giorgione on the external paintings of the Fondaco dei Tedeschi in Venice by 1507–08.

In 1505–07, Dürer was paying his second visit to Venice, and the one building he certainly visited, probably frequently, was the Fondaco dei Tedeschi. There he will have encountered his fellow countrymen, and, indeed, he painted for the German merchants resident there his Madonna of the Rose Garlands, which is now in Prague.

Giorgione, and Giovanni Bellini himself, enjoyed in that decade an unparalleled liberty in the way their patrons, notably Isabella d'Este, encouraged them to use their own imaginations in the choice of features in their pictures. Hence small paintings such as Giorgione's *Tempesta*, whose subjects have puzzled onlookers ever since.

Christ with scythe:
Titian's Noli me
tangere *(c.1514)*

Young Titian is no exception: the banner of Christ's victory in this painting has been replaced by a scythe. It is a light and modest scythe, a ceremonial rather than a working tool, but Titian's Christ has won it from death in fair combat. One of the first things Dürer did when he got back to Nuremberg was the small woodcut *Passion* of 1511, where he introduced the figure of Christ the Gardener. In the same way that Dürer's Christ among the Doctors remembers Leonardo, this surely reflects the Titian, not usually dated quite so early as Dürer's visit to Italy, but suggesting direct contact. The gesture of Dürer's Christ is more conventional, his stigmata more conspicuous, but, in both Titian and Dürer, the crouching Magdalene raises her right hand towards Christ in a gesture as much of blessing as of supplication. Her left hand most powerfully suggests a direct connection: in both compositions she has collapsed on the ground, and is partly supporting herself on her left hand, splayed across the top of her ointment jar.

Dürer, always of a down-to-earth and Teutonic way of thinking, however exalted his subject-matter, has replaced a delicate scythe (fit only to trim the most willing grass) by a workmanlike spade. A spade of the same practical form had been wielded by Adam in the 14th-century glass of the west window at Canterbury Cathedral. That Adam was setting about his job of feeding his wife and the future people of the fallen world. This second Adam, however, comes back from an even more daunting task, the harrowing of hell.

Among the taunts with which God measures the distance between himself and Job (chapters 38–39) is the challenge: "Canst thou bind the unicorn with his band in the furrow? Or will he harrow the valleys after thee … Wilt thou believe him that he will bring home thy seed, and gather it into thy barn?" (KJV) Here is the Saviour, the pure unicorn, who, 400 years after Job, has harrowed the valley of death and garnered the seed of life.

This image of the "harrowing", or the "ploughing", words as old as the English language, is very different from the more conventional idea of the descent into hell or limbo. That, frequently portrayed by Titian's master's brother-in-law, Andrea Mantegna, was of Christ striding into hell's mouth, or a cave; sometimes, as in Byzantine or Anglo-Saxon art, shown with him striding over the broken gates.

A scythe or a spade would have been no help in effecting that entry, so to speak, by the front door. Harrowing does not compare with Orpheus's journey to find Eurydice. It is not keyhole but open-heart surgery, open-cast mining, or full archaeological uncovering, as opposed to exploratory trenches. This Gardener has dug all the way, has brought light to the darkest places of *accidie*, the medieval mortal sin of total despair.

So, what does Rembrandt make of this idea, which he seized on the crest of his country's passion for flowers? He set about the subject of *Christ the Gardener* immediately he had Dürer's *Little Passion* in his hands. We have three drawings by him around the subject, the most hesitant showing Christ standing abruptly, with no classical curves, behind Mary as she stares into the empty tomb. There is the hat and the spade over his shoulder, but the artist has hesitated over the gesture of the Risen Lord.

He started by sketching Christ's right hand, outstretched in welcome. Clearly, Rembrandt feared that was too casual, and drew over it in harder strokes of the pen a more formal gesture of blessing.

In another sketch, Christ leans in a classical pose against a rock, and the huddled Mary shrinks from him. Her retreating companions are conspicuous against the empty hill of Calvary, and Rembrandt is already suggesting the City of Jerusalem in the distance. The picture, signed and dated 1638, was probably painted for his friend, the sick-visitor, teacher and poet, Herman Frederick Waterloos.

It has pasted to the back a rather bad poem by another friend, J. de Decker. Here, Jerusalem is shown with twin stoned towers, Jachin and Boaz, soaring from the courtyard of the Temple ("Destroy the Temple and in three days

Following Titian: Rembrandt's Christ appearing to Mary Magdalene *(1638), now in the British Royal Collection*

I will raise it up" John 2.19). They rise in the first dazzling sunlight of Easter behind one who, bearing his spade, face shadowed by a wide-brimmed hat, is indeed a gentle and weary gardener, at rest upon the seventh day.

Two angels are much at ease in a cave tomb that recalls the kind of garden grotto that first became popular in the 1620s. The foreground is filled with luxuriant foliage, and the approach is defined by the curves of low-cut box hedging that edged the patterned flowerbeds so popular at the time.

The Magdalene has made no mistake. This indeed is *Christ the Gardener*, son of the Father who planted a garden eastward in Eden, and put the first man there to dress it and keep it. As the Father had walked there in the cool of the evening, so now the Son walks in the first dawn. As we muse on Christ the Gardener, we are coming in these latter days to realise that the garden we were asked to dress and keep is not just the plot of soil we individually own and rigidly control (or otherwise), that it may bring forth petunias and begonias and nothing we do not label and command, but the whole surface of this miraculous planet that we have so recklessly plundered.

So, we turn to Lancelot Andrewes's peerless sermon of Easter 1620, of which there is only space here for a few snatches:

"For in a sense, and a good sense, Christ may well be said to be a gardener, and indeed is one … The first, the fairest garden that ever was, Paradise. He was the gardener, it was of his planting … And ever since it is He that as God makes all our gardens green, sends us yearly the Spring and all the herbs and flowers we then gather, and neither Paul with his planting nor Apollos with his watering could do any good without Him … He it is who gardens our 'soul' too …

"Christ rising was indeed a gardener; and that a strange one, who made such a herb grow out of the ground that day as the like was never seen before, a dead body to shoot forth alive out of the grave … He it is that by virtue of this morning's act shall garden our bodies too, turn all our graves into garden plots; yea will one day turn land and sea and all into a great garden …

"He that was lost is found again, and found … not a dead body but a 'living soul' … and that might Mary Magdalene well say … he quickened her that was as good as dead.

"You thought you should have come to Christ's resurrection today, and so you do. But not to his alone, but even to Mary Magdalene's resurrection too. For in very deed a kind of resurrection it was wrought in her, revived as it were, and raised from a dead and drooping to a lively and cheerful estate. The gardener had done his part, made her all green on the sudden."

(2007)

Donne's extravagant grace of a feast-fast

Mary Ann Lund traces John Donne's intermingling of
the Annunciation and the Passion

IT HAPPENS only a few times every century that Good Friday falls on the
same day as the Annunciation, 25 March. It has happened just three times
in the 20th century (1910, 1921, and 1932) and twice in the 21st (2005 and
2016). And it won't occur again until 2157. If, as the Archbishop of
Canterbury suggests, all Churches agree to fix the date of Easter within the
next ten years, it will never happen again.

It might seem unlikely that an oddity in the Church calendar should
prompt a poem, but, just over four centuries ago, on 25 March 1608, it did
exactly that. For John Donne, the coincidence of the two holy days provided
a fertile opportunity for literary reflection.

Whereas we might think about the liturgical practicalities of transferring
the Principal Feast away from Good Friday, Donne's "Upon the Annunciation
and Passion Falling upon one Day" asks us to pause, and to see what happens
when we keep the two days together in our minds.

Donne had been born and brought up a Roman Catholic, and perhaps
that inheritance attuned him to Mary's perspective. He pictures her vividly,
alone at home, receiving the Angel Gabriel's greeting, *"Ave"*, and in the
crowd at Golgotha, where she hears her son's final words from the cross,
"Consummatum est".

The Church of England that he entered as a young man — and in which
he would later be ordained — gave him another important prompt. The
Book of Common Prayer's collect for the Annunciation asks God to "pour
thy grace into our hearts; that, as we have known the incarnation of thy Son
Jesus Christ by the message of an angel, so by his cross and passion we may
be brought unto the glory of his resurrection."

DONNE begins his poem tenderly, telling his own "frail body" to fast
because his soul has a double feast today, celebrating Christ both here and
gone again ("hither and away"). It is a running theme, that God is always
slipping out of the poet's reach. Christ is not yet born in the flesh, yet he is
already dead on the cross.

A symbolic circle represents the multiple images of Christ. As fully God,
he is eternal, just as in a circle the "first and last concur", or meet; and, as

fully human, his physical presence mirrors that shape, because the extremities of the human body — feet and outstretched arms — touch a circle's circumference (as the Vitruvian Man figure drawn by Leonardo da Vinci, shown here, so memorably illustrates).

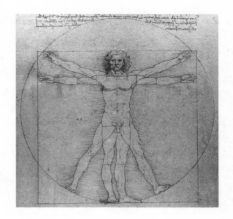

And there is a third emblematic circle that hovers behind these two: the communion wafer. Donne was aware of the centuries-old debate over whether it was right to celebrate the eucharistic feast on Good Friday, the most solemn of fasts; so the eucharist is elusive in this poem.

The poet's soul "eats twice" by meditating on the Annunciation and Passion, but does he also take the bread and wine of the communion table? Perhaps the poem itself provides the eucharistic moment, intensely concentrating the whole gospel story, and sharing it.

DONNE presents us with a dizzying succession of images and ideas — sometimes even verging on the absurd. Christ, the bridegroom of the Song of Songs (5.15), who is "excellent as the cedars", becomes a tree that grows itself, then falls, in a kind of surreal time-lapse photography. The creator becomes the subject of his own creating ("put to making").

Mary ages rapidly within a single moment. Like the other "she" in the poem — the poet's soul — the virgin mother carries her own contradictions. Christ is just beyond her grasp: "promised her, and gone". Simultaneously expectant and bereaved of her child (the meaning of being "in orbity"), a sword has pierced her soul, even as she conceives.

"All this and all between this day has shown": it is not just those two moments that the day marks. What seems like a linear story from birth to death becomes twisted round itself through the mysterious workings of the incarnation and atonement. In his sermons and poems, Donne loved the mental contortions of seeing a flat ("plain") map of the world, and imagining that the furthest right side of the sheet joined up with the left, as it does on the globe.

Here, the map symbolises the way devotion works as "the abridgement of Christ's story". Reading the Bible, public worship during the cycle of the Church year, and private moments of reflection: all these bring the events of the gospel into a single place and time.

IN THE second half of the poem, Donne widens his gaze to the place of the Church. Unable to resist reminding us that he had a good legal education, he treats the Church as "God's Court of Faculties" (the ecclesiastical court responsible for legal dispensations such as special marriage licences). So he praises it for "joining these" two days in a less-than-typical union.

There was an ancient Church tradition that the annunciation and crucifixion happened on the same day of the year, but Donne prefers the idea that the Church deliberately wedded the days to give them a new sacred dimension.

The Church is a guide — but not a perfect one, Donne hints. Shakespeare, his contemporary, had described love as "an ever-fixed mark" and a "star to every wandering bark". But Donne had been to sea, and knew that the Pole Star was not fixed at all, but shifted its position ever so little in the night sky.

So he leaves open an acknowledgement that the Church may stray, too, even while he suggests that, like the Pole Star, it is still the most dependable way of navigating. As it steers, so it illuminates.

Donne's powerful conclusion is that the Church offers this cosmic coincidence of days to imitate a God who stands outside time, who sees all the world's history — from the creation to the Last Judgement — at once. This double feast-fast is the Church's reflection of extravagant grace.

But is it for one day only? The poet insists that it is not. The treasure that he gathers wholesale ("in gross") on 25 March can be spent over the course of his life. And it becomes a treasure to be distributed, too. The first half of the poem is between the poet, his "frail body", and his soul; but, in the second half, he starts speaking about "us".

What the poem invites us to do is to participate in this rare, ancient conjunction of days, where the Church "join[s] in one Manhood's extremes".

Upon the Annunciation and Passion Falling upon one Day

Tamely, frail body, abstain today; today
My soul eats twice, Christ hither and away.
She sees him man, so like God made in this,
That of them both a circle emblem is,
Whose first and last concur; this doubtful day
Of feast or fast, Christ came, and went away.
She sees him nothing, twice at once, who is all;
She sees a cedar plant itself, and fall,
Her Maker put to making, and the head
Of life at once not yet alive, yet dead.

She sees at once the virgin mother stay
Recluded at home, public at Golgotha;
Sad and rejoiced she's seen at once, and seen
At almost fifty, and at scarce fifteen.
At once a son is promised her, and gone;
Gabriel gives Christ to her, he her to John;
Not fully a mother, she's in orbity,
At once receiver and the legacy.
All this, and all between, this day hath shown,
The abridgement of Christ's story, which makes one
(As in plain maps, the furthest west is east)
Of the angels' Ave, and Consummatum est.
How well the Church, God's Court of Faculties,
Deals, in some times, and seldom joining these!
As by the self-fixed Pole we never do
Direct our course, but the next star thereto,
Which shows where the other is, and which we say
(Because it strays not far) doth never stray;
So God by his Church, nearest to him, we know,
And stand firm, if we by her motion go;
His Spirit, as his fiery pillar, doth
Lead, and his Church, as cloud; to one end both.
This Church, by letting those days join, hath shown
Death and conception in mankind is one;
Or 'twas in him the same humility,
That he would be a man, and leave to be;
Or as creation he hath made, as God,
With the last judgement, but one period,
His imitating spouse would join in one
Manhood's extremes: He shall come, he is gone:
Or as though one blood drop, which thence did fall,
Accepted, would have served, he yet shed all;
So, though the least of his pains, deeds, or words,
Would busy a life, she all this day affords;
This treasure then, in gross, my Soul, uplay,
And in my life retail it every day.

(2016)

The best to the brave

Robert Browning's defiant poem about death points to the heart of Easter, says **David Bryant**

Prospice by Robert Browning (1812–89)

Fear death? — to feel the fog in my throat,
    The mist in my face,
When the snows begin, and the blasts denote
    I am nearing the place,
The power of the night, the press of the storm,
    The post of the foe;
Where he stands, the Arch Fear in a visible form,
    Yet the strong man must go:
For the journey is done and the summit attained,
    And the barriers fall,
Though a battle's to fight ere the guerdon be gained,
    The reward of it all.
I was ever a fighter, so — one fight more,
    The best and the last!
I would hate that Death bandaged my eyes, and forbore,
    And bade me creep past.
No! let me taste the whole of it, fare like my peers
    The heroes of old,
Bear the brunt, in a minute pay glad life's arrears
    Of pain, darkness and cold.
For sudden the worst turns the best to the brave,
    The black minute's at end,
And the elements' rage, the fiend-voices that rave,
    Shall dwindle, shall blend,
Shall change, shall become first a peace out of pain,
    Then a light, then thy breast,
O thou soul of my soul! I shall clasp thee again,
    And with God be the rest!

I RECENTLY started to watch Mel Gibson's film *The Passion of the Christ*. Halfway through the notorious ten-minute scene of the scourging, I turned it off, unable to stomach the reality of the crucifixion drama and its innate cruelty. I found myself longing for the familiar and soothing words of "When I survey the wondrous cross", and hankering for the colourful Stations of the Cross hanging on the church walls, and their artistic softening of the horror that was Golgotha.

This epitomises society's assessment of death. We want it to be wrapped in a garland of solemn music, cushioned with whispered platitudes, and softened by silence and the reverential tread of the undertaker. Even our language surrounding death is deprived of its sting. We rely on euphemisms: "He has passed away"; "I have lost him."

Robert Browning, in his short poem "Prospice" ("looking ahead") puts forward a different approach to death, one fired with optimism and hope. He views it as an experience to be faced full on, and not hidden away in some dark corner. For him, it is that point in life when "the journey is done and the summit attained". Indeed, it is a rite of passage that leads directly to the glory of Easter.

It was a tangle of threads that led Browning to this conclusion. His grandfather was a wealthy slave-owner in St Kitts, and his father, after a brief visit to the sugar plantations, returned as an ardent abolitionist. His mother was a devout Nonconformist and musician, and the gifted young Robert soon became multilingual, a writer of poetry, and a keen natural historian.

This mellow Christian background was rudely shattered when Browning was given a volume of poetry by Shelley, who was an atheist. Browning rapidly dropped his theistic beliefs and incorporated his new philosophy into his poetry. This led him to write somewhat facetiously of a beautiful spring morning when larks were on the wing and snails on the thorn. "God's in his heaven, All's right with the world."

An even more rigorous disposal of religion came when Browning was asked if he considered himself to be a follower of the Christian faith. He is alleged to have replied with a "thunderous" no.

In 1845, all this changed. Robert was introduced to Elizabeth Barrett, a semi-invalid and poet who lived in isolation in Wimpole Street, in London. Her days were spent in a stultifying atmosphere of guilt and oppression brought about by her obsessively possessive father.

"I am not of a cold nature and cannot bear to be treated coldly," she wrote wanly. Her grief was compounded when her brother Edward died in

Then a light: engraving of Elizabeth Barrett Browning, based on a photograph by Macaire Havre taken in 1859, two years before she died

a sailing accident in Torquay. As a result of the shock, she became a recluse. Robert's arrival threw her into ecstasies, and inaugurated one of the world's most dramatic and celebrated love affairs.

His ardent letters underline the intensity of his passion for her. "Words can never tell you ... how perfectly dear you are to me, perfectly dear to my heart and soul." Again he wrote: "You have given me the highest, completest proof of love that even one human being gave another. I am all gratitude ... that my life has been so crowned by you."

The couple were married secretly in 1846 in Marylebone Parish Church, from where they fled to Pisa and subsequently to Florence, away from Elizabeth's father's crushing hand. There they became part of a famed literary circle.

There was another offshoot from this romance. Browning recanted his atheism, and returned to the Christian fold, admitting that Shelley's works had led him to an unwholesome self-absorption. He appears to be working through these arguments in his poem "Christmas Eve and Easter Day" (1850), the first poem that he published after his marriage.

The publication of Darwin's *On the Origin of Species* (1859) did not shake his faith. He saw this scientific achievement as a bridge connecting human-kind with the divine, and a partial explanation of the profound mysteries of God's world.

He came to believe in the immortality of the soul and the immanence of God. He viewed the Christian ethic as one of perpetual striving within the world towards the attainment of something better. From this period comes his magnificent poem "Saul", in which the harpist, David, reveals to King Saul the reality of salvation through Christ.

In 1861, after 15 years of marriage, the unthinkable happened, and Elizabeth died. Browning moved with his son Pen to London, and for a while his life became "as grey as the London sky". It was out of this dark night of the soul that his great poem "Prospice" (1864) was born.

THE POEM begins with an eye-catching challenge, a gauntlet thrown down to those who seek to sanitise the final earthly hours. "Fear death?" Browning does not shy from the earthly finality of death, nor deny that it contains more than an element of the unknown, even the fearful. He describes it as "the fog in my throat", "the mist in my face". He personifies death as "The Arch Fear [standing] in a visible form".

Halfway through the poem, the mood changes, and a hint of optimism creeps in. True "a battle's to fight ere the guerdon be gained."

But this last fight is the best. He wants to taste the whole of it. He wants to face it heroically, with that indomitable human spirit shown by great men of the past. He is eager to taste "the reward of it all".

The final stanzas are incomparably powerful. At the point of death, when all seems lost, a miracle kicks in. "For sudden the worst turns the best to the brave." All the horror and fear fades away, the black minutes come to an end, and the nightmares fade to nothing.

At this point, the stunning reality of bodily resurrection strikes home, and he is restored to his dear Elizabeth. "Then a light, then thy breast, O thou soul of my soul! I shall clasp thee again."

The final line is a summation of Browning's faith at that time of his life, a distillation of the traditional Christian credo. "And with God be the rest!"

I once saw the reality of "Prospice" played out on a cancer ward when I was a part-time hospital chaplain. A sapling-thin, shrunken farmer was sitting on a bed, grey-faced. "How are you?" I asked, realising the banality of my words.

His reply was calm: "The consultant tells me I have three months to live."

"And are you frightened?"

He looked at me long and hard. "All my life I have worked on a farm, and seen life and death. It is the way things are."

"And when the time comes?"

He smiled. "I am a religious man, Vicar. All will be well."

This is the heart of the Easter message.

(2009)

243

Author details and index

Numbers in square brackets refer to pages where the author's work appears.

Graham James was Bishop of Norwich from 1999 to 2019 and is now an Assistant Bishop in the Diocese of Truro. [60–3]

Simon Jones is Chaplain and Fellow of Merton College, Oxford. [64–7, 147–50]

Simone Kotva is Postdoctoral Research Fellow at the Faculty of Theology, University of Oslo. [125–7]

Michael Lloyd is the Principal of Wycliffe Hall, Oxford. [212–14]

Mary Ann Lund is Associate Professor in Renaissance English Literature at the University of Leicester. [236–9]

Robert Mackley is Vicar of Little Saint Mary's Church, Cambridge. [6–9]

Terence Handley MacMath is an Anglican priest in Dorset, and a writer for the *Church Times*. [160–3]

Rachel Mann is Area Dean of Bury and Rossendale, and a Visiting Fellow of Manchester Met University. [169–72]

Mark Oakley is the Dean of St John's College, Cambridge. [68–70, 95–8]

George Pattison is Professor of Divinity at the University of Glasgow. [215–17]

Michael Perham (1947–2017) was the Bishop of Gloucester from 2004 to 2014. [187–91]

Ben Pugh is Lecturer in New Testament and Applied Theology at Cliff College, Sheffield. [54–7]

Timothy Radcliffe OP is a Roman Catholic priest and Dominican friar, and former Master of the Order of Preachers from 1992 to 2001. [29–35]

Hugh Rayment-Pickard is Chief Strategy Officer and co-Founder of IntoUniversity. [128–32]

Jonathan Romain is a rabbi, writer and broadcaster, and director of Maidenhead Synagogue. [10–13]

David Scott is an Anglican priest, poet, playwright and spiritual writer. [40]

Steven Shakespeare is Professor of Continental Philosophy of Religion at Liverpool Hope University and an Anglican priest. [51–3]

Katharine Smith is a freelance writer and author and an Anglican Reader in Bishops Lydeard in Somerset. [166–8]

Jo Spreadbury is Canon Precentor of Portsmouth Cathedral. [197–8]

Peter Stanford is a writer, journalist and broadcaster, and was formerly editor of the *Catholic Herald*. [20–4]

Barbara Brown Taylor is an American Episcopal priest, professor, author and theologian. [151–5]

Angela Tilby is a Canon Emeritus of Christ Church Cathedral, Oxford, and Canon of Honour at Portsmouth Cathedral. [199]

Peter Townley is the Archdeacon of Pontefract in the Diocese of Leeds. [93–4]

Pamela Tudor-Craig (1928–2017) was an eminent British medieval art historian. [25–8, 230–5]

Robin Ward is Principal of St Stephen's House, Oxford. [133–6]

Martin Warner is the Bishop of Chichester. [1–5]

Samuel Wells is vicar of St Martin-in-the-Fields in London and Visiting Professor of Christian Ethics at King's College London. [43–6, 81–5]

William Whyte is an Anglican priest and Professor of Social and Architectural History at the University of Oxford. [36–9, 89–92]

Edward Wickham is a Fellow and Director of Music at St Catharine's College, Cambridge, as well as founder and conductor of the vocal ensemble The Clerks. [206–9]

Tom Wright was Bishop of Durham from 2003 to 2010 and is now a senior research fellow at Wycliffe Hall, Oxford. [109–13]